Pieces of
My Puzzle

Shirley,

Keep adding pieces
to your puzzle.

Karin Wrelinski

Pieces of My Puzzle

A Personal Journey Through the '50s, '60s, '70s and Beyond

By Karen Wielinski

LIBRASTREAM

BUFFALO, NEW YORK

Rights and Permissions: kwauthor17@gmail.com

www.OneOnTheGround.com • www.karenfwielinski.com

Cover/Book Design: Leslie Taylor, Buffalo Creative Group

ISBNS: 978-1-68061-039-0 (Trade Paperback)
978-1-68061-040-6 (Ebook)

Publisher's Cataloging-in-Publication Data
(Provided by Paula Perry of Cassidy Cataloguing Services, Inc.)
Names: Wielinski, Karen, author.
Title: Pieces of my puzzle : a personal journey through the '50s, '60s, '70s and beyond / by
    Karen Wielinski.
Description: First edition. | Buffalo, New York : Librastream, [2023]
Identifiers: ISBN: 978-1-68061-039-0 (Trade Paperback) | 978-1-68061-041- 3
        (Hardcover) | 978-1-68061-040-6 (Ebook) | LCCN: 2023931655
Subjects: LCSH: Wielinski, Karen. | Families--New York (State)--Buffalo--History--20th
    century. | Buffalo (N.Y.)--History, Local--20th century. | Catholic schools--New
    York (State)--Buffalo-- 20th century. | Adolescence--New York (State)--Buffalo-
    -20th century. | Coming of age--New York (State)--Buffalo--20th century.
    | Aircraft accident victims' families--New York (State)-- Clarence Center--
    Personal narratives. | Resilience (Personality trait) | Senses and sensation. |
    LCGFT: Autobiographies. | Personal narratives. | BISAC: BIOGRAPHY &
    AUTOBIOGRAPHY / Cultural, Ethnic & Regional / General. | BIOGRAPHY
    & AUTOBIOGRAPHY / Historical. | BIOGRAPHY & AUTOBIOGRAPHY /
    Personal Memoirs. | BIOGRAPHY & AUTOBIOGRAPHY / General.
Classification: LCC: F129.B853 W54 2023 | DDC: 974.7/96--dc23

LIBRASTREAM
BUFFALO, NEW YORK

First Edition
Printed in the United States of America

Dedication

Dedicated with love to my grandchildren,
the newest branches on our family tree:
Lydia, Caden, Curtis, Rowan and Gavin.

Table of Contents

Foreword
Preface

Grandchildren

Work

Thoughts on Homes

The Five Senses

Writing

Doug

Epilogue

Acknowledgements

About the Author

The Douglas C. Wielinski Memorial Scholarship Fund

Foreword

Courage, determination and faith must have been guiding Karen Wielinski as she wrote *One on the Ground* a few years ago. What an accomplishment that was, to face the brutality of the Flight 3407 tragedy and its aftermath head on, recounting how she and her girls restored some order to their lives amid the emotional toll of that first year. Those of us in her Tuesday writing group were privileged to have a front row seat during its creation. Not only was the book a paean to her husband, Doug, but the proceeds from its sale have annually funded scholarships for deserving high school graduates who, like her husband, value history and technology and will pursue careers along those lines in college.

Would anyone have blamed Karen if *One on the Ground* had become the only book she ever wrote? After all, she laid bare so much pain and grief that she was certainly entitled to step away and never commit another word to paper or computer screen.

But an amazing thing happened during the creation of her first book. She reaffirmed the goodness of life even as she was dealt a terrible blow. Those who have attended her many talks about the book have witnessed the affirmation she embodies firsthand.

In the process of creating *One on the Ground*, Karen became a writer and a storyteller. And storytelling, as we know, becomes an itch that needs constant scratching.

Even before *One on the Ground* went to press, she was plumbing the depths of her memory—of childhood, adolescence, courtship, marriage, parenting and on—to find nuggets to share. Week after week in our writing workshops, she illuminated characters, houses, adventures of her past. Parents Clarey and Margie, sister Barbara, Schwabs and Schoenwetters, aunts and uncles, Buffalo's once proud East Side, Uncle Nick the artist, St. Mary of Sorrows Roman Catholic Church, Bishop McMahon High School, the non-prom, first jobs and her future husband, Doug Wielinski, the many moves to Eden, Cincinnati, Amherst, Clarence and East Aurora came alive. And, of course, the girls—Kim, Lori, Jessica and Jill—each unique and wonderful, shined through her stories as do the grandchildren who are now enriching her life.

As much as *Pieces of My Puzzle* tracks the trajectory of Karen's life so far, it's not really an autobiography or a memoir. It's, as she says, pieces of the whole puzzle. Beyond family, she writes about writing and about the five senses, about the responses to *One on the Ground* and the good will it has generated and about a life that has been, to quote Nat King Cole, unforgettable.

Enjoy *Pieces of My Puzzle*, then get ready for the third book, which won't be far behind.

Rick Ohler,
East Aurora, NY
2022

Preface

On February 12, 2009, my life literally collapsed around me when Continental Flight 3407 crashed into our home on Long Street, Clarence Center, New York, killing my husband, Doug, and 50 souls on the aircraft. My daughter, Jill, and I were in the home at that time and somehow miraculously survived.

After that tragic event, I documented our story in my book, *One on the Ground*, published in 2017.

In that book, I make several references to puzzle pieces. A month before the crash, Doug had purchased old black-and-white puzzles from the 1920s that were given out to Buffalo Bisons baseball fans. We spent hours putting the puzzles together as a family, and on that terrible night, one remaining puzzle sat on our dining room table waiting to be completed. Jill sketched a puzzle piece for a tattoo she would eventually get and it became the inspiration for the engraving on Doug's tombstone. My daughter, Lori, discovered an old email from her dad that she had received while living in Brooklyn, NY. His dad was born in Brooklyn and Doug felt perhaps Lori could do some research in archives there to discover "another piece of our puzzle."

The Pandemic of 2020 rocked our lives and jigsaw puzzles became an obsession for me. They kept my mind occupied and sharp during months of isolation.

On reflection, I feel our lives are just like puzzles. Many pieces combine to shape who we become. We harvest experiences that teach, influence, and most of all, touch us in many ways.

What follows is my personal puzzle that started to take shape in 1951 on the East Side of Buffalo, New York, an area bordered by downtown Buffalo to the north and west, the I-190 and Kensington area to the south and Cheektowaga to the east. At that time, the city bustled with a stream of Polish and German immigrants including my great-grandparents. Spurred on by the Erie Canal and well-planned railway systems, the city thrived.

During my childhood, I was surrounded by a loving family whose lives were centered around the Catholic faith. In the turbulent '60s, our city began to change. The opening of the St. Lawrence Seaway played a big role in that change, as it cut deeply into Buffalo's industrial power. Many also feel that the construction of the I-190 highway and the Kensington Expressway (that both run from downtown Buffalo to the suburbs) destroyed many communities in their paths, as they severed neighborhoods in two.

The '70s and '80s brought new experiences for me. I entered the workforce, found love, married in 1979, and began a beautiful family. Doug and I quickly became parents to four girls: Kim, Lori, Jessica, and Jill. We also found ourselves transplanted to Ohio in 1983 and did not return to the Buffalo area until 1997.

When I open a box of puzzle pieces I am faced with a mystery, a conundrum, a challenge. The results often amaze me, just like life itself.

My puzzle pieces include family, schooling, children, grandchildren, work, homes, and writing. The senses of touch, taste, sight, hearing, and smell also play an important role in developing sections of my puzzle.

Of course, Doug's death and the crash of Flight 3407 are also a large part of that puzzle. You will find references to that experience here, but since specific details are given in *One on the Ground*, I felt I should not repeat that story in this gathering of essays. I hope my memories will transport you to the '50s, '60s, '70s, and beyond, and perhaps even help you recall your own jigsaw puzzle of life.

I have been discovered, cultivated, lost, and rearranged like puzzle pieces throughout the years. They are held together by faith, trust, wonder, and most of all love. I take comfort in knowing that my puzzle picture remains unfinished for now. The framework is sturdy and will hold so much more.

Please note: date written follows each piece.

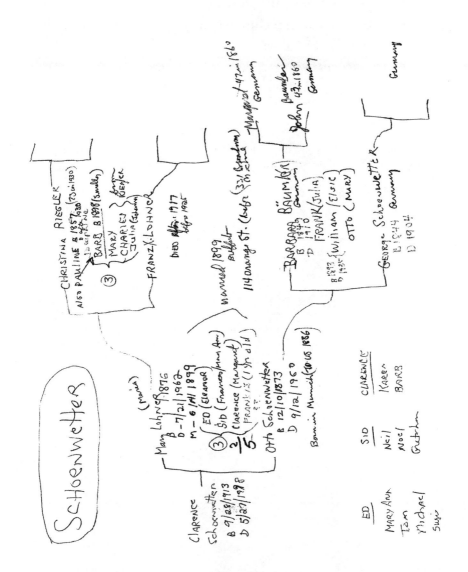

The Schoenwetter Family Tree

(thanks to Doug for this contribution)

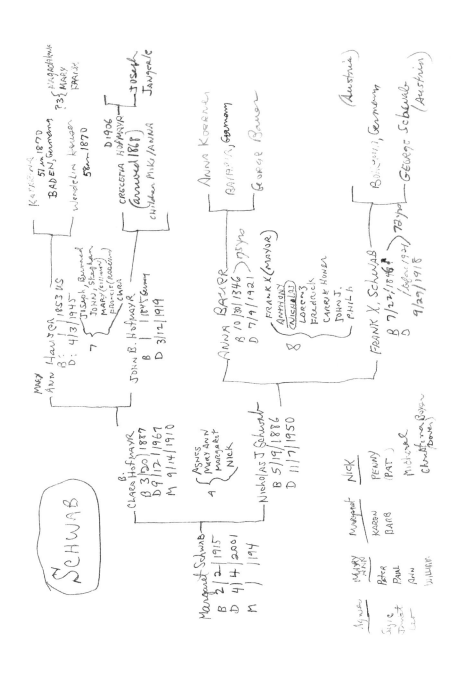

The Schwab Family Tree

(thanks to Doug for this contribution)

Family

"Like branches on a tree, we all grow in different directions, yet our roots remain as one."

~ Author Unknown

The Comfort Zone

I sought counseling after the crash of Flight 3407. In one of my sessions, my counselor encouraged me to find a "comfort zone" or "safe place" to mentally retreat to when facing a reoccurrence of distress or panic caused by the twist of fate dealt to me. Conjuring up this "safe place" was difficult, since she instructed me that this haven could not include any experience that involved my husband of thirty years, as his death was part of the tragedy. It was a dilemma, as my happiest times were with him and he most assuredly was my comfort. I did, eventually, find memories of my grandmother's small home at 221 Herman Street on the Buffalo East Side, a fitting "comfort zone."

Grandma was an important influence in my life. She was an independent woman, before it was fashionable to be so. She was filled with a love of life and for her family. There was nothing she wouldn't do for her children.

Grandpa Schwab, who passed away shortly before my birth, and Grandma had lived in their little house on

Grandma's House on Herman Street

1

Mr. and Mrs. John Hofmayr
request the honor of your presence
at the marriage of their daughter
Clara
to
Mr. Nicholas J. Schwab
Wednesday morning, September fourteenth
nineteen hundred and ten
at nine o'clock
St. Ann's Church
Buffalo, N. Y.

Nick and Clara Schwab

Herman Street for years, raising four children. They transformed a garage in the backyard into an art studio for my Uncle Nick, and then it was expanded into a house for his young family, and later for my parents.

Closing my eyes, I can still see Grandma. A tiny woman, barely five feet tall, strong willed and filled with vitality. To a small child, one of the amazing things about her was her hair. She always kept it neatly braided on top of her head, but on rare occasions, I saw it when she let it down, cascading well beyond her waist. Visions of a young girl in the 1900s with flowing brown hair, pursued by a youthful suitor, came to mind. She finally gave into modern styles, and cut it shortly before she passed away at age 81.

I spent a good deal of my childhood days at Grandma's house. Her kitchen was filled with the wonderful smells of cookies, birthday cakes, and German specialties, such as apple kuchen. Some days when I returned from school, she'd greet me with a kuchen all my own. To this day, I regret that we never found her recipe. There always was a snack waiting, either in her kitchen or old-fashioned pantry, to satisfy the hunger of a couple of children.

"All good things come in threes," she'd say, when handing out cookies or candy. That's an adage I use to this day.

From the kitchen, a narrow stairway led to the attic, once my Uncle Nick's bedroom and his first art studio. We considered ourselves lucky when we were allowed to go up and explore the boxes and drawers containing treasures from the past. It was always amusing, and amazing, to find old newspapers

Cousins: Tina, Peter, Barb, Leo, Karen, and Janet on velvet couch

and compare styles and prices from years ago.

We spent many an hour in Grandma's cozy living room, either sharing a special program on the then new medium, television, or just watching Grandma crochet one of her beautiful afghans or make delicate lace. A maroon, crushed velvet couch was the focal point of the room, but my favorite was the big blue chair, big enough to cradle me while I took a quick nap or paged through Grandma's old magazines.

Those magazines supplied many pictures for school projects. Old copies sat neatly piled next to a chest of drawers in the spare bedroom. It was an interesting room, where early pictures of my mother, aunts, and uncle were displayed. A daybed was there, always available for overnight stays. Grandma faithfully lit a vigil light before a large statue of the Blessed Mother on another dresser in that room. A woman of strong faith, she felt her prayers were answered with its help.

In the dining room, she kept her "magic" sewing machine where she created fashions perfect for dolls found under Christmas trees. She also was our head seamstress, altering outfits for a growing girl. In one drawer of her credenza, she kept tasty mints or caramels in an old tin, ready for little hands to discover. Another drawer held a scrapbook of my Great-uncle Frank Schwab who was Mayor of Buffalo in the 1920s. What a feeling of pride and amazement I always felt gazing at the memento that chronicled the life of a famous relative. I received that scrapbook from my parents, and I regret that only a few pages survived the devastation of the crash.

Grandma's woodshed sheltered our precious bicycles. We were always in trouble if, after making Grandma open the back door to get them out, we didn't ride them for more than ten minutes. The woodshed was not only my father's workshop, but mine too, for creative school projects.

Official babysitter, Grandma was always there to lend a hand. In emergencies, such as the time my front tooth was chipped off in a backyard incident, she took command. She had the job of calming both me and my mother, and continually reassured me I wouldn't be "ugly," as I tearfully lamented.

Barb and me with a pumpkin friend. Grandma's woodshed door can be seen in the background

When reality begins to feel insurmountable for me, I mentally revisit my special childhood, and all the wonder and joy that Grandma brought to it, and yes, the little girl who originally visited back in the 1950s and '60s still finds her home to be a much needed "comfort zone" and "safe place."

Originally written 1983, updated in 2009

My Parents, Clarey and Margie

Margie considered her reflection in the mirror: twenty seven years old, chestnut brown hair, high cheekbones, and just a touch of make-up. Her eyes, though, still held the pain. Could it possibly be two years since her idyllic life as a newlywed was abruptly taken from her? A brain tumor took the life of her husband Chuck Trapp; their life together ended before it even began. She walked away from the mirror, turned slightly to make sure the seams were straight on her stockings, and walked out to the kitchen.

Her mother, Clara, was putting the finishing touches on dinner. Margie was living back with her parents; there had been too many memories in the apartment she had shared with Chuck.

"You look nice. Are you sure you do not want a quick bite before you leave?" Clara asked.

"No, there will be plenty of food at the party," Margie replied.

She had always been popular with the guys, and after a respectable time of mourning, there had been a few dates. Her heart was just not in it though.

Tonight, her sister, Agnes, and brother-in-law, Leo, were picking her up. They would join her other sister and brother-in-law, Maryann and Norbert, for a gathering to welcome home Clarence Schoenwetter. Norbert and Clarence both grew up on Sherman Street. Clarey, as his friends called him, spent the last four years in Europe, after being drafted into the Army. Although Margie knew little about Clarey, she thought it might be interesting to hear

Dad in uniform

about his European experiences in World War II.

At the party, Margie observed the crowd. There were a few familiar faces, but the majority came together as couples. A pang of loneliness swept over her. She noticed a nice-looking guy in the corner. That might be Clarence. In an instant, their eyes met; perhaps it was gravity that hesitatingly pulled them toward each other.

The above is a fictional depiction of how my mother and father met. Unfortunately, I cannot recall my parents volunteering all the details. I do know they met after Dad returned from his stint in World War II.

Dad was pretty much a confirmed bachelor. I asked him how Mom managed to snatch him up. Grinning, he replied, "Guess I was shell-shocked!"

Mom and Dad on their wedding day

They were married on April 19, 1946. It actually snowed a bit that day.

Mom and her first husband did not have any children, so she was thrilled when she became pregnant. My sister, Barbara, arrived in 1948 and enjoyed the unencumbered life of an only child. My arrival on the scene in 1951, no doubt, turned her life upside down. There was a picture of me tearing

Birthday party for my sister Barb. Cousin Suzy, left of Barb, Mom, and cousins Penny, Ann, Paul and Billy. 1950

up her Valentines, as she looks on in horror. Things improved, and we managed to get along after that.

We were pampered and spoiled, and there is no doubt in my mind that we were loved. On Christmas they lavished gifts upon us. Our summer birthdays allowed celebrations on the large concrete area next to the house on Herman, where grandparents, aunts, uncles, and cousins joined the fun.

Marty Glouse and Clarey at Glouse's Deli

During most of my childhood, Dad worked for Glouse's Delicatessen on Broadway, near St. Ann's Church. I am thrilled to have a picture from that era, showing a young Clarey with Marty Glouse. Any good "deli" of that time included a glass case of

Clarey at Glouse's

penny candies. Glouse's was no exception. My favorite purchase was always a little pie tin, which included a tiny spoon for eating the sugary concoction. Whenever I see old-fashioned candies, I always look for this childhood favorite, but I haven't found it yet.

Wanting to better provide for his family, Dad eventually went to night school and obtained his boiler and engineer license.

As most little girls do, I idolized my dad. He could do no wrong. I liked to accompany him as he ran errands in the old Chevy.

Occasionally, Dad took me with him to pick up his paycheck at the Simon Pure Brewery. Prior to working at Simon Pure, he worked at the Phoenix Brewery. Along with Dad's stories on how he kept things running smoothly, I also have a vague memory of tales involving entrance into the huge beer vats to help scrub them clean.

Dad did our grocery shopping, which often included a ride to Loblaw's farther down Genesee Street toward Bailey. The store was in front of the Wonder Bread factory, and you could always catch a whiff of the bread baking. As a Brownie, I took a tour of the facility, and received not only my own tiny loaf of Wonder Bread, but a plastic rain bonnet, folded neatly into a case. It didn't take much to make us feel special and happy.

Sometimes we took a trip to the Niagara Mohawk office on Fillmore Avenue in the Broadway District. While Dad attended to business, my sister and I perused the pamphlets lined up in a display: little books explaining how to stay fit and healthy or manage utilities economically. On the way out, we usually were allowed to slip a penny into the gumball machine; I hoped the luck of the draw would not result in a black licorice reward (ugh!).

Looking back, I do not remember Dad or Mom spending what today would be considered "quality time" with us kids. When it came to play time, my sister and I entertained ourselves. I have no recollection of them reading books to us, playing games, coloring, or indulging in our imaginary activities. Hopefully, my girls will have some memories of me sharing their playtime, or at least smile remembering the considerable amount of reading that went on prior to bedtime.

To his credit, Dad did help me on a few school projects. He brought out a wooden crate, sent to his mother while he was in Europe, and filled with letters, postcards, and pictures. I always loved an opportunity to share those experiences with him. For a project on foreign countries, he let me include some of those postcards and photos of France in my project.

There are only a few things I truly regret losing in the crash. That box is one.

I love this note that did surface from the Long Street site:

Dear Kim, Lori, Jessica & Jill:

How are you girls? Hope you are being good for Mommy & Daddy. Better be, or Grandpa will get the bug after you. Here he comes…got you.

The "bug" was also referred to as a "cootie" (perhaps after the children's game). For as long as I can remember, Dad entertained

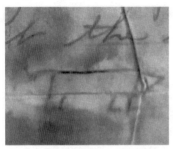

us with the cootie. He drew the culprit with a long rectangular body, a triangular head, curly tail, and four legs. Sometimes the cootie would sport dots inside his body. Dad and Uncle Ed brought the cootie to life by setting four finger tips on a table and raising the middle finger up as its head. The cootie then scooted up our

Cootie discovered on a letter from Dad that was retrieved from the Long Street site.

arms. I loved that tradition and continued it with my girls.

One advantage of having children is that you have an opportunity to relive your youth. The passage of time dims our remembrance of childhood joys. As I watched Dad with my girls, I recaptured the silliness and laughter he gave to me.

I do have pleasant memories of sitting next to my mom in our old Chevy and placing a sleepy head in her lap. The steady beat of her heart usually lulled me to sleep. Even if I was not asleep, I pretended, so I could stay snuggled against her, and get Dad to scoop me up in his arms and carry me carefully into the house.

As Mom prepared for an occasional night out with Dad, I often sat in a large chair in the corner of their bedroom and watched as she selected her jewelry from a small pink box carefully placed in her dresser drawer. She had a long, delicate silver chain that held an amethyst which sat in a lovely square setting that enhanced the violet/red hue of the stone. That was my favorite, along with a colorful brooch with matching clip earrings. The drawer also held a pair of white cotton gloves, which she always wore when she slipped on her nylons.

When our interest in boys began to develop, Mom helped encourage our efforts by allowing us to have co-ed Christmas parties. My mother's clever decision to serve holiday cookie-cutter sandwiches filled with egg salad and tuna fish, and have a small 45 rpm record player spinning the newly discovered Beatles' tunes eased the awkwardness of those boy/girl encounters.

People liked Margie, and confided in her. I recall many phone calls Mom received from her friends and family. She had the gift of soothing those in need.

Mom was a people person. She always remembered birthdays and anniversaries, and kept small card shops in business with her regular purchases. Just the simple action of sending cards made her happy.

Part of Mom's ritual included the ladies' pinochle club. About twelve ladies took turns holding monthly gatherings in their modest homes. Mom's sisters, Maryann and Agnes, along with two of Aunt Maryann's sisters-in-law (Neil and Irene) were in the group, along with Mrs. Whitman, whose husband was a policeman like Uncle Leo. My cousin, Ann, also joined the group. The other attendees are a blur to me.

When it was Mom's turn, she set up card tables in our large living room, covered with quilted green and silver tablecloths with elastic edges securing them to the tables. She dusted and placed folding chairs around the tables. A box of bridge mix, along with a slim box of chocolate thin mints, were a special treat only when the ladies were coming. Perhaps they drank beer, high balls, or ginger ale, and no doubt finger foods were available. Their voices blended together into an incoherent babble. When we received a tape recorder one Christmas, my sister and I hid in a bathroom and taped them. When played back, it was impossible to comprehend what was being said.

The ladies kept this traditional game alive for many years until illness and death decreased their numbers.

Besides caring for her family, Mom did branch out into other endeavors.

As a young woman, she worked at Adam, Meldrum, and

Anderson (AM&A's) in downtown Buffalo. Like most women of that era, she stayed home when we were small. She did, though, do telephone soliciting at home for the American Progressive Insurance Company several days a week. I can still hear her cheerfully saying, "Hello, my name is Margie with the American Progressive Insurance Company. We have a new, low-cost insurance plan…" She would line up calls for the salesman, writing details on little pads. My sister and I liked to scoop up a pad and mimic her role of solicitor.

As we got older, Mom returned to the outside business world, first as a stock girl in an elite, upscale women's dress shop, Mabel Dannahy's, on Delaware Avenue. She really enjoyed that atmosphere, and could often get discounts on clothing like my sister's senior prom dress. It was a long, fitted knit garment, white on top with a pink skirt, totally unique and not a cookie-cutter design. And, it was suitable to be altered to a sensible length for after the prom.

Since Mom never did get her driver's license (she was too nervous to handle the stress of driving), she counted on the bus or my dad for transportation. As my sister and I obtained our licenses, we became her chauffeurs.

Mom was disappointed when Mabel Dannahy's eliminated her stock girl position, but she moved on to a job with an office supply company on Main Street. The company was on the second floor in a building between Tupper and Pearl Streets. The office manager had a nephew who it seemed was the perfect age to be introduced to my sister. That meeting took place, but there was no spark.

My memories seem to center more on faith-related events. We accompanied Mom and Grandma Schwab every Friday for the Novena of Our Lady of Seven Sorrows at St. Mary of Sorrows Church, also known to parishioners as Seven Dolors. Admittedly, by the age of twelve, I was eager to attend these services. I wanted to see if the boys I had crushes on would be the altar boys.

Mom belonged to the Ladies Holy Rosary Society and sometimes I accompanied her down Herman Street to collect dues from members. Since she was friendly and talkative, it was an excellent job for her.

Mom and Dad never considered missing Mass on Sunday. They sang in the choir and participated in all religious activities offered by the church.

Besides being a member of the choir, Dad bowled with the guys from the church Holy Name Society. In later years, he and Mom traveled to the Adirondacks with the aunts and uncles, and they became members of the Senior Citizens Group.

Friendship was important to Dad, and he kept in touch with childhood buddies: George Wolf, Casey Ronas, and Rudy Kirsits.

Growing up, we saw little of George, who was the best man at my parents' wedding. George, a lifelong bachelor, had no children. We enjoyed numerous summer visits with Casey and Rudy's families. Casey's children, Casey Jr. and Mary, were younger than my sister and me.

Rudy had five boys, several who were our age. I can only remember three of their names: Donny, Bobby, and Richie. We referred to them as the "Golden Boys." A perpetual tan, combined with blond hair, enhanced their good looks. I cannot speak for my sister, but I looked forward to those summer visits and always harbored the hope that one of them would actually be interested in me. Of course, that never happened, but a girl could always dream.

The Buffalo breweries declined in the '70s, as did the neighborhood where Dad worked. He always worked the swing shift and was becoming more and more uncomfortable during those overnight periods. He decided to switch jobs and secured a position at the Millard Fillmore Gates Circle Hospital in their engine room.

It had always been obvious to me that Mom was a very nervous person, although she did not present that characteristic to others. Her quivering chin was an outward sign, and the presence of a prescription bottle of green liquid tucked away in a kitchen cupboard was often retrieved to ease her tension. It was somewhat of a shock, though, to learn Dad could retreat into depression.

His anxiety at work crept into our home. He would sit and barely talk or eat. It was difficult for me to see such a change, a part of his personality never before exposed. In the long run, it was decided that an earlier than expected retirement would ease his dilemma. It was the tonic he needed.

It took persistence on my mom's part to move the family away from our East Side neighborhood in the late '60s. Dad was reluctant to take a financial risk. The $30 per month that he paid Grandma Schwab for rent was hard to give up. Mom felt her teenage girls needed a safer neighborhood though, and she had always dreamed of owning a house. She won that battle and we said goodbye to Herman Street and hello to Hagen Street near the Buffalo city line.

The emotion my dad displayed at my wedding in 1979 touched me. After the ceremony, as we gathered in the church vestibule, I saw tears fill his eyes. His baby girl was embarking on a new life.

Mom, Dad and Kim

My parents were enjoying retirement and thrilled when their granddaughters arrived.

However, a big change occurred in Mom's personality after Doug and I moved to the Cincinnati area. Her battle with obsessive compulsive disorder (OCD) began. I have read that the onset of this affliction can be caused by trauma. A daughter's departure, along with those long-awaited grandchildren, could have been the catalyst.

Mom with Lori and Jess

A physical illness is easy to understand, but it is a struggle to comprehend a mental illness. Mom had good periods where it seemed she had beaten that illness.

"It's a great life, if you don't weaken." I can still picture her uttering those words of wisdom. She and my dad were visiting us in Loveland, Ohio, following the birth of our third daughter, Jessica. Seated on a lawn chair, Mom wore her usual summer garb: sleeveless, floral blouse and, unbelievably, peddle-pushers over pantyhose. She must have felt contentment as she watched her older granddaughters, Kim and Lori, play on the backyard swing set and frolic in their small plastic pool.

Unfortunately, the years following that idyllic summer day saw my mother plunge deeper into the depths of OCD. She would never win the battle with that relentless foe.

We returned to Buffalo for visits and stayed with my parents. Mom hardly communicated and barely spent time with the girls, retreating, instead, to her bedroom. Yet, when it came time to leave, she complained that we couldn't stay longer.

OCD's hold on Mom was strong. It was difficult to witness her decline and to see how it enhanced the aging process. Dad did everything for her. She lived with demons in her head.

On one visit, I came downstairs to give one of the girls a bottle in the middle of the night. I was shocked to see Mom standing at the bathroom sink continuously washing her hands. She would not budge; she was completely stiff. I went to get my dad. He slept in the bedroom, lights blazing. As always, he made light of the situation and proceeded to literally pry her from the sink. The entire encounter will always remain imprinted in my mind and heart.

She barely communicated with us and often would mutter, "No sin, no sin." What sins did she need to ask repentance for? "Mom," I would say, "If you have any sins, they are washed away because you are living your Purgatory now."

I often wonder if Mom enjoyed her adult daughters or her grandchildren amidst her illness; not that I was aware of, and that made me so mad. Sometimes, I just wanted to shake her and beg her to try harder, to try to enjoy life. Mental illness is so hard to understand and I had to realize that, because of the OCD, she was unable to beat her demons.

If something positive came from her struggles, it is the hope that I will quickly recognize any tendencies I might have of entering the darkness that consumed her life. She gave me that; she gave me the will to grab on to life, and the determination to not let a moment slip by. That resolve would make the Margie of my childhood happy.

I hold another letter from Dad that was written to us after we moved to Cincinnati. His words were written on wrinkled pieces of paper with blue ink, smeared and faded, not from time, but from tragedy. They too were retrieved from Long Street. I could sense between the lines his struggle to deal with Mom's problem:

No, we didn't get to the family picnic, Mother did not feel up to going. She does not care to go any place; no club, no Senior Citizens (I go alone)—just church and maybe McD or 4 Seasons (restaurant) *after church, then back home."*

In a note to the girls, he wrote: *"Grandma is good some days. Say a prayer for her when you go to bed."*

Despite the undertones of sadness, Dad enjoyed sending messages to the girls:

Thank you for my birthday card & gifts. It sure was nice. Kim, how is the lunch at school? Very good I hear. Lori, I liked your little note on the back of Mommy's letter. You are doing real good. Jessica are you a good girl? Jill I hope you are using the potty? Will write again.

Lots of love & kisses,
xxxxoooo
Grampa & Gramma

Dad's constant care of Mom took its toll. A rare call from Mom informed me that Dad was acting odd. When he got on the line, he sounded belligerent and incoherent. He refused to call a doctor. I felt helpless hundreds of miles from him. I immediately called my cousin, Paul, in Buffalo. He took charge, visited Dad, and assessed the situation. Dad had suffered a stroke, and was hospitalized.

Doug was out of town so I made arrangements for the girls' care and headed to Buffalo. Decisions had to be made immediately. It was obvious that Dad could no longer take care of Mom. They needed to be with us in Cincinnati. Within weeks, my parents' house was on the market and they were living with

Doug and me.

We made the difficult decision to place Mom in an assisted living environment. I had plenty of guilt over separating my parents and placing her there.

Grandpa and his girls: Lori, Jess, Jill and Kim

We built "Grandpa's wing," and Dad became an integral part of our lives. Looking back, I am glad the girls got to know their "Papa." He adjusted to the craziness of living with four little girls and definitely enjoyed having his own sanctuary at the back of the house. My responsibilities increased as I made sure he could make visits to Mom several times a week.

When we knew a job move to Buffalo was imminent, the plan included taking Dad with us and moving Mom to another facility in that area. It was not meant to be. One afternoon while I was at work, Dad suffered a massive heart attack at home. The girls were with him. I remain amazed that the girls (ages 11-15) kept relatively calm. They called 911 immediately and ran to neighbors for help.

At the hospital, my sister and I were asked if everything should be done to resuscitate Dad. We said, "Yes." It was a decision we later regretted. We should have let nature take its course. Dad did survive, but he was miserable.

Doug, the girls, and I made the move to Buffalo. It fell on my sister's shoulders to be my parents' main support in Ohio. Another layer of guilt was laid on my shoulders. We do what we can. The following May, on Jill's birthday, Dad left this earth. Mom followed two years later.

It is sad that my girls will only remember my mom as someone who "existed," and not that chestnut brown-haired young woman who, with Clarey again, found a life filled with love. I am thankful, though, that they could share fun and laughter with their "Papa."

My Aunt Maryann, Mom's sister, who later in life married my dad's brother, Sid, said many times: "What wonderful, caring men those Schoenwetter boys are." Although I remember little about Grandma Schoenwetter, I do know she was a quiet and gentle woman. Her boys inherited those qualities.

Dad enjoyed the simple life. Possession-wise he required and asked for little. A shared glass of beer and some cheese and crackers with Mom each evening brought him happiness. He taught me that sometimes less is more.

My cousin, Jan, recently told me, "In my mind's eye, I can see the twinkle in your dad's eye, and remember his quiet, sweet sense of humor." That is a good way to recall Clarey.

He is missed, but somehow the closing from one of the retrieved letters written before his birthday, leaves me with hope:

> *Well, that's about it for now, more later. I'll see if I feel any older after tomorrow, I don't think so.*
>
> *Bye awhile.*

3/8/13 & 10/7/13

A Question/Grandpa

A distant memory of one so small,
in my eyes he stood ten feet tall.

Beer poured in a frosted mug,
me settled next to him for a hug.

The whiff of cigar smoke in the air,
brought comfort not to be compared.

A cigar band slipped on my finger,
this happiness would surely linger.

Oh, so gentle and soft spoken,
the German accent now forgotten.

Sickness brought a wedge to separate;
our time cut short by fickle fate.

The County Home was his destination,
for a child there was little explanation.

Visitation rights denied,
"Wait in the car." I complied.

The warmth was gone…I felt so cold,
left without him, me just nine years old.

Where was my laughing, robust grandfather?
In the coffin looking thin and young, more like my father.

3/23/12

*Author's Note: My Creative Writing moderator, Rick Ohler, suggested
that I turn this poem into prose. Here is that essay.*

Grandpa

It was my first experience losing someone I loved, but it was hard for me to feel remorse for the man in the coffin. Since his illness, I had not seen my 88-year-old grandpa in some time. In my mind, he was still a robust, jolly immigrant from Germany. Now in 1960, I barely recognized the man in the coffin. He looked thin, young, and resembled my father.

Born in 1872, my grandpa, Otto Schoenwetter, came to the United States from the Black Forest region of Germany at age fifteen with his parents and brother, Frank. He entered the upholstery trade while still in his teens, and later was employed at the Pierce-Arrow Motor Car Company and the Pullman Company. He married my Grandma Mary Lohner in 1898 and they had five sons: Ed (called Tom), Frank (called Sid), Clarence (my father), and two who died as infants.

The family lived on Sherman Street on the East Side of Buffalo. I have very vague memories of the house. My grandpa would have been seventy-nine when I was born, and as my grandma eventually lost her sight to glaucoma, they sold their home shortly after that.

Grandpa loved his beer and was one of the regulars at the local pubs on Broadway near their home. My dad told me, "We'd have to go over to the tavern and tell Pa that

*Uncle Ed, Uncle Sid, Grandpa and Grandma Schoenwetter, Dad, and
unknown girl*

Ma wanted him back home for dinner."

Pinochle was one of Grandpa's delights. There were
regular get-togethers with the guys on Sherman Street for
a game or two. Dad and his brothers liked to hold pretend
"Masses" and would interrupt the game to distribute
"communion" to the card players.

The brothers took turns having Grandpa and Grandma
live with them after the home on Sherman was sold. Our
dining room was transformed into a bedroom for them.
My mother's nerves could not handle the situation for
long and they were quickly moved elsewhere. Grandma's

Grandpa and Grandma Schoenwetter

health was failing and she was taken to the Wende Nursing Home.

Grandpa visited us often. He'd sit on the couch, stein of beer in one hand and cigar in the other, and I would snuggle next to him. I know I felt warm and secure there, but I cannot remember any conversations we might have had or even the sound of his voice.

Although my dad talked fondly of his days growing up, I do not believe he had an especially close relationship with his father. I think my grandpa worked hard to keep the family living comfortably and found relaxation with his tavern friends. Family time was no doubt limited. I regret I never thought to ask my dad about this.

Grandpa's health also declined and he too ended up at Wende. My sister and I accompanied our parents there, but were never allowed to visit. Children were not permitted in his ward, so we patiently waited for our parents out in the car. At least I was spared from seeing Grandpa's rapid decline.

In the beginning we could visit my grandma. Dad always took a thermos of hot tea and we stopped at the bakery for pastries, a treat for Grandma. She was not in a critical-care ward and remained at Wende until her death

Grandma Schoenwetter, Barb, and me

in 1962.

There would be no more hugs and nestling with my grandpa.

It was difficult looking at the man in the coffin. He really did not resemble the grandpa I knew. Death was a new experience, hard to comprehend, and difficult to accept.

The funeral was at St. Ann's on Broadway. I have memories of that church, but none of the funeral. It's funny what you remember: wearing my first high heels and nylons to Mass there and avoiding the sculpture/ picture of Purgatory at the back of the church. That always creeped me out!

Several years ago, Doug and I went to Mass there one Sunday. Yes, Purgatory still resided at the back of the church. I marveled at the beautiful craftsmanship of the pews, railings, and confessional booths. Much of the work was done by the German parishioners. The Mass felt more like a Baptist than a Catholic service, but it was spiritually uplifting to me. As I sat there, I wondered how many of my relatives had been a part of that church. It was emotional and I hoped Doug wouldn't notice the tears in my eyes.

Grandpa's spirit certainly surrounded me that day. I was snuggling next to him, smelling that cigar smoke, and waiting for him to hand me a cigar band for my finger.

Me with Grandma and Grandpa Schoenwetter

My Sister, Barbara

In July 1982, my sister Barbara, Barb to me, sent her family and friends a six-page letter updating us all on a seven-month journey she and her then husband, Adrien, had been experiencing. They had traveled through fifteen states and Mexico on Adrien's Harley Davidson motorcycle. After covering 16,000 miles, they settled in La Mesa, California. It was a new adventure for her, one that would be added to her long list of endeavors since she became my big sister back in 1951.

She enjoyed the uninterrupted attention bestowed on an only child for three years. An example of the chaotic world she had been forced to enter when I arrived on the scene is evident in a photo where I appear ready to pull her hair.

Being a sibling did have its advantages, though. There was always someone around to play games with such as Monopoly, Chinese Checkers, Go to the Head of the Class, Uncle Wiggly, or Bingo. We

Dad, impish me, and Barb

also spent time coloring in our individual Mickey Mouse Club coloring books. To this day, Barb loves coloring. We liked our dolls and loved a game or two of rummy or pinochle. Our imaginations kicked into high gear as we imitated mothers trying to keep our babies quiet during pretend Mass or sang along with

our parents' records of *The Sound of Music* or *The King and I,* envisioning ourselves on a Broadway stage.

I never got lonely. She was always there. We shared a bedroom and sometimes we held hands at night with the intention of seeing if they remained together in the morning. I'm not sure if they did but the memory of the tenderness remains.

Barb at 5 years old

Some siblings might have rebelled against the necessity of having to include a little sister in all their activities. As children, I can only recall one instance where she tried to give me the slip. She and her friend decided it would be fun

to hide from me. I was distressed by this slight, but they had second thoughts about their scheme, reappeared, and allowed me to play with them again.

As we got older, we still kept each other company, but we branched out by either entertaining ourselves or making new friends of our own.

For Barb that friend

The remains of a photo of Barb and me in our Halloween costumes, but our joined hands reminded me of our sleeping experiment.

Dad, Barb, and me, Herman Street, around 1956

was Connie. Barb was in seventh grade, and as she and I sat on our grandmother's front porch, we noticed that a girl kept riding her bike up and down the street. She was new to Herman Street. That was the beginning of a friendship between Barb and Connie that lasted a long time. Connie lived with her mom and dad in the upstairs apartment of the house next door to my Aunt Maryann. Although Barb and Connie mainly did things on their own, occasionally I was allowed to join them.

I recall sitting in Connie's bedroom watching her and Barb perform the song "Sisters" from *White Christmas*. There is also a vague memory of Connie's downstairs neighbor's cat having kittens and the three of us being allowed to get a peek at them.

Because she was older, I was always envious of what my sister could do. She was pretty young when she joined other kids at St. Ann's parish on Broadway where they allowed roller skating

Connie, Barb, and me at Lori's wedding

in the school gymnasium. One Christmas, Barb received her own skates. They came in a red, white, and blue case. She couldn't have been more than nine or ten at the time. I do not recall ever going skating there. Either I was too young or she needed her own time without me tagging along.

I looked forward to the days when I would be old enough to belong to Junior Achievement, CYO (Catholic Youth Organization), or get a job and make actual money. Junior Achievement was an organization that encouraged local businesses to work on projects with teens. They brainstormed, made a product, and then sold it. I recall Barb's group working on a retractable extension cord apparatus. Why do I remember that? Anyway, it was marketed, but I am sure only parents and other relatives bought them from the kids. I can't say I ever saw such an item like that for sale in the hardware store.

The CYO provided opportunities for teens in the parish to get together. There were meetings, dances, baseball teams, and an annual visit to the Crystal Beach Amusement Park in Fort Erie, Canada, during the summer. Unfortunately, by the time I was old enough to join this group, participation had declined, and when I was fifteen, we moved out of the neighborhood. I was too shy to join a similar group in our new parish.

Barb, Connie, and Connie's cousin all worked at a credit agency in downtown Buffalo during high school. I was so impressed with that accomplishment. The thought of making money was very appealing to me, and how fun to dress in business attire, skirts or

Teenage Barb 1963 & 64

dresses, as women were not allowed to wear slacks in the 60s.

When I was finally 16 and had obtained my working papers, officially required by New York State for 16-year-olds, I hoped to join the girls at that office. Unfortunately, they had enough full-time employees to fill their needs.

I followed in Barb's footsteps when I chose to attend Bishop McMahon High School. She was a senior when I was a freshman. Around that time, I was beginning to appreciate hanging around with my friends instead of my sister all the time. I was starting to need sibling separation.

McMahon took all of those girls interested on a trip each year to

Barb and me in front of our dining room window on Herman St. in 1966

either Philadelphia, Montreal, or Washington DC. Seniors always looked forward to their special trip to New York City, but usually did not go on the other trip scheduled for that year.

I was eagerly

awaiting my first trip to Philadelphia freshman year. As there were still openings for students to go, at the last minute, Barb decided she would go too and stay in my room.

Although I still feel guilty about it, I was crushed and disappointed that she was going. This was my chance to do something on my own. I wanted the experience to be uniquely mine. It worked out all right in the end; I wasn't glum during the whole trip and one of my friends shared our room too.

After some tense driving lessons with my dad, Barb took over my training sessions. Her willingness to do so was severely tested one day when I handed her the directional signal stick from her car. It had somehow come off as I used it. Despite this setback, she continued to allow me to borrow her Ford Falcon after I received my license.

Barb was the organizer and leader. I was usually the follower and that was fine with me. She was also a good traveling companion.

We took a West Coast trip and toured San Francisco, Los Angeles, Yosemite National Park, and Las Vegas, which included a plane ride to the Grand Canyon. I'll never forget sitting in the Las Vegas airport, waiting to leave for the Grand Canyon. We had to

Bus Driver Dave, Barb, tour guide Jon, and me on our California and West Coast adventure

tell an attendant our weight to make sure we were within the weight limitations for the plane. It was memorable.

I was only 20 at the time and not the legal age to gamble or drink in Vegas, so I placed few bets during our time there, as I feared getting arrested. I did risk having a few drinks though.

Barb never had any trouble attracting boys or men, as was demonstrated on that trip. By the time we reached Los Angeles, she was meeting the tour guide for drinks in the bar. Perhaps there is more to that story, but I was not privy to details.

After I graduated from high school, Barb planned excursions for us. We would fly to New York City on a Friday night and spend the weekend catching three Broadway shows and shopping at Macy's. Perhaps we were still stuck in a conservative post-Catholic schoolgirl state; we never hit the nightlife in the big city, but we always had a great time.

Our last big trip together before my husband Doug entered my life, was a Canadian West Coast adventure with Connie, her cousin, and a friend. We started out via rail in Toronto and continued the tour by bus from Calgary. We had a wonderful time visiting Banff, Lake Louise, Vancouver, and Victoria Island.

Me and Barb on the Canadian Railway

Much to our mother's lament, at the ages of 28 and 25, Barb and I decided it was time to spread our wings and rent an apartment in Hamburg, New York. Our planned moving date came a few short weeks after Buffalo's memorable Blizzard of '77. After spending time snowed in with our parents for several days, the timing to move to our own place seemed perfect.

We made the most of our freedom and enjoyed doing things our way at the Lake Heights Apartment complex without parental interference.

Barb had been working at the Federal Reserve Bank on Delaware Avenue in downtown Buffalo since graduating from Bishop McMahon High School. It was a great place to work. She started as a "trotter" in the mail room and eventually held a position in accounting. The bank provided many perks for their employees. Occasionally, I was able to go there for lunch in the large, upscale cafeteria, and I joined her in some of the after-work events that were offered to the workers. We were loyal fans of the bank baseball team and participated in field trips to Pittsburgh for a baseball game (my first time going to a professional game), Sabres hockey games, plays, and picnics.

During the Blizzard of 77, her job was considered essential, so she was picked up at the corner of our street and traveled to work in a limo.

Besides taking the plunge and moving to our own apartment, Barb also decided to change jobs. She found employment at the WGR television office in their accounting department for two years. I always thought working for the media industry would be my dream job, so I can say that I was a bit jealous of her entry into that field.

Adrien and Barb's wedding

The summer after we moved into our apartment, my life happily changed when I met my future husband, Doug. Barb was a considerate roommate, making herself discreetly absent during Doug's many visits to the apartment, and our cuddling time on the couch.

Although she had dates, Doug and I were married before Barb met her first husband, Adrien. He was a French Canadian living in St. Catharines, Ontario, and swept her off her feet. He was definitely more liberal than our family. That trait was reflected in the location of their wedding, which took place outside at Chestnut Ridge Park.

They lived in St. Catharines after their marriage, but soon began their motorcycle adventure.

Barb's life was the complete opposite of mine. I started raising children, and in a way, she started "raising Cain." Theirs eventually was an open marriage that sometimes included dating others. When we visited them in California, I was shocked to see that light switches were covered with a certain male appendage, and I was not quite prepared to witness Adrien walking around the apartment in just his Speedo. All this didn't fit into my lifestyle, but I could accept the situation if it fit their life. My friends were always asking me for updates on Barb's life. They said it was better than watching a soap opera.

Barb began to consider adding a new chapter to her life shortly before her 40th birthday. Over dinner one night while visiting us in Cincinnati, she casually mentioned to me that she and Adrien had decided to get divorced. Apparently, she had become disillusioned with her California lifestyle. She wanted to be near family again, and as she did not want to move back to Buffalo, she decided she would give Cincinnati a try. Doug cleared out a portion of his collection room in our basement, carving out a private space for her bed and dresser, and he made a wooden clothes rack for her.

While she hunted for a job, my friends welcomed the fact that she was willing to babysit for their kids while they did their errands. I am sure she did not lament saying goodbye to that occupation when she secured a position with the Federal Reserve Bank in downtown Cincinnati. Fortunately, they agreed to accept the time she had spent with the bank in Buffalo, extending her tenure and increasing her eventual retirement pension.

Barb stayed with us for seven months, which gave her time

Barb confronts being 40

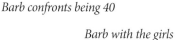

Barb with the girls

to bond with my girls. On each of their birthdays, she treated them to dinner at Friendly's and took them over to Johnny's Toys where a special key unlocked the Birthday Castle door that allowed them to retrieve a gift.

When asked to reflect on her days with us, Barb also remembered coming home from work and finding supper ready. It was probably the only time I was organized with dinner plans. To impress my sister with my efficiency in culinary skills, I posted a menu on the refrigerator listing the weekly fare.

It was wonderful to have family with us to celebrate birthdays and holidays, something we missed since moving away from Buffalo. As Barb caught her reflection in the bathroom mirror on her birthday, these red lipstick words jumped out at her: "This is what 40 looks like!"

Since my dating experiences were limited, I always told my girls as they got older, they should consult with Aunt Barbara if they had any dating questions. During her time living with us, we met some of her beaus.

One was a bit younger than she and separated from his wife. He came over to our house one night for dinner. I remember this event because I hollowed out a pumpkin and served stew in it. He was a nice guy, but since he worked for a Catholic institution that frowned on the thought of divorce, they had to be very discreet about their relationship. Needless to say, that did not last long.

Barb had moved to an apartment closer to downtown Cincinnati when, through a work friend, she met another nice guy from Kentucky. He owned a boat and he and Barb cruised down the Ohio river and secured a spot to view the big, annual Cincinnati Labor Day fireworks display. He also invited Doug, the kids, and me to his cottage for a fun day on the river. He was a quiet guy and I guess that relationship ended when he could not commit to a more permanent status.

Barb liked to attend singles' dances, and one night, she met a guy from Monroe, Ohio, named Bill. He was divorced, had two grown girls, was a truck driver, and owned a nice property about four hours away at Lake Cumberland, Kentucky.

Barb and Bill's wedding

They began to see a lot of each other, and Barb called one day in 1991 to tell me that she and Bill were getting married at the Newport Town Court Building in the morning before work. I had mixed emotions about what seemed to be a sudden decision. They hadn't known each other that long, and I wondered how this change would affect our relationship. Despite my doubts, I went to the Court Building to lend my support. Things turned out okay though. They recently celebrated their 30th anniversary.

They lived in Monroe for a while, and then permanently moved to the Lake Cumberland location, making many friends and enjoying the beautiful lake with their boats. They eventually retired to Clearwater, Florida.

Barb was living in Monroe when we moved our mom and dad from Buffalo to Loveland, Ohio. She visited Mom in assisted living and then the nursing home. She and Bill took Dad, who was living with Doug and me at the time, to the lake some weekends where he loved riding in the boat.

When it became apparent that Doug would be accepting a new job in Buffalo, our initial plan was to take Dad with us and locate a nursing home for Mom there. Dad then suffered a heart attack and moving him and Mom no longer seemed to be an option. After we moved, Barb became our parents' main support. I felt guilty about leaving her in that position, especially as she watched their decline before their deaths.

Unexpected changes occur in life and Barb and Bill faced a horrific event in 2004. While driving into town, Bill and his son-in-law were struck head-on by a young man high on drugs and alcohol. The son-in-law hit the windshield and escaped serious injury, but the engine came toward Bill and pushed him into the back of the truck. He was pinned down and surrounded by dripping gasoline. Help arrived quickly and he was extracted from the vehicle. He spent weeks in the hospital. He had lost teeth, damaged his eyes, and his left foot and ankle had been shattered.

Unfortunately, the damage to his foot and ankle was severe. When he developed a staph infection, Bill's leg had to be amputated below his knee. With therapy and lots of loving care from Barb, he adjusted remarkably to living with a prosthetic.

Supportive. That definitely describes my sister, and this was again illustrated following the crash of Flight 3407 in 2009. The day after the tragedy, she and Bill arrived in Buffalo to help us in any way they could.

During our childhood, teenage, and early adult lives, Barb and I were always close. As the years went on though, our relationship has definitely changed. We live such different lives, but I have always found that when we do see each other, our sisterly bond still exists and we can easily rekindle the feelings we held for one another in the past.

Although the COVID-19 pandemic darkened our lives in 2020, I feel it has strengthened my relationship with my sister. During that time, we started to video chat and talk on the phone more than we had done in years.

Life is a constant series of changes, but the core of love never really disappears. I am thankful that I disrupted Barb's life back in 1951.

11/16/20

Barb and Karen, 2018

The Haugs

It has been a long time since I found myself on Best Street. As a child growing up on the East Side of Buffalo, I traveled down that city street often. Herman Street, where I lived until I was fifteen, ran from Broadway to Best Street. We had to walk only one block down Herman to reach Best.

If we crossed Best Street, Humboldt Park (now Martin Luther King Park) stretched out before us. Of course, this was frowned upon by our parents and off limits until we were at least ten or eleven.

The Buffalo Museum of Science occupied part of the park. I took art classes at the museum for several years and have a faint recollection of attending art shows, sitting in the auditorium and hoping I might win an award for my creations. Sadly, my artistic endeavors did not warrant such rewards.

A huge dinosaur that greeted visitors in the main hall was one of my favorites, as were the Native American dioramas.

Once or twice, we attempted to ice skate on the frozen shallow pond at Humboldt Park. We strapped on hand-me-down skates, unfortunately a few sizes too big. Despite several layers of socks, our ankles flopped about and Olympic dreams of gold medals vanished.

War Memorial Stadium, affectionately referred to by Buffalonians as "The Rock Pile," was located at the corner of Dodge and Best Streets. People could easily walk from my

Herman Street neighborhood to watch Buffalo Bisons and Buffalo Bills games. I can recall going to one Bills game, but by the time I had the ways and means to soak in the atmosphere of the old stadium, the football facility had moved to the suburbs of Orchard Park, New York.

Most of my trips down Best Street were taken to visit my Aunt Agnes and Uncle Leo Haug's home on Johnson Street. Their two-family home faced the imposing wall of the Good Shepherd Home for "wayward girls." My sister and I harbored the fear that any misbehavior on our part would result in a stop at that facility's front door, a fear my mother occasionally reinforced.

Aunt Agnes was my mother's youngest sister. Her union with Uncle Leo produced three children: Suzanne (Suzy), Janet (Jan), and Leo Jr. Leo was a few months older than me and we grew up as classmates at St. Mary of Sorrows School.

Grandma Schwab and the Haug family 1950s

My aunt, uncle, and cousins lived in the lower flat of the Johnson Street house and Uncle Leo's parents lived in the upper flat. I have no recollection of Grandma Haug, but Grandpa Haug was a part of my extended family during childhood and teenage years. I probably never had a real conversation with him, but I recall him as a happy man, quietly joining us for any gathering.

We always entered the house from the side door and took the short, side staircase up to the kitchen. The dining room was off the kitchen. You could reach the bedrooms and bathroom by following a hall to the right of the dining room.

Leo's bedroom was to the left and contained a variety of toys not found among mine, a fort with cowboys and Indians and a two-story tin garage. I relished the chance to play with these toys, usually reserved for boys.

We easily created our own entertainment. We inserted a paper sail attached to a wooden toothpick into a brand new bar of Ivory soap and took imaginary voyages as our vessels floated in the bathroom sink.

A built-in linen closet separated Leo's room from his parents'. Our house on Long Street included a similar closet, and I loved that it reminded me of that house on Johnson Street.

We never dared go into Aunt Agnes and Uncle Leo's bedroom, but peeking in, at least to a child's eye, it seemed huge.

Fr. Wangler, Leo, and me at our communion party on Johnson St.

Suzy and Jan's room was located at the end of the hall. During large family gatherings, all the guests' coats were tossed on their full-size bed. Occasionally, I pretended I was sleepy so I could lie on that bed and be lulled into a state of semi-sleep, a sort of limbo reached while clinging to the babble of adult voices as the sandman sprinkled me with sleeping dust.

When you returned to the dining room and walked toward the front of the house, you reached the living room. It was a comfortable gathering spot. Uncle Leo, a Buffalo police department patrolman, kept his gun high on a shelf in the closet off the living room. We never thought of examining it.

I am always amazed at what memories we retain from our childhood. That closet appears in my mind on one other occasion. Aunt Agnes opened the door and retrieved a paper doll set left over from my cousin, Janet's, birthday party. She gave it to me and I was thrilled. That set was probably the first paper doll I had ever received. I wasn't exactly sure who Patti Page was, but she kept me occupied for hours as I carefully cut out gowns and peddle-pushers to dress her up.

Instead of a porch, the Haugs had an enclosed front parlor. The outside was covered with bricks. My mom tried several times to get her driver's license. She gave up because of those bricks. She ran into them on an attempt at pulling into that driveway. Unfortunately, her nervous reaction overcame any future desire to drive.

Suzy and Jan were several years older than me, so I did not have much interaction with them growing up.

Once, though, I spent some time with my cousin Suzy watching her paint in the Johnson Street basement. I felt quite privileged spending time with her as her brush strokes captured the thoughts swirling in her mind onto the easel.

It also gave me a chance to look at a beautiful wooden dollhouse that resided in the basement. I am sure, in its prime, it might have sat in Suzy and Jan's bedroom. My small, tin dollhouse could not match the splendor of this abode for miniature dolls. Years later, this much loved toy continued to enjoy adventures created by the hands and imaginations of not only Suzy's children, but her grandchildren.

All the Haug cousins are creative individuals, artistic and

unique in many ways. Suzy has her painting and crafts; Jan has a spiritual awareness, a beautiful singing voice, and writing ability; Leo possesses musical and artistic talents.

Suzy worked for the Buffalo Federal Reserve Bank before marrying Tom Barrett. They have four children. Her oldest

Stacy and me

daughter, Stacy, lived in Indianapolis while we lived in Cincinnati. The relatively short distance between the two allowed us to visit often and we developed a close relationship that strengthened the bond I have with Stacy.

Over the years, Suzy and I have been lucky to spend time together. We visited her homes in San Jose, California; Kenneth Square, Pennsylvania; and

Jan and me

Baltimore, Maryland, and enjoyed many good times and memories.

Jan has remained in the Buffalo area. She was a teacher and was involved in the wholesale food industry for many years. She married young, had three daughters, divorced, and remarried. She lost her husband, Mike Frappier to cancer. Jan and I are now not only widows but dear friends. She has become a fan of my writing endeavors and a great critic, which highlights her own writing abilities.

Leo has worn many hats: pharmaceutical salesman, photographer, real estate agent, and bartender. New York City has been his home for more than thirty years. I admired his ambition to take a career leap at the age of fifty. He obtained his teaching degree and was a science teacher at the Bronx International High School before retiring. Our time together is limited, but always welcome.

As for Aunt Agnes and Uncle Leo, they lived full and happy lives together for over fifty years.

Aunt Agnes and Uncle Leo
(photo by cousin Leo Haug)

Uncle Leo passed away in 2001 at age 87. Although he worked for Morgan Linen and the Iroquois Brewing Company in Buffalo, his career as a Traffic and Accident Division patrolman in downtown Buffalo lasted 37 years. This line from his obituary captured his true spirit: "He was well known to everyone from corporate executives to street vendors." The electric smile and enthusiasm he shared with his family also was extended to those he met during his work hours. I remember Uncle Leo as a storyteller and singer who could entertain us all. He was a big man with a big heart.

Aunt Agnes physically left us shortly after her 90th birthday. Her spirit remains. Again, her obituary captured her essence: "She was one of those special people who lit up any room she walked into with warmth, kindness, and good cheer." She worked for the Dixie Hat Shop, which might explain her love of hats, almost her trademark. She also worked for the L.L. Berger Company, which no doubt cultivated her keen eye for a bargain.

To me, Aunt Agnes retained her beauty, both inside and out, as she aged. We should all age so gracefully. Her kindness in letting the girls and me live in her home following the tragedy on February 12, 2009, endeared her to me even more.

The summer of 2013, I drove down Best Street. When the big wall of the former Good Shepherd Home loomed before me, I glanced down Johnson Street. I was stunned to find only one house left standing on that once populated block.

I later learned that my cousins, Jan and Leo, also drove down Johnson and they confirmed that the one house remaining was theirs. It is a testimony to the Haug family's love. Jan feels my Uncle Leo's spirit protects that legacy.

I think that makes perfect sense.

Original Date 3/3/13

Aunt Maryann and the Uncles

My Uncle Nick was Clara and Nicholas Schwab's first child. My mother, Margie, arrived in 1915, followed by Maryann and Agnes. Of the siblings, Mom and Aunt Agnes resembled the Schwab lineage, and Aunt Maryann and Uncle Nick, represented the Hofmayr side of the family.

Aunt Maryann on her wedding day with sister-in-law Irene and my mom

Even as a young child, I remember Aunt Maryann always having white hair. There are pictures, though, that show it once was brown. She always wore glasses; I never saw her without them.

Like my husband Doug and me, Maryann met Norbert Becker at a local baseball game. They were married at St. Ann's Church in 1939 and had four children: Ann, Paul, Billy, and Peter. Their family lived at 243 Herman, just down the street from us on the East Side of Buffalo. We were a close-knit family. Everyone went to St. Mary of Sorrows Church, and all the children attended the

Aunt Maryann and Uncle Norbert

parish school together.

Most of the parties I recall from my early life took place at the Becker's home. There were gatherings following Christmas Midnight Mass and Holy Saturday Mass. Despite the fact that Aunt Maryann had attended Mass on those occasions, a full spread of food appeared, as if by magic, on her dining room table when we arrived after 1:00 a.m. There was also a gathering at their house on Memorial Day where my aunt and uncle's friend, George Raucher, cooked up a large vat of clam broth. He never shared his secret recipe with anyone.

Aunt Maryann was the picture of domesticity: canning, baking, sewing, and cleaning. My cousin, Ann, remembers

Aunt Maryann and Uncle Norbert with Ann, Paul and Peter

seeing her mom down on her hands and knees scrubbing floors. The family maintained a small plot of land in Colden, New York, where they grew crops to fill those canning jars.

Ann had a bedroom on the main floor of the house and the three boys shared a room in the attic that was especially cold in the winter.

The Becker kids: Billy, Paul, Ann & Peter

Becker kids all grown up: Ann, Paul, Billy & Peter

My sister, Barb, and I slept in Ann's bedroom when I was about seven years old. We were sent down the street to Aunt Maryann and Uncle Norbert's house during my mom's hysterectomy operation and recovery period. They kept us occupied, as did our 4 cousins. One night, I was allowed to walk with my cousin, Peter, to the corner drug store where we purchased a pint of ice cream. Uncle Norbert cut a generous square for each of us. This treat helped ease my concern about Mom . I also occupied my time hitting the keys of their old typewriter: *"Now is the time for all good men to come to the aid of their country"* an exercise that promised to increase typing speed, which no doubt was useful when I started my secretarial career many years later.

The woodshed behind their kitchen held a bookshelf where I often found myself leafing through "The Lives of the Saints." I stared in disbelief at one saint (whose name escapes me now) who had been beheaded by an unfriendly native. This horrible end,

*First day of school for cousins: (front) me & Barb;
(back) Billy, Ann, Paul & Peter*

illustrated in color, remained embedded in my mind long after I placed the volume back on the shelf.

I was learning that life was not all rosy; saints were beheaded and mothers needed operations. As a small child, I took comfort in the fact that at least Mom recovered, even if she had lost some body parts during her operation.

A fireman's uniform also hung in the Becker's woodshed. Although Uncle Norbert's short stature did not enable him to serve as a regular fireman, he was welcomed as an auxiliary

*Christmas celebration at the Beckers: Barb, Gayle
(Peter's wife), me, Leo, Jan, Mom, Aunt Agnes*

member of the department. He happily served in that capacity, directing traffic and assisting when and where he could during emergencies.

He also proudly served as a Knight of St. John. They described themselves as a men's semi-military organization, protecting and promoting the Catholic faith in their parishes. Aunt Maryann was in the Ladies Auxiliary. I was always impressed when I saw them in their uniforms.

Uncle Norbert also nurtured jade plants in the woodshed. His green thumb helped provide sturdy plants he shared with family members. Every time I see a jade plant, a vision of Uncle Norbert comes to my mind.

In elementary school, I lamented the fact that my rate of growth exceeded that of the boys in my class. I remedied this reality by slouching to hide my height. Uncle Norbert noticed my attempt to "shrink," and bellowed, "Shoulders back, chest out!" I cowered in fear and immediately pulled my shoulders back, and what little chest I did have, out.

Uncle Norbert did not want any wife of his working, a rather common attitude in the '50s and '60s. One day, though, Aunt Maryann donned her good blue coat, hat, and gloves and announced to her family that she was determined to find a job. She returned home having secured a secretarial position at the Wilson Warehouse. She later worked at the R. B. West Meat Packing Company.

Although I am sure Uncle Norbert protested this change in his life, he probably appreciated the extra money that Aunt Maryann's decision brought to the family's income, supplementing his salary from the Phoenix and Iroquois Breweries. Always looking for ways to provide for his family, my cousin Peter recalls that his dad collected newspapers from the neighbors to recycle for cash.

Our family joined in a big celebration commemorating Aunt Maryann's and Uncle Norbert's 25th wedding anniversary. Shortly after, their peaceful life was rocked when not once, but twice, their home was robbed while they were attending a novena at St. Mary of Sorrows. Some of the anniversary gifts were stolen, as was a strongbox hidden in a closet. To the best of my knowledge, no one was ever arrested for this invasion into their lives, although the box was discovered that spring, one block away from Herman Street. Their papers remained in the box, but any cash that had originally been tucked away for safekeeping was gone.

While in his thirties, Uncle Norbert suffered a heart attack. I never witnessed any signs that would have indicated he had heart issues after that event. But in 1969, another heart attack took his life. He and Aunt Maryann had just moved into a new home on Lisbon Avenuc.

For Aunt Maryann, another chapter in her life was about to begin. Dad's brother, Francis, was known to most people as Sid. Coincidentally, Sid married a woman also named Frances. I knew her as Aunt Sis. The couple had three children: Gretchen and twins, Noel and Neil. Gretchen was a bit older than her brothers, and when Dad went to Europe during World War II, she sent him letters.

Aunt Sis died suddenly when I was in elementary school. She had just picked up her grandson from Gretchen's house. She was discovered slumped over the wheel of her car as her grandson sat quietly in his seat.

The twins were in high school at the time, and their mother's death made them rebellious in their youth. They settled down, though, when they both served in the military.

Uncle Sid remained single for many years until he met one of his aunt's younger sisters. Ruth was a sweet woman and the mother of a daughter and son. Sid and Ruth married, and I became friends with Ruthi, her daughter. I enjoyed many happy times with their family. Eventually, Sid and Ruth separated and divorced.

After that, my mother decided to play matchmaker. Of course, Maryann and Sid already knew one another, but Aunt Maryann was reluctant to date anyone. Mom conveniently managed to get them together for a breakfast date.

Things progressed quickly, and my Uncle Sid married my Aunt Maryann in 1971. Mom and Dad were their attendants and the reception took place at The Old Orchard Inn in East Aurora. Aunt Maryann was a big fan of "Hawaii 5-0," so she was thrilled that they honeymooned in the 50th state.

Clarey, Sid, Aunt Maryann, Fr. Schroeder, and Margie

They settled into married life on Lisbon Avenue, and all their children embraced their new brothers and sisters. The blended families shared weekend getaways where there was much laughter, and the indulgence of drinking a Manhattan or two. It is evident by their smiles that Maryann and Sid were very happy.

They had fifteen wonderful years together that ended suddenly on Halloween, 1985, when Sid suffered a fatal heart attack.

Aunt Maryann and Uncle Sid

When we lived in Loveland, Ohio, my cousin Ann, her husband Kenny, and Aunt Maryann visited us. Alzheimer's was slowly creeping into Aunt Maryann's life, but as she had done in the past, she told me, "Grandma Schoenwetter raised some wonderful boys."

The disease did eventually rob Aunt Maryann's memories of her life with her two husbands. It was painful for her children to witness her slipping away from them. I recall my cousin, Ann, telling me how she had to visit her mom as a friend and not as a daughter. That eased the pain and stress Aunt Maryann felt when she was unable to remember her past.

Hopefully in the end, it brought her a bit of peace.

4/15/19

Uncle Nick

He had thrown down the gauntlet and my cousin, Leo, and I had accepted the challenge.

Uncle Nick, my mother's brother, would give $50 to the piano virtuoso who could master George Gershwin's "Rhapsody in Blue." My ability at the keyboard was limited, and despite an effort to master the piece, my interest and patience waned shortly after my efforts netted only a slow rendition of the first few bars. Leo, who seemed to be a natural musician, won the challenge, although I later

Uncle Nick as a young man

learned he never did receive the reward.

I was about 13 when this event occurred and that challenge was probably the first time my Uncle Nick had actually acknowledged my existence. He was basically an enigma to me.

The only son of Nicholas and Clara Schwab, Uncle Nick was considered a prominent Native American artist and historian.

His artistic endeavors began at 221 Herman Street in Buffalo and his first studio was established in the family garage. That space eventually was expanded into his home, and when he moved to the suburb of Orchard Park, my parents started their family in the house behind my Grandma Schwab's home. Perhaps some of his artistic vibes were passed on to me during the first 15 years of my life.

The brewery industry flowed through Schwab heritage. My great-uncle, Francis X. Schwab, was a brewery owner who became Mayor of Buffalo from 1922 to 1929. My grandfather, Nicholas Schwab, also worked for the breweries.

The brewery was an important element of my uncle's life too.

The Iroquoios Indian

As a youth, he cleaned and installed beer taps. His biggest legacy was the creation of the Iroquois Brewery's Indian head logo while he was their vice president in charge of advertising. The brewery's original logo, based on the Indian head penny, was replaced by his classic portrait of a Plains Indian. Products with his logo are still considered collector's items today, including a series of Native American portraits commissioned by the brewery.

Growing up, my mother told us stories about Uncle Nick and his long-time girlfriend, Suki. There were many pictures of his stylish girlfriend in the old black-and-white family photos. She was not fated to become Mrs. Nicholas Schwab though. On a business trip, Uncle Nick met and was smitten with my Aunt Marie who had a daughter named Pat, and their marriage quickly followed. Aunt Marie's daughter became my cousin and the family grew as they had three children: Penny, Michael, and Tina.

Their home in Orchard Park was a destination for many family outings. A weekend visit presented an entirely different way of life to us. At one point, Uncle Nick kept deer in a fenced corral attached to his garage. His property also included two ponds where we were allowed to take rides in a rowboat. Ornate wrought-iron furniture mixed with our canvas folding chairs and water flowed from the mouths of garden statues.

Uncle Nick welcomed his family, but he was not overly visible during these visits. Aunt Marie usually was not feeling well and was out of sight.

We were rarely allowed in the large house. I do recall a modern kitchen, but my favorite area was a storage space underneath the main staircase. When opened, it exposed a child's wonderland, complete with dolls, stuffed animals, and a small table ringed with chairs where creative and imaginative ideas could unfold. This paradise was my cousin Tina's retreat and I would have been content to play in this toyland during every visit. Tina was just a year older than me, but she was an "old soul" who left childish ways behind her long before I did. Unfortunately, the opportunity to share this hidden treasure did not arise often.

The addition of a German Ratskeller, a basement bar or restaurant, allowed more access to the house. Perhaps inspired by a ratskeller that served as a tasting room in the Iroquois Brewery, Uncle Nick created this cozy spot in his basement.

Large windows encircled his studio in the house, allowing natural light to illuminate the room. Although I knew that early in his career Uncle Nick followed the classic style of Norman Rockwell, I recently learned that he personally knew Rockwell. Apparently, the famous illustrator and painter spent time in my uncle's studio. When a separate building was constructed for a new studio, Uncle Nick recreated a structure similar to Rockwell's studio in Stockbridge, Massachusetts.

The American West came to life for those walking into one room in the new studio; life-size murals depicting Native American life were painted on the walls. One can only imagine the time and talent that my uncle devoted to that project. Sadly, the studio is gone now and what became of the murals remains a mystery.

Examples of Uncle Nick's Native American prints

Uncle Nick captured the rugged life of Native Americans in his portraits. Deep lines on faces indicated longevity and exposure to harsh weather elements. Native American culture and pageantry were illustrated by colorful, feathered and beaded garments, complemented by elaborate headdresses.

In his later years, Nick traveled out West and was inducted into the Cowboy Hall of Fame in recognition of his lifelong study and paintings of Native Americans.

With the demise of the Iroquois Brewery, Uncle Nick became a research and development director for an advertising firm in Florence, Kentucky, and made his home across the river in Cincinnati, Ohio.

There was no doubt in my mind that Uncle Nick was a talented painter, but he was a private person who appeared gruff and impersonal to me. His sisters would gush over and flatter him whenever he appeared, but I cannot recall him ever giving any expression of affection toward them.

Doug and I moved to the Cincinnati area in 1983 and I hoped we could connect with Uncle Nick and get to know him better. It was not to be; he died in December 1982 prior to our move. We did visit Aunt Marie and were able to enjoy many of Uncle Nick's paintings throughout her home.

Unbelievably, Doug had the opportunity to bid on several of Uncle Nick's paintings during an auction in Cincinnati. Many of the works, including a few in the Rockwell-style, were beyond our budget. Doug was able to purchase two: a small portrait

Uncle Nick's painting

depicting explorers on the brink of the Grand Canyon and a larger canvas of a bear attacking a Native American Brave. We placed the painting at the bottom of our open stairwell in the

Paxton-Guinea home, where a flood light illuminated this dark, both in color and subject matter, representation of life on the plains. Looking back, I realize that perhaps this was not the most upbeat art to expose to my small girls. When I questioned them recently about this, they assured me that the painting did not cause them any distress.

I also inherited an 8 x 10 charcoal portrait of my Great-grandmother Hofmayr sketched by Uncle Nick.

Unfortunately, both the Grand Canyon painting and the portrait were lost in the destruction of our Long Street home. The Native American canvas was in the garage and once again hangs in my home in East Aurora.

My desire to write about Uncle Nick was fueled by discussions with my cousin Paul Becker. About ten years older than me, Paul had opportunities to see a more personal side of Uncle Nick, and even spent time during the summer working at his Orchard Park property. One of Paul's goals was to explore the role Uncle Nick played in the Golden Age of breweries in Buffalo, an appropriate subject in modern times, when craft breweries are making a comeback.

I can see the influence Uncle Nick had on Paul. He also lived in Orchard Park and completed his own ratskeller. Standing in this new gathering spot, I could begin to see that perhaps Uncle Nick created his ratskeller to provide a place of comfort and camaraderie for his family and friends.

My sister sent me a random collection of letters my mother wrote to Barb while she lived in California. How coincidental it is that several of these pieces of correspondence referred to the death of Uncle Nick.

I felt badly about Brother Nick and the fact that I didn't see him this year, but Aunt Marie said every week that he looked like a shriveled old man more and more, and that it was best to remember him when he was well. I guess she was right. We will miss him, but do have a lot of happy memories from the past…he is at peace…and would not want to live with a stroke and being in a rest home which would have been next.

I do not recall Uncle Nick being a religious man. I recollect him complaining about length and ritual during my Grandma Schwab's funeral Mass. Reading my mother's description about his memorial service came as a surprise:

> *Uncle Nick's memorial Mass was beautiful. A good group of friends and relatives were there. Mike (Uncle Nick's son) brought a beautiful picture Uncle Nick drew last year of a communion chalice and host…it was so great. The priest placed it in front of the pulpit. Everyone admired it. Uncle Nick made frame and all…the organist played "Edelweiss." I cried and was very shook, and others were too. It was his favorite song. The priest had a beautiful homily too about him being an artist and all the memories he left behind in his paintings. It was very impressive.*

We humans all have complex personalities. We share the gift of ourselves with those we meet, but often expose only a few layers of that mystery. Although Uncle Nick did not present himself to me as an approachable and loving uncle, and gave me the illusion of being more a business man than family man, he continuously strived to perfect his talents and those of others. After all, wasn't he trying to make my cousin Leo and me reach deep within our abilities to perfect "Rhapsody in Blue?"

My cousin Paul's death in 2020 put an end to the quest to bring Uncle Nick's story to the forefront. But, working with a local publication about antiques (New York Pennsylvania Collector), Paul was able to locate one painting. My cousin, Michael, was given that piece from his father's past.

After a friend read one of my more poignant essays, he quoted

Ralph Waldo Emerson, "In art, the hand can never execute anything higher than the heart can imagine."

When my eyes absorb the beauty and detail Uncle Nick created with his brush strokes, I can now see that he revealed images held within his heart, and perhaps he was a far gentler man than the one I remember.

1/16/14, updated 8/18/19

Aunt Eleanor and Uncle Ed

As a child, my whole world revolved around the East Side of Buffalo, New York. Especially in the '50s and '60s, family, friends, church, school, and even my dad's job were within walking distance of our home at 221 Herman Street.

My Aunt Eleanor and Uncle Ed Schoenwetter, though, lived on Sheffield Street in South Buffalo, and that involved a short car ride. To me, that was an adventure. We passed the looming Republic Steel factories where white and black billowing plumes of smoke snaked their way into the sky. At times, we pinched our noses to escape the putrid smell that seeped into our car. There was one point near the plants where we crossed a bridge over water. For some reason, that crossing filled me with fear, and I was always relieved when we reached the other side without tumbling into the murky steel plant water.

South Buffalo was traditionally known for its large Irish-American community and Aunt Eleanor met that criteria. She was small in stature and had a feisty nature often associated with the Irish, especially those with the maiden name of O'Neill.

I always called him Uncle Ed, but many people called him Tom. His real name was Edward, and there is no clear explanation as to why he went by two different names. He was the oldest of the Schoenwetter brothers. I always remember him as being tall and thin with a wide smile on his face and a sparkle in his eyes.

The couple married in 1941 and had four children: Susie,

Aunt Eleanor and Uncle Ed's wedding

Tom, Maryann, and Michael.

As it seemed to be in all families during the '50s and '60s, the week after Christmas was a time to visit almost every relative you had. We made the rounds religiously, and of course that included a trip to South Buffalo. There were also parties where we celebrated c o m m u n i o n s, graduations, and engagements.

Aunt Eleanor's Irish nieces were often present at these gatherings. As a young, rather Plain Jane-type of girl myself, I was so envious of these beautiful teens with red hair.

Although they lived in South Buffalo, Uncle Ed was still active in his childhood parish, St. Ann's on Broadway.

I remember he sometimes stopped over at our house after attending a weekday Mass at St. Ann's. He always brought sweets from one of the local bakeries that dotted the neighborhood, including long doughnuts spread with a sweet frosting and sprinkled with almonds or pecans.

I referred to my aunt as being feisty, but my cousin, Maryann, was surprised when I used that adjective to describe her mom. "She was only feisty when it came to protecting Susie."

Susie was born with Down syndrome. I wondered if she was subjected to the bullying that is so common in today's world. I have learned that nothing was further from the truth. Susie

Uncle Ed and Susie as a toddler

ruled her turf and the neighborhood kids gathered on the Schoenwetter's front porch on many a summer day. They knew Susie shared her collection of coloring books, crayons, and comic books.

As you walked into their house, you entered a living room with a fireplace. The shelves around that fireplace were filled with Susie's collection of treasured items. There was a specific place for each thing, and she could always tell if someone had moved something and replaced it in the incorrect spot.

I recall that when Doug and I visited the family with our two-year-old daughter, Kim, Susie carefully selected a coloring book for Kim. She had strict control over her possessions, but she was always willing to share.

There was a grocery store on the corner of Sheffield and South Park Avenues. Aunt Eleanor often gave Maryann and Tom a dime to purchase new comic books for Susie. "She didn't care which ones we chose," Maryann told me. She couldn't read them, but she loved flipping through them. The brilliant colors swirling on those pages must have danced before her eyes.

There is some regret in the family that those comics were not saved over the years. Old copies of "Archie," "Little Lulu,"

"Nancy," or "Superman" might be worth money these days.

Susie could always be spotted with a bottle of Pepsi and a box of Kleenex. Those were definitely two of her trademark accessories.

She always used a rainbow of colors when she filled her coloring books, but after Aunt Eleanor died in 1985, Susie only used black crayons. It seemed to be her way of expressing her grief. She did venture out from her home, attending classes and events through People, Inc. over the years.

Uncle Ed continued to lovingly care for Susie as long as he was able. Maryann and Tom welcomed Susie into their homes

Uncle Ed and Susie

until she was placed in a nursing home due to failing health. By then, Susie would not have even realized where she was. She died at the age of fifty-five, which is remarkable for a Down syndrome baby born in the '40s. In the '80s, the average lifespan of a person with Down syndrome was only 25 years. Today, the average is approximately 60 years.

Her sister and brothers caring for Susie continued the lessons the siblings had learned from their parents. Taking care of loved ones was an important and natural part of life for my aunt and uncle.

When my Grandpa Otto and Grandma Mary Schoenwetter sold their home at 300 Sherman Street in Buffalo, their three sons took turns caring for their parents. I recall our dining room being transformed into a bedroom for them, but my mother's nerves did not allow that scenario to last for too long.

Aunt Eleanor and Uncle Ed took on most of the responsibility for their care. They gave up their bedroom on Sheffield and added a folding bed in a front parlor for themselves. Their care of my grandparents lasted for several years, until my grandparents were admitted to the Erie County Wende Nursing Facility.

Grandpa Otto had long frequented the neighborhood taverns near the Sherman Street homestead. He was pleased to find a tavern at the end of Sheffield and went down for one beer in the late afternoon. My cousins often had to go and bring him home for supper. It wasn't because he would drink too much, it was just that his memory was fading, and he would forget to go home.

In their later years, my dad and mom did many social activities with Mom's sisters and their husbands. That also included my Uncle Sid Schoenwetter. Although Uncle Ed probably was invited to some events, my cousin, Tom, told me that Uncle Ed felt badly about not being invited to more of the couples' gatherings. That does make me sad, and as a widow now myself, I can understand the feelings that might have crossed his mind at that time.

Doug and I moved to the Cincinnati area in 1983. My mother kept us up to date on our cousins. She and Aunt Eleanor were very close. After Aunt Eleanor's death, and Mom's struggle with OCD, we lost our main connection with the Schoenwetter cousins.

Their families continued to grow. Maryann had two children, Tom had four, and Michael one.

Moving back to Buffalo in 1998, I again became a part of that side of my family. I attended showers, weddings, church events and lunches, and they were invited to our home.

They all supported us after the crash of Flight 3407. In particular, my cousin Michael and his wife, Marty, attended Doug's memorials and wake. In the months that followed, they eased me back into a social life by inviting me to dinners and Shakespeare in the Park productions. I continue to be thankful to them for their support at that sad time in my life.

It's true that my relationships with my South Buffalo cousins were not as close as my bond with the East Side cousins, but I am grateful that despite that fact, we remain connected today.

In a sense, they broadened my world. I learned there was more to life than what I experienced in my childhood neighborhood. There was a big world waiting for me to explore.

1/6/14

Holy Week

"Oh sacred head surrounded by crown of piercing thorns…"

When the congregation lifts their voices during the Lenten season, I am transported back in time. I see myself as an eight-year-old sitting in a pew at St. Mary of Sorrows church on Genesee Street, on the East Side of Buffalo…

Above the altar, there is a huge mural depicting saints. I am certain that they watch over antsy children at Mass, which perhaps includes me, due to my wavering attention span during services.

My family will be attending services all through Holy Week. On Holy Thursday after Mass, we will visit seven churches.

Every neighborhood seems to have a Catholic Church. It takes a while to get to the churches, so we will have to drive to them. Mom doesn't know how to drive, so Dad will be at the wheel. When I grow up, I am going to learn how to drive a car.

We will definitely visit St. Ann's on Broadway where Dad was an altar boy. I wonder if some little girl had a crush on him when he was little. I have crushes on several of the altar boys.

At the end of Holy Thursday Mass, everything will be taken off the altar, and all the crosses will be covered with purple fabric.

We will be staying a bit to pray and then go to the other churches, which stay open way past my bedtime.

On Good Friday we will go to another service, which will remind us of the visit to Gethsemane. I have an actual picture of Jesus' time there. My Grandpa Schwab died before I was born, but I have one of his Mass cards. A picture of Jesus at Gethsemane is on the front of that card.

I like when the priest walks the covered crucifix down the aisle of the church on Good Friday. He stops three times and uncovers a small part of the cross each time. Then, we get to go up to the altar and kiss the cross. I like to kiss Jesus' feet.

On Holy Saturday, there will be an evening service that includes midnight Mass. I am not allowed to go to that until I get older. Part of that service includes the baptism of people who are becoming new members of the Catholic Church.

One year, my cousin's fiancée was a candidate. I remember Mom telling me how beautiful she looked as the blessed water flowed down her long platinum hair.

I bid farewell to this flashback from my youth, as another familiar hymn fills the church.

Faith is tough at times, and I still have some doubts about religion. As a child, I figured everything would be easier to understand as I got older. That is not necessarily true for me. But, despite doubts that occasionally arise, that basic belief I had as a child still resides in me. The important thing for me is the feeling of comfort I receive sticking to familiar traditions. No matter how much my life changes, the repetition of Catholic Church practices peacefully soothes me.

That must count for something.

3/27/18

St. Mary of Sorrows

Good Friday

I found myself in a traffic jam inside the Broadway Market in Buffalo.

This stagnant human cavalcade stood amid colorful vegetables, lush fruits, tempting baked goods, and assorted poultry and meats.

What else could one expect on Good Friday, the busiest day of the year for the market?

Crowd at the Broadway Market

Small children received a bird's-eye view of the scene while perched on their fathers' shoulders. Those in the middle of the pack, myself included, realized the opportunity to break free to the outside track and actually purchase Famous Horseradish, Weber's Mustard, Lewandowski's Produce, or Pierogies By Paula was quite impossible.

My current pause in movement did give me time to reflect on this historic market. Immigrants setting foot on our fair land made their way to the industrial and farming opportunities available in Buffalo. They wished to preserve their Eastern European traditions and heritages and continue their Old World customs. The Broadway Market opened in 1888 and family-owned-and-operated businesses continue to be passed from generation to generation, providing customers with some of Buffalo's best loved foods.

There was finally movement in the crowd and I inched my way through the market. Sights, sounds, and smells heightened my whole experience.

Vibrant colors met my eyes: pastel hues were evident around every corner as "Peep" heads emerged from their chocolate-encased bodies, and festive bows were tied around chocolate bunnies and lambs nestled among mounds of colored jelly beans and foil-wrapped eggs. Ukrainian Easter eggs, with their intricate designs, caught the attention of many shoppers. Tomatoes in various shades of orange and red appeared to have been buffed to achieve a brilliant shine.

An organ grinder was tucked in a corner cranking out tunes. A straw hat on

Chocolate Peeps and Tomatoes

his head, suspenders, and a bow tie complemented his outfit. Although his monkey sidekick was mechanical, the total package made me smile.

A middle-aged musical troupe performed on a stage in the middle of overflowing booths, entertaining the crowds flocking around them. The process of buying and selling periodically stopped as people hummed tunes and tapped their feet to the beat of the music.

The whiff of freshly baked bread almost made me salivate in anticipation of sinking teeth into crunchy crusts encasing soft white, wheat, or rye.

I wanted to find a seat on a silver stool at the diner counter and enjoy a morning treat of bacon and eggs. A line of others with the same idea wrapped around the corner; that experience would have to wait for another time.

It was difficult for me to walk by the booths filled with chocolate goodies waiting to be picked up by the Easter Bunny to fill so many empty baskets. Catholic tradition calls for limited food consumption on Good Friday, so I could only savor the delicious smells.

I grew up on Herman Street, about a mile or so from the Broadway Market. The area around the market was a bustling retail destination back then. As I emerged from the market this Good Friday, it was hard for me to realize that the Broadway-Fillmore district I now encountered was a far cry from its glory days. Of course, much has changed in over 50 years. Population has declined, malls captured the attention of potential customers, and once busy stores turned into dilapidated buildings and were eventually torn down. Empty lots now dot the landscape and graffiti expresses the emotions of those living in the once proud Polish and German neighborhoods.

As a child, neither I nor my parents spent much time at the Broadway Market itself, but the vicinity surrounding the market was a popular destination for us kids. It took us about 20 minutes to walk there, but there were always things to catch our attention along the way.

One path found us walking down either Genesee or Sycamore Streets, turning right on Fillmore Avenue. There was a lot to see along that wide avenue. An array of photos was displayed in the window of the Fox Lee Dance Studio. I imagined how exciting it would be to take dance lessons, wear colorful costumes, and have your picture in a window for all to see. It was definitely a luxury my family could not afford. Little girls' eyes always lit up while passing the various bridal shops on Fillmore: Clara Milas, Ceils, and Frances Bridal showcased the latest wedding fashions in their large window displays.

We often walked directly down Herman Street and turned left onto Broadway. One of the main stops along that route was Liberty Shoes. I do not recall ever buying shoes, but we did buy our nylons there. The nylons were not openly displayed. Customers had to approach a long counter and experienced salesladies produced slim boxes of nylons in various shades. Of course, they wore gloves to avoid a snag in the fine material. If you were lucky, you purchased the last pair in the box, which meant you got both the nylons and the box.

The invention of pantyhose liberated ladies from nylons and the need for dreaded garters. Those tiny garter hooks easily broke and left the wearer afraid to move, lest the remaining hooks also break and risk the embarrassment of nylons slipping down your legs and sagging around your ankles.

The intersection of Broadway and Fillmore was the official start of the shopping district. We had our choice of two big department stores: Sattler's and Kobackers. Sattler's was the most popular destination. Their catchy advertising radio and television tune of "998 Broadway in Buffalo, 998 Broadway" was easy to remember.

I can still recall making some special purchases in those stores. Finding myself in possession of considerable cash for a

Old Sattler's ad

seven-year-old following my Communion party, I decided to treat my family members. I believe I bought something for everyone, but can only remember one purchase in the two big shopping bags I carried home: a Corning glass juice set that included a pitcher and four small glasses. Can you imagine letting a seven-year-old walk that distance alone in this day and age? I grew up in a much safer era that allowed kids considerable freedom.

When I graduated from eighth grade, again in possession of additional cash, a trip to Kobackers "netted" me my first tennis racket. It actually did not get much use until I began to work at National Gypsum in 1969 and my boss gave me lessons.

I purchased many of my first record albums at Sattler's. I rushed there whenever a new Beatles album was released. I can still see that department on the first floor next to the escalators with a soft-serve ice cream stand by the wall.

I will now illustrate what a "dorky" teenager I was. My friend, Cindy, and I once went to Sattler's to see the King Cousins. *The King Family Show* aired on ABC in the late 1960s and included the very good-looking children of the King Sisters, a popular singing group during the big-band era of the '40s and '50s. Cindy and I were very disappointed that our favorite "cousins" were not available to sign autographs that day. We were instead greeted by unknown cousins.

Woolworths and Neisser's were both large 5 & 10 cent stores. We spent considerable time at Neisser's luncheon counter, enjoying chocolate milkshakes, mixed and served in large silver blender cups, enough for several glasses of the frosty delight. No thick consistency for me, I liked mine thin and slippery as silk.

These 5 & 10 cent stores provided many tropical fish for my dad's tank, and a bright yellow canary which sang lovely tunes until we placed a mirror in its cage. Apparently, the shock of seeing its reflection caused him to never sing again. We later learned that mirrors were fine for parakeets, but not canaries. Ironically, our canary was named "Lucky."

It had been years since I had visited the Broadway area. Now in 2013, I stood on Broadway contemplating my youth, and decided to walk a few blocks to Fillmore Avenue. I wanted to retrace steps I would have taken so long ago. Was the library building still standing on Fillmore?

I loved that library. The second floor was completely devoted to children's books. "Graduation" to the first floor adult section was a big step. Somehow, I always felt a sense of pride presenting my carefully chosen books and library card to the librarian. I watched as she placed the card, tucked into the back pocket of each book, into a large machine to record my lending transaction and stamped a due date on the card.

The walk down to the library building was considerably longer than I remembered, and took me almost to Paderewski Drive (named for the pianist, composer, and political spokesman for Polish nationalism). I was happy to see the stone edifice continued to stand tall, but there were no signs to indicate its current purpose.

The avenue was desolate, and walking back to Broadway, I questioned the safety of undertaking this journey on my own.

I walked a bit faster and saw the old army recruiting building, along with a small attached office space once the home of a post office.

One of the original McDonald's restaurants was on Fillmore Avenue. Its arrival was quite a coup for the district. My friends and I occasionally scraped together enough cash for a hamburger, fries, and milkshake (not as good as Neisser's). That familiar building remains, but now is a Cricket phone store.

Norban's, described itself as a "self-service department store" and was also on Fillmore. Long rows of clothing in every shape and size greeted customers. We slipped on potential purchases over our clothes. I do not believe they had fitting rooms. It remains but a memory now.

Arriving back at my SUV, I could not resist the urge to take a drive down to Herman Street. There were so many empty lots on our block, including my first home, 221 Herman. My memory conjured up a vision of my grandmother's small home at the front of the lot with space for two automobiles next to the house. The white picket fence once more opened up to a grassy area and I pictured our green and white house at the back of the property. The old ship continued to sail at the top of an awning shading the dining room window.

I have no idea why the ship was there. I like to imagine, though, that it symbolized new courses being charted, and the hope by residents of 221 Herman that they would experience smooth sailing toward a safe harbor during their voyages.

I noticed the driveway entrance was still visible, but then realized that there were actually two driveways remaining. That empty space included not only our lot, but that of our neighbors, the Goettelmans. Their lot included a narrow house with three apartments and a small house in the back. Did all those buildings really fit in that space?

Who were some of our other neighbors? Henrietta Moeller lived next door. I do not believe she ever married and therefore

Current lots of 221 and 219 Herman. Grandma's and our home were on the left.

would have been considered "an old maid" back then, not a flattering term. Other names that entered my mind included the Felschows, Bostwicks, Barones, and Tryons. What became of them all?

Before heading home, I turned right on Genesee Street past empty lots that once housed the Liberty Bank, Weber's Furniture, and a large housing unit referred to as the "tenement," an apartment building filled with immigrant families, none of which I ever knew.

It gave me comfort that, in spite of all the emptiness in the old neighborhood, our church, St. Mary of Sorrows is still a constant (although it has been transformed into a Community Education Center), as is the parish elementary school.

I had not planned on making a pilgrimage to my childhood home that day. It was a spur-of-the-moment decision, and really did make for a very "good" Friday.

7/15/13

Family Travels

On a bus tour of Wyoming County, New York, with members of my writing group, we made our way into the cottage area of Java Lake. I had to smile. The last time I was down this road I was about seven years old. Mom, Dad, my sister Barbara, and I were going to spend a week at the lake.

Unlike families today who seem to travel great distances during vacations, in the 1950s our family vacations usually consisted of day trips to Niagara Falls or Crystal Beach, along with the summer luxury of going to the Glen Park Amusement Park on our birthdays. A week at a lake was quite a treat.

Grampa Schoenwetter with his cousins John and Taya and Grandma Schoenwetter

Barb, right, and me at Java Lake

The cottage belonged to my grandfather's cousin, Taya, and her husband, John. The old Chevy climbed a steep hill to the cottage. I remember little about the inside, but recall a glider in the backyard that my sister and I enjoyed.

A family photo showed us sitting on the glider in our shorts sets, identical except for color: one red, one blue. Although we were three years apart, my mother seemed to enjoy dressing us in matching outfits. Perhaps she had a secret longing for twins. Our bowl-cut haircuts in that photo bore a strong resemblance to the "Buster Brown" shoe trademark of the '50s.

We could easily walk down the hill to the lake, swim caps perched on our heads, carrying our beach towels covered with penguins (certainly an odd symbol for a beach towel). My beach towel remained a constant in my life, but was another casualty of the crash. Like my parents, neither my sister nor I knew how to swim. Their fear of the water was transferred to us. We only waded in. I have a memory of somehow getting into water over my head once and my sister pulling me up by my swim cap. The trip up the hill took a bit more effort and I disliked walking barefoot on the stones. My sister reminded me that, at one point, our father helped push our mother up the hill.

I can't remember a single meal we ate during that stay or how we kept ourselves occupied. I do remember assembling cut-out crafts, which we had excitedly obtained free from a cereal box promotion.

Dad helping Mom up the hill

It must have taken all the strength my mother could muster to manage a week of cottage life. She was a true city girl. This lifestyle probably didn't come easily to her, but she prevailed.

The next stop on our bus tour brought us to a dairy farm and I was transported back to my cousin's farm in Langford.

One of my family's day trips often included a ride out to the country. Aunt Mary was my Grandmother Schwab's sister. She had settled on a dairy farm in Langford with Uncle Louie. He passed away before I was born, but in the '50s Aunt Mary was still the strong leader of her family and busy canning, cooking, and making sure the farm was in good running order. After her death, the farm was inherited by her son, John, and his wife,

Dad helping Mom up the hill

Aunt Mary and Mom (above); Dad, Uncle Leo, and John

Elaine. Their two children, Johnny and Charlene, were close in age to my sister and me.

Hot summer days seemed cooler at the farm, which was

perched atop a hill and reached by ascending a long, steep driveway. There was always something to do. We took long walks in the fields, sliding under barbed-wire fences. It seemed I had an uncanny ability to step into any muddy hole or fresh cow manure we came across. We weren't able to enter the barn often, unless John allowed it. We did, however, get to visit with the cows, chickens, or cats who resided there. If the weather prevented our walks, we occupied ourselves playing school or flipping through the Sears catalogs.

Many family reunions took place at the farm. We were also allowed to bring along friends and

Thanksgiving, early 1960s:
Barb, Johnny, Charlene, and me

boyfriends. I remember one of my cousin Leo's friends, Wally, romping along the hills with a towel on his head singing, "The Hills Are Alive" as he pretended to be Maria from "The Sound of Music."

We attended church dinners with the country cousins in Langford. Nothing beat the homemade pies that ended the meals.

When my sister and I first had our learner's permits, we were allowed to add the experience of country driving to our skills. Our cousins joked and feigned fear as we pulled up or down the farm hill. We became adept at driving on the hills and pushing the floor button to activate the "brights" at night.

Generation after generation found the farm a happy retreat from our lives in the city. The hard life took its toll on cousin John, though. We were living in Ohio, but on one trip back to Buffalo, Doug and I decided to take the girls to the farm. He wasn't the rugged John I remembered as a girl, but a man struggling to breath with an oxygen tank close by. He still had his quick sense of humor, though, and commented to the girls that their mother always seemed to get into trouble on those country walks.

The girls were delighted to check out the barn, especially as a new litter of kittens had recently arrived. When we were ready to leave, Jill tried to smuggle a tiny, white kitten into the car. Luckily, the little castaway was discovered and returned to its brothers and sisters in the barn.

The visit meant so much to John and it was difficult to see the tears in his eyes as we left. I am thankful we had the chance to see him that one last time.

Eventually, the economy and hard work involved in running a farm resulted in the sale of the property. I visited with Johnny and his mother, Elaine, when they moved to Springville, New York. It was so strange to pull up to their apartment building instead of driving up a country hill to their farm house. They were the same down-to-earth people that I remembered, though. Yes, older, but when I listened to their voices, I could see them as they were in

Langford, welcoming us for a day in the country.

One day, I retraced the route of those family visits to the farm. Finding the old homestead, I was disappointed to see how the farmhouse had been painted an aqua-blue and the large front porch had been completely enclosed. The barn looked the same and several outbuildings had been added to the property. Despite the disappointment I felt in the changes, it was comforting for me to see that it remained an active farm.

I was thankful that the bus tour had given me a trip back to good times.

5/20/21, updated 8/17/21

An Overdue Visit

Following the premature birth of my little granddaughter, Lydia, in 2012, I traveled quite a bit on route 33, better known to Buffalonians as the Kensington Expressway, to visit her at Sisters Hospital in Buffalo.

Pine Ridge Road marks the city line between Buffalo and the suburb of Cheektowaga. When we were teenagers living on Hagen Street, Pine Ridge was our limit when it came to riding our bikes. It marked the spot where we turned around and headed back home.

The Pine Ridge exit reminded me that it had been some time since I had visited my parents' grave. I decided to postpone my journey home one day and veered to the right.

As kids, we were familiar with the cemeteries on Pine Ridge. Growing up, we made regular pilgrimages to visit deceased relatives. The majority of these ancestors resided in the German-American Cemetery. My parents faithfully maintained flowers at the Schwab and Schoenwetter grandparents' graves.

We often stopped at my great-grandparent's, the Hofmayr's, graves. They were Grandma Schwab's parents. Great-grandpa Hofmayr had designed the bleeding heart on their headstone. My mother was certain that the artistic talent in the family, especially that of my Uncle Nick, who worked in advertising for the Iroquois Brewery, was inherited from Great-grandpa Hofmayr.

Their gravesite was not far from my Schoenwetter grandparents' resting place. A small, flat stone was also near them. Dad told us two of his infant brothers were buried there. Once Doug and I visited the grave and had to free that stone from the grass that obstructed it from view.

"It will only get lost in the grass again," Doug reasoned, "so why don't we just take it for our garden?" I vetoed the idea, as that proposal seemed a bit sacrilegious to me.

In addition to the German-American Cemetery, we also stopped at the Mount Calvary Cemetery. My mother's first husband, Chuck, was laid to rest there. They were married only a few years when he died from a brain tumor. His relationship with my mother caused me some concern when I was a small child. I spent time trying to figure out how his existence would play out in heaven. Who would my mother love more? Surely, my dad would hold the more important role.

Once, we lingered in the Mount Calvary Cemetery after dusk. We had not heeded the entrance sign that explicitly warned that the cemetery closed at dusk and found our departure blocked by the locked gate. Since I was not a big fan of the cemetery treks, this development sent panic coursing through my veins. Would we have to sleep in our car, or would we have to find some mausoleum where we would huddle together in fear of spirits? A caretaker quickly came to our aid, and squelched any unwanted adventure.

On this long overdue visit, I located the Schwab-Schoenwetter gravesite without any difficulty. I turned into the main entrance, bore left at the roundabout, and found the stone right by the road. It seems interesting to me that Grandma Schwab's grave is in front of the stone and my parents rest behind, the mirror image of their homes on Herman Street.

I am sure that my lack of visiting my parents' gravesite does not please my mother. I really should make more of an effort just to make her happy. At least today, I had fulfilled my duty. I apologized for not visiting sooner, discussed the amazing fact that now I was a grandmother, and ended with a prayer that, "their souls and all the souls of the faithfully departed rest in peace."

Meandering up and down the roads, I was unable to locate my Schoenwetter grandparents' grave. I recall seeing some prayer cards retrieved from the Long Street site. If I can just remember where I put them, hopefully they will provide a clue.

I was reminded of the cemetery's significance in Barbara's and my experiences as novice drivers. If we could handle navigating the narrow cemetery roads without knocking down any tombstones, we could handle the city streets.

For my parents' generation, visiting gravesites of loved ones was a given, a duty they were glad to fulfill. I do not think I am an exception when it comes to my lackadaisical approach. Life is fast-paced for my generation. Cemetery visits are not high on our list of priorities. My parents always remain in my heart and are included in my prayers. I just do not feel the necessity to make that trip to the cemetery. Then again, perhaps all those visits to cemeteries as a child burned me out.

Doug's remains are in the Clarence Fillmore Cemetery, and I make a point of visiting on special occasions: our wedding anniversary, his birthday, the anniversary of the crash, and just when I need an additional boost. I have arranged to have a pot of geraniums blooming there throughout the summer.

My girls do visit their dad's grave from time to time. They lovingly left flowers at the site following their weddings.

Shortly after the crash, my daughter Jill posted a haunting picture she had taken at her dad's grave. She sat with her back resting on the stone, and the pain etched on her face broke my heart.

How touched I was one day, shortly after Kim and Lori gave us the news that they were both pregnant, when Jill mentioned she had stopped at the cemetery. "I told Dad about the babies," she softly told me, and again my heart ached.

Directly behind Doug is the grave of the husband of a woman from the Clarence Women's Club. She told me that she and her family bring chairs and stay awhile to visit. She feels it helps her grandchildren remember their grandfather. Sorry Doug, there is no way I would consider that. I can think of better ways to keep your memory alive with our grandchildren.

When he was 6, my grandson Rowan made a bucket list of things he wanted to do when he visited Buffalo. Visiting Papa's grave had made his list. Lori and Chris had discussed Doug's passing with their boys, and so we went to the gravesite. They stood at the stone and pointed out the puzzle pieces depicting things Papa enjoyed that were represented by a bat, hockey stick, and hammer. Before we left, Rowan asked if they were allowed to kiss the stone. Lori suggested that, since the stone might be dirty, perhaps he could blow a kiss toward it. That little guy kissed his hand and then, ever so slowly and tenderly, passed his hand over the stone, causing my eyes to well with tears.

Dusk was approaching that day back in 2012 when I visited Pine Ridge, and I did not want to repeat our episode of being locked in the cemetery. Of course, now almost all the wrought iron fencing that rimmed the cemeteries has been removed. I smiled as it occurred to me that today's open living space in homes even extends to current cemetery trends. Besides, if the remaining gate was locked, I could easily just step out to the road and call someone on my cell phone for assistance.

I knew, just like I did on those bike rides to Pine Ridge long ago, it was time to head home.

9/6/12, updated 11/20

School Days and Teenage Years

"You're off to great places. Today is your day!
Your mountain is waiting,
So get on your way!"

~ Dr. Suess

St. Mary of Sorrows (SMS)

I had better write them down, these snippets of memory that flash through my mind.

Awaking at 2:30 in the morning, I suddenly seem to be reminiscing about my days as a schoolgirl during the '50s and '60s at St. Mary of Sorrows School, located on Rich Street near Genesee on the East Side of Buffalo. What brought this on? Had I been dreaming of the old neighborhood?

St. Mary of Sorrows School

There was never any debate regarding what to wear to school. We donned blue jumpers and white short-sleeve blouses every day. Blue beanies were also necessary for church, until chapel veils, small circles of lace placed on your head, became fashionable.

The letters SMS were sewn onto the uniforms. Initials seemed to be a reoccurring theme at the school. No doubt, many students monogrammed JMJ in an upper corner of their papers imploring Jesus, Mary, and Joseph for guidance in picking the correct answers on a test, or writing an essay that would result in an A+.

My sister Barbara and I walked the three blocks to and from school.

The old A&P sat on the corner of Herman and Genesee. It was fun to watch deliveries slide down to the basement of the grocery store on a ladder device that lookcd like it was wearing roller skate wheels. We hopped over it and continued on our way.

We checked out the windows at the florist shop, and I would check if the statue of Theresa, the Little Flower, still stood among the floral displays. Hopefully, it would remain there until I saved enough allowance to buy it. I found it amazing that this saint joined a convent as a teenager at just 15.

Zwack's Delicatessen was directly across from the church on Genesee. We peered through the glass on the display cases that held tasty penny candy, including wax lips and bottles filled with sugary liquid. A nickel or dime netted a small brown bag full of treats. We were constantly on the alert for any new packs of Beatles cards that arrived, first printed in black and white and later in color. I hoped there would be no doubles of cards already in my collection in these new packs. Squeeze cups of sherbet were also a good buy for a nickel. On rare occasions, I bought a cupcake-like confectionary that had a denser consistency than your average cupcake, and actually looked more like a muffin top drizzled with thin frosting. Oh, how I could go for one of those right now.

During the winter months, we had to walk down to the school basement where messy boots (zip-ups trimmed in fur) had to be removed before heading to our classrooms. Surely defying today's safety codes, an incinerator seemed readily available for anyone's use.

As I reflect on that basement, memories silently drift through my mind. Once I had concealed myself behind one of the pillars and entertained my fellow classmates with a hand puppet crafted from an old sock, while singing an updated version of "The Twelve Days of Christmas." Kids always hoped to win the big door prize, perhaps a new transistor radio, at our yearly school bazaar held in the basement. We took turns tossing a circular ring at wooden sticks. If the ring slipped over the stick, we were able to take the stick home with us. Our parents usually took the stick away from us, as they feared we would poke someone in the eye with it. Members of the parish were invited to view "The Life of Christ," shown as a serial during Lent. Girl Scout Christmas parties allowed us to visit Santa on the basement stage. One year Santa, who I knew was my friend's father, told me "Good things come in small packages," as he handed me a cool, and very grown-up, orange pen and pad set.

The first floor of the school housed kindergarten through third grade and included one fifth grade. The remaining grades were housed upstairs. There was no official gym. Physical education classes, just called "gym" back in those days, were held outside or in the basement, with lunch tables removed. Originally, there was a separate building next to the school with bowling alleys and space for gym class or Girl Scout meetings. That building was demolished following a fire in the late '50s and replaced with a parking lot. About the only things I remember about gym class are playing dodge ball and having hands checked to see if we were biting our nails.

Throughout my elementary days, I had boyfriends. Let me rephrase that. I had "crushes" on boys who were unattainable, but I still swooned over them. I was sure Robert would gallantly retrieve my dropped handkerchief in first grade. Apparently, gallantry was dead and my handkerchief remained on the floor. Paul seemed to be interested in me, and we even talked. That was nipped in the bud when he moved out of town. Gary, a Ricky Nelson look-alike, was the boy for me as a pre-teen. He was cousin Leo's friend, but unfortunately, he liked two of my girlfriends instead. Interestingly, a few years ago I discovered that Gary was married to one of the secretaries in the Clarence School District where I used to work.

Schwab cousins Leo and Peter attended SMS. Leo and I always seemed to be in the same classroom. One day I noticed him looking at me. I asked him, "What are you looking at?" He replied that my hair looked golden with the sun shining through it. Even though he was just a cousin and not one of the boys I liked, that remembered remark still makes me smile today.

Peter was in my sister's class and one of the older boys who had the distinction of being allowed to deliver the cartons of milk to classrooms each morning. Whenever we saw each other in the hallways, Peter would say, "Hey, Skinny," to which I'd reply, "Minnie!" That was me, thin as a rail, Skinny Minnie.

Several of my old report cards have resurfaced. It is interesting to see what "Character Traits" we were graded on at school: obedience, cooperation, orderliness, self-control, attention, and protection of property. My grades averaged in the high eighties to mid-nineties. It appears that my worst year was grade one, where I received several Cs, including one in English. Hey, I ended up being a writer, so deal with that!

I can remember most of my teachers' names.

I had watched my sister go off to school for 3 years and was quite happy to finally be following in her footsteps. Mrs. F was my kindergarten teacher. She was young, and had flaming red hair, and as I was soon to learn, a temper to match. One morning, after drinking my warm carton of milk, despite a mad dash to

First day of Kindergarten, 1956

the restroom, I got sick at the front of the classroom. I received a very loud, angry reprimand.

My fear of getting sick again and making people angry stayed with me for years. Forget about eating breakfast in the morning or picking up another carton of milk. Forget about staying in Girl Scouts and attempt camping. I bowed out of some school outings because of that fear, and when I did attempt to break the fear habit and actually go on trips, nausea was always a close companion.

How much of my childhood was lost because of one morning in kindergarten?

I probably needed some psychological help, but I never did talk to my parents about my fear. I kept my thoughts and feelings locked up inside of me.

It is sad to think that one person's actions toward someone who was only 5 years old could have such a lasting effect. It is also sad to think that I continued to let that action cause such distress. Until I met my husband, Doug, I still struggled with that fear.

Sister Hortence was my first grade teacher, although according to my report card, she was replaced by Sister Athanasia. Sister Hortense taught us to sing "Ave Marie," which I proudly sang to my Grandma Schoenwetter on a visit to the Erie County Nursing Home. Glaucoma had stolen her sight shortly after I was born.

Me in 1st grade

My sister and I occasionally joined my parents for a drive to the nursing home. I was happy that I could bring Grandma a song and some joy.

After Sister Hortence left, we were all given TB tests, which explained her sudden departure.

I really do not remember Sister Athanasia, except for a botched art project. We were supposed to draw and cut out a dog on a folded line, so it could be opened like a card. My attempt resulted in two separate pieces. I realized my error, and was so nervous while I waited in line to hand in my design. I thank Sister for her understanding. I received no harsh reprimand. I did, however, receive a C in art.

Sr. Clarisa taught second grade. The big event that year was First Communion. In anticipation of receiving the Sacrament, we were prepared for the daunting entrance into the confessional booth. What lurked behind those velvet curtains? Hearts beating, we knelt inside waiting for the light to slowly emerge as Father slid the black screen open and we confessed our laundry list of sins. Confession was almost a weekly part of school activities. Could 7-year-old children possibly have so many sins to confess? By the time May rolled around, we were spiritually ready.

We were also ready materialistically. My mother and I went to Kobacker's in the Broadway shopping area to buy a Communion dress. We also bought a plastic purse, rosary, scapular, prayer book, and veil from the nuns during a rare visit inside the

Communion Day

convent. Grandma Schwab placed a rosary on her window sill to ward off rain, and when the day arrived, we were blessed with sunshine. All went well, except that panic arose in me as the host became stuck on the roof of my mouth. Although I knew I should not touch the host, I secretly used my finger to release it. Oh, the guilt I felt, actually for years, until I gathered up the courage to confess my sin to Father during confession. He assured me God would forgive me, which was a great relief.

Miss Minklein was my third grade teacher. She was fresh out of college, young and stylish, and a big change from the nuns in their starched habits. The third graders presented a Christmas pageant that year, and I won the role of Mrs. Claus. I wore a red housecoat and a white wig my mother fashioned out of cotton. That was my first, and last, theatrical endeavor as the opportunity to perform never arose again.

I saw a death notice for Miss Minklein a few years ago. She never married and had taught in the Williamsville School District for over 25 years. It was a surprise to learn that one of the ladies from the Clarence Women's Club was a friend of hers and they had discussed me following the crash. It's a small world. How nice it would have been to reconnect with her.

Mrs. Barczak taught fourth grade. Her sister taught one of the third grades, which we kids found hard to believe, as they looked nothing alike. Mrs. Barczak taught me a life lesson. Once when I used my finger to point to someone I was talking about, perhaps referring to Miss Manners, she gently pulled my arm down and said, "Never point your finger at someone."

For Halloween that year, I dressed as a hula dancer and was quite thrilled with my grass skirt. One of the boys in my class, I think his name was Paul, told me I looked beautiful. I should have realized that a girl isn't often told she is beautiful, and boys who give such compliments should jump right to the top of the "crush" list.

A healthy Sister Hortence returned as my teacher in fifth grade. No memories come to my mind during that year. I do see that I received several Bs on my report card for "Self Control." I would love to know where I exhibited a lack of self control, as I basically still had a fear of authority back then, and cannot imagine myself being out of control or disrespectful.

Sixth grade was my favorite year. Again we had a lay teacher, Miss Schewe. She wasn't as stylish as Miss Minklein, some would even have called her a "plain Jane," but she knew how to make learning fun.

In Social Studies we had to research a country of our choice. For me that was France. My father opened his wooden box of World War II souvenirs and his maps and pictures were incorporated into my report. I was sure that memorabilia, along with the extra effort I put into drawing a picture of the Eiffel Tower on the cardboard cover, earned me an A on the report.

Another project involved making a musical instrument. It didn't have to work, it just had to look like it. My choice was a miniature piano. Production of the instrument began in my grandmother's woodshed, as Dad cut the wood to fashion a small upright piano. I felt somewhat guilty when I received an A for that project, as my father really got carried away and basically took over construction. I just didn't know how to tell him I wanted to make it myself.

That year the Bishop was making the rounds for Confirmation. Although eleven was a young age to be confirmed, we prepared to receive the Sacrament. I felt sure I would feel this spiritual surge when filled with the Holy Spirit. I waited, but cannot say I felt any different afterwards. I felt some disappointment, and perhaps a bit of relief. How would an eleven-year-old pre-teen handle such a burst of spirituality? Theresa the Little Flower, my favorite from the flower shop, would have known what to do with that inspiration.

Again a nun did double duty, as Sr. Florissa was my teacher in both seventh and eighth grades. I have two vivid memories of Sr. Florissa.

The first is seeing this diminutive nun being backed into the lockers by a cocky, disrespectful boy. She eventually got the upper hand and threatened to have one of the parish priests talk to him.

November 22, 1963, marks my second remembrance. Sr. Florissa had stepped out into the hall to talk to one of the priests. As soon as the door closed, thirty kids began talking and fooling around. Within minutes, Sister opened the door and emotionally told us, "You act this way when our President has been killed?" The chaos was replaced with stunned silence. We would always remember where we were and Sister's words on that tragic day.

In seventh grade, I teamed up with eighth grader, Eric, to sell the Catholic paper, *The Echo.* I think the sisters arranged this to combine our sales. Eric and I walked up and down Herman Street selling subscriptions. We must have been pretty persuasive, as we won the contest and the right to spend a day downtown. Winners from other parochial schools joined us for lunch at The Swiss Chalet, followed by a screening of "*It's A Mad, Mad World.*" That was quite the treat. Eric and I got along fine, and here too, I probably should have put him on my "crush" list.

One sunny day in eighth grade, I was chosen to accompany the school principal on a bus excursion down Genesee Street to the Wonder Bread factory. I have no clue why we went there, but it was exciting to be the girl who could cut classes and be sister's companion. I must have talked about this adventure with my girlfriends after school.

Pam was probably my first "real" girlfriend, one you talked to on a daily basis and spent all your free time with. Our friendship

  started around fifth grade. She was an only child and lived in a flat above her grandmother. We always seemed to play at her house. She had a terrific attic that inspired make-believe and secret clubs. Each

Pam   Me

of us had one Barbie doll, unlike my daughters who seemed to have an entire community of them. We created fashions for our Barbies from scraps of material found in our parents' rag bags. I tried not to eat at Pam's house; her mother always put butter on sandwiches (ugh!).

On Monday afternoons, SMS kids had afternoons off while the public school kids had Religious Ed classes. Usually this meant a walk to Broadway, which included a trip to the library, and a stop at Neisner's, Sattler's, or Woolworth's. It was a big event when McDonalds was built on Fillmore Avenue. Pam and I purchased chocolate shakes and French fries.

When I turned 12, I could go DOWNTOWN on the bus. There was a problem, though. Pam was allowed to walk to Broadway, but she couldn't go downtown. Another friend, Cindy could. We started spending more time together. I guess I was a fickle friend to Pam, because soon Cindy was my new best friend.

Cindy's dad owned George and Eddies, a tavern and supper club at the corner of Herman and Sycamore Streets. She and her family lived above that establishment, which to me was exciting. I was in awe of her mother, who was completely different from most moms of that era. She just had a classy air about her. She dressed like a model, while other moms dressed in house dresses. Cindy's mom also did not put butter on sandwiches. Every now and then, she would take us down to the tavern back room and grill up some of the best hamburgers.

Some years ago, Verlyn Klinkenborg, Cindy's then brother-in-law, wrote about George and Eddies in his book *The Last Fine Time*. Reading that book brought back memories of the times spent in that apartment above the tavern. I've connected with Cindy on and off over the years, but once we graduated from SMS, attended different high schools, and moved away from the neighborhood, our friendship ended.

My graduation from SMS came at a time when the neighborhood was in a state of decline. It was the turbulent '60s. The glory days of St. Mary of Sorrows were drawing to a close, but at least school children can still be found in the parish of my youth. The church was saved from demolition and is now

The King Urban Life Center. It is also being used as a Head Start educational site for the neighborhood children.

Amazing what memories can be unraveled at 2:30 in the morning. I wonder if tomorrow night I'll wake up with memories of high school?

1/22/12

Author's note: In November of 2018, I had the opportunity to visit The King Urban Life Center and Head Start school. Benches no longer lined the floor of what was St. Mary of Sorrows church. In their place, offices have been partitioned off, but the beautiful stained-glass windows remain, as does the original ceiling. I was there with several of my Schwab cousins, and we were allowed to take a spiral staircase up to the old choir loft that is now a library. When I was part of a children's choir at SMS, I never realized how amazing the stained-glass windows were in that loft area. As an adult, I find them breathtaking.

Inside SMS church then (above) and now (below)

Back to SMS with cousins Peter, Alison & Paul Becker.

We then walked over to our parish school. To my delight, the memories I outlined in this piece seemed to be spot on. Coat racks now line the hallways in front of the classrooms, but everything else was so familiar to me. Even the incinerator is still in the basement. I was so thrilled to have had the chance to revisit the church and school that were such a big part of my childhood.

In recent years, I have been reunited with my friend, Pam. I apologized for probably not being the best friend during seventh and eighth grade. I so appreciate that she is back in my life and a regular dinner companion.

Pam, Leo and Me

The High School Years

Three of my eighth grade St. Mary of Sorrows classmates and I slid into the front church pew, chapel veils haphazardly thrown on our heads. Our presence at Mass that morning was a last-ditch effort to perhaps reap some blessings before taking our entrance exam at Bishop McMahon High School.

I certainly felt some pressure. Everyone knew that our scores would determine where we would be placed in the freshman class of 1965. There were four homerooms and the top girls would be grouped together in Room 101. My sister, Barb, who was a senior

Bishop McMahon High School

that year, was in the top group every year. It was a tough act for me to follow.

Along with my sister, two cousins had also attended Bishop McMahon's business school. I considered defying tradition and thought I might attend Archbishop Carroll High School, which was geared toward college entrance preparation. My rebellious streak faded, though, when I went to an open house at McMahon. Even then I loved historic architecture and the school captured my heart.

The large brick mansion was located at 888 Delaware Avenue, in an area near downtown Buffalo known as "Millionaires' Row," when it was designed by architect E. B. Green in 1903. It was the home of Buffalo attorney, politician, businessman, and Pan-American Exposition Director Charles W. Goodyear. The mansion was sold to the Catholic Diocese of Buffalo in 1950, when it became Bishop McMahon High School.

An article in the January 16, 1952, *Courier Express* written by Katherine Smith informed readers that, "In the house where once outstanding socialites of this city and of the nation were received, today 490 girls are taught such practical accomplishments as typing, shorthand, and bookkeeping, and educated in the fundamentals of business and business law. High school English and social studies also are taught."

I survived the tension of the entrance exam, and followed in the footsteps of those girls. I even managed to secure a spot in Room 101. I joined the other freshmen clad in my kelly green skirt, discreetly falling below the knees; white, button-down-collar blouse; and green sweater. Luckily, changing styles eliminated the green vest previously issued to the girls.

As a child of Buffalo's East Side, I was surrounded predominantly by German and Polish families. McMahon's proximity to Buffalo's West Side introduced me to girls with last names like Miceli, Amato, Rubino, Piazza, Grizzaffi, and Rotundo. In my eyes, many of the girls were streetwise, and some even had boyfriends. At

My senior photo

that point in my life, the closest I came to having a boyfriend was going to Crystal Beach Days with the church CYO group and hanging out with Paul Schweigert for the day.

During those four years of high school, straight hair with a whisper of a flip displayed at shoulder length was a popular style for most of the girls. Short hair teased at the crown adorned other girls, accented with a strip of hair sweeping on to the cheek ending in a perfect point. I attempted to keep my wavy hair in a somewhat straight style, and as evidenced in yearbook pictures, was not overly successful. My senior year photo captured my method of growing out my bangs by combing them back and securing bobby pins to the curls that fought to be free.

We all had our senior pictures taken at Adam, Meldrum, and Anderson's Department Store, better known to locals as AM&A's, in then bustling downtown Buffalo. Everyone wore a silky white, long-sleeve blouse that buttoned in the back. We could choose what color we wanted the blouse tinted for our eight by ten portrait: mine was yellow. These portraits were displayed on a wall in our parents' homes until they could be replaced by a wedding picture.

The music room, chapel, and library of the school were on the first floor of the mansion. The eleven bedrooms upstairs were converted to accommodate classes, and a large, two-story addition was added to the back of the building. The mansion classrooms were reserved for the seniors, and one of the senior privileges

spiral staircase

was the right to use the beautiful spiral staircase that rose from the foyer to the upstairs classes.

The curriculum at McMahon had grown to include physical education, math, and science. Math came easily to me, but my skills and knowledge in physical education and science were questionable. I never attained the coveted "President Kennedy Physical Education Award," lacking the strength to do pull-ups. How much strength could a 90-pound girl possess? Biology was especially challenging for me. It was cool that classes were held in the old carriage house, but having to dissect frogs prior to lunch did not sit favorably with me. I have to admit that my poor frog was not dissected; he was destroyed. I will never forget my utter surprise when I opened the mail one day in June and discovered that I had actually passed the Regents Biology exam by one point.

I doubted my choice of schools when I started to learn typing and shorthand; coordination for typing and attempting to decipher my scribbles of shorthand seemed limited. *If this didn't work out, I could switch to Carroll, right?* It all clicked, though, enough that I could make a living as a secretary (although some previous bosses might question that statement).

An interesting mixture of nuns and lay teachers taught us. Some left lasting memories.

Sister Angeline provided our musical education. Perhaps because of her stern disposition, my four years in her music classes did not result in many memories. In addition to the school song, only one other song lingers, and I recently found myself going to *Google* and typing in "The Happy Wanderer."

"Oh, may I go a-wandering
Until the day I die!
Oh, may I always laugh and sing,
Beneath God's clear blue sky!

"Val-deri, Val-dera,
Val-deri,
Val-dera-ha-ha-ha-ha-ha
Val-deri, Val-dera,
My knapsack on my back."

Why? Why would that song stick in my mind some forty-five years later? "Val-deri, Val-dera" must have caused the melody to remain in my memory.

Miss Erickson taught history. She was a pretty woman and always wore her long brown hair up in a French twist. Her personality could best be described as bland. She entered the classroom, sat down, and started reciting history. There was no time given for comparison to current world events, or for questions of any kind. Just straight text. If you copied down and memorized every word she said, you breezed through her exams.

She did deviate from her classroom lesson plan one time. For some reason, a large empty box had been placed in our classroom. As a joke, my friend, Liz, hid in the box, and once Miss Erickson was seated at her desk and began her usual monotone lesson, Liz popped out of the box. Any consequences Liz incurred were worth the look of surprise on Miss Erickson's face.

Liz savored the free-and-easy approach to life. I, on the other hand, always felt the need to stick to the rules; some would refer to that as being a goody two shoes when it came to authority. It only seemed natural that Liz coaxed some of that trait out of me. Sure enough, Liz and I were reprimanded by Miss Erickson for talking in class. It was a big step for me to come out of my shell.

Liz liked to tease me. The best illustration of this occurred at our senior retreat. My loafers mysteriously disappeared on the first day of the retreat, and to my embarrassment, were presented as gifts during the offering at Mass. During that weekend, I also found articles of my clothing attached to tree branches. It may not sound like it, but Liz was my friend, a friend I still keep in touch with to this day.

Liz and I also kept in touch with Sister Pat, our homeroom teacher sophomore year. She originally was called Sister Victor. The Sisters of St. Francis were in the midst of change in the '60s. When their members entered the convent, they left behind their old ways, and that included their names. By our sophomore year, the nuns not only reclaimed their names, but their restrictive habits were adjusted to reflect modern times. This

Liz, Sr. Pat, and me

meant their starched head pieces were relegated to the past. The students at McMahon speculated what the nuns would look like with their hair exposed. It took everyone some time to adjust to the nuns appearing with short veils, framed by varying textures of hair, and wearing jumpers settling just below their knees. Over the years, Sister Pat became quite stylish, as she was allowed to abandon the habit and veil altogether.

In the years following graduation, Liz and I joined Sister Pat and Father Trotta (who led our senior retreat and resembled Gene Kelly) at Fort Niagara Park in Youngstown, New York. Father Trotta was a dean at nearby Niagara University. We enjoyed picnics, munching cheese and crackers, and sipping wine as we sat on a grassy knoll and gazed out at Lake Ontario with Toronto in the distance. Although I still occasionally see Sister Pat, unfortunately I have not connected with Father Trotta in years.

Miss Pilus, a sturdy woman born and raised in Nebraska, taught business law. Again, I did not retain any principles of business law, but still use one of her frequently used phrases, "I said to myself, self..."

I loved doing reports, traveling downtown to the library and searching through index cards to locate magazines and books to delve into my topic. How exciting was it to use microfilm? Luckily for me, Mrs. Iannone made us tackle several reports for economics and sociology. This hands-on technique of learning was just what I preferred, and I always scored an A+. Mrs. Iannone was a nice change of pace from the nuns and single women who taught us; she was married and had two small sons. She was a positive role model who illustrated that a girl could have a career and a family.

Affection for libraries resulted in my volunteering at the school library. Sister Adeline, who must have been at least in her eighties, was the head librarian. For four years, I dusted shelves, straightened, and covered books. As I worked, I made mental notes of the books I wanted to read in the future, and more than once, stopped and flipped through the pages, traveling to different times and places.

Sister Joan taught English and was known for her pop quiz on "*It's Halloween, Charlie Brown.*" I had failed to watch that classic cartoon when she sprung that quiz on my class during junior year. Luckily, I had watched when it debuted in 1966, so memory served me well and saved the day.

Mrs. Bonn, a mother of six, was chosen to remind the girls of the Catholic doctrines on sexual behavior. I recently had the opportunity to flip through the sex education curriculum taught today; no stone is left unturned. While that topic is introduced in

Outside Senior entrance, Me, Donna Stange, and Marilyn Galley

middle school today, in the '60s this naïve Catholic girl did not have her eyes opened until sophomore year. There we sat in the beautiful reception hall, a place that in the mansion's past was lavishly decorated for the wedding of Esther Goodyear, watching a film on reproduction. It was at that moment that I clearly learned the true meaning regarding the coupling of men and women. I cannot say what my perception was prior to that day; things were sketchy, and I certainly could not ask someone for details. Reality, though, made me break out in a cold sweat.

I retained quite a bit of naïveté during those high school years. I was unfortunately what could be described as a nerd. Being a member of the Sodality (explained in the yearbook as fostering "*devotion to Jesus through Mary by means of personal holiness and apostolic work*") and taking on the role of sacristan, having "*the honor and privilege of keeping Our Lord's home in perfect order,*" were not exactly after-school activities of the cool girls. Those girls were cheerleaders, active in the Pep Club, Student Council, or participating in a sport.

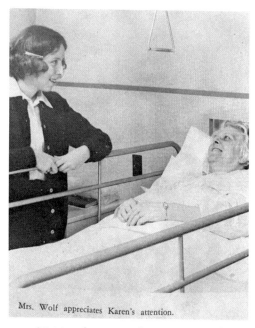

Mrs. Wolf appreciates Karen's attention.

Visiting the nursing home with a much better hair style

Hopefully, the Lord did not mind that the main reason I became a sacristan was the opportunity it gave me to meet the boys from Bishop Ryan High School, who came on Fridays to serve for Mass in the gym. They, of course, did not realize that I existed.

My main job in the Sodality was visiting the elderly at the Nazareth Nursing Home. It was a somber task and reinforced my own mortality. There was not much of an opportunity to talk to the residents, as the majority were always sleeping. My usual duty was trying to get them to eat. To this day, tapioca pudding or custard, the only food my charges would eat, brings back memories of the sadness I felt on those visits.

Two teachers encouraged me to break out of my shell.

English teacher, Mrs. Shirley, demonstrated the enjoyment I could derive from the written word. She walked into the classroom in her practical suit and casually perched herself up on the desk as she expanded my knowledge of literature. She was the moderator of the National Honor Society and I was informed the summer of my junior year that I would be the president during my senior year. It was quite an honor, but also a responsibility. I had to keep my grades up. What if I wasn't able to do that? Could a National Honor Society president be impeached? I never found out, and was able to remain on the Honor Roll senior year.

As president, I was encouraged to make the senior lounge

area a comfortable retreat for my fellow students. A small library was added to the space, along with an area where the girls could display their artwork. I contributed drawings of Robert Kennedy and Abraham Lincoln.

When it was revealed that I would be the Class of 1969 Salutatorian, Mrs. Shirley worked with me on my speech, approving my choice of a topic. I illustrated how my 4 years at McMahon had introduced me to people who always would be a part of me. I used that experience and theme when delivering a speech at the dedication of the Long Street 3407 memorial in June of 2012.

Toward the end of my junior year, I was surprised when asked by moderator Sister Ann to join the 1969 *Memo* yearbook staff as co-editor. I debated whether I should take on the responsibility,

Working on the yearbook

doubting my ability to get the job done. I took the plunge, which turned out to be one of my best decisions. I loved the excitement of the yearbook process: helping set up photo sessions, cropping photos, preparing copy, and meeting deadlines. Our lay moderator, unfortunately I cannot remember his name, saw my enthusiasm and suggested I reconsider my decision not to attend college and instead pursue a career in journalism. In the end, I did not divert from my planned future, but I hope he would be pleased to know that I finally fulfilled the pursuit of the written word in my endeavors today.

Our efforts resulted in a yearbook whose theme was "Teach Me" that won a city-wide award during a banquet at the Statler

Hotel. I don't remember what the award actually was, but I'll never forget the memory of our excitement at winning.

School trips were an important part of my high school experience. I visited Philadelphia, Montreal, Quebec, and Washington D.C.

During one trip, my friend Paulette looked at me and laughingly said, "Do you know that you have bird eyes?" She was right. When I close my eyes, the lids meet in the middle just like a bird's. The top lids for most people meet at the bottom of the eye. It's true. Check it out.

Sophomore year, we traveled to Canada for the 1967 Montreal Expo. The first days of the trip were exciting, but then I became ill and spent the majority of the time in bed while in Montreal. I improved enough to visit Quebec, which included a stop at the shrine of St. Anne de Beaupre. Two girls sneaked out of their hotel room and hooked up with a couple of Canadian sailors. This could not be tolerated, and the girls were promptly sent back to Buffalo in a cab, accompanied by one of the nuns, where their parents found themselves with quite a tab.

During the junior year trip to Washington D.C., I bucked authority, and uncharacteristic of my reputation as a goody two shoes, failed to obey the nuns' explicit command to NOT walk down the steps of the Washington Monument. Two friends and I figured we had plenty of time. Who thought it would take so long? The descent took forever. The nuns and our fellow classmates were waiting in the bus for us and very unhappy. Luckily, such action did not receive the same punishment as the girls in Quebec; we received a reprimand, but nothing more.

Our class never made it to New York City senior year. The behavior of the classes before us in the Big Apple ended that senior privilege.

Social events added fun to those years. An annual Harvest Festival brought families together, and the father-daughter dance was a popular way to get dads involved in their daughters' lives.

There were school dances, where we eagerly hoped some boy would ask us to dance (never happened) and of course, the much anticipated proms.

I nervously asked a neighbor to escort me to my junior prom, and after he said, "Yes," I lived in a constant state of panic. *What would we talk about all night?* The week of the prom, he called to say he had mono and could not go. My mother and sister were devastated, but I was relieved.

Senior year, being turned down by the only boy I considered a good prom candidate (he already had too many proms to attend), I decided to go with a friend of my cousin. During the prom, he asked me if I thought my sister would go out with him. I was OK with that, as I only considered him a friend, but my mother and aunt were horrified that he would ask that question.

High school definitely broadened my horizons. I was exposed to a wide variety of personalities, obtained knowledge that would guide me toward a career, and I was challenged to take chances and step beyond my level of comfort. The progression of time, and the sudden change it could bring, was also thrust upon me by the death of a classmate.

One Monday morning, as I prepared to get off the bus, the driver said, "It will be a sad day for you girls; one of your classmates was killed over the weekend."

It came as a shock, and I quickly learned that a senior had gone hunting with her friend and their boyfriends. She was accidently shot by her own boyfriend. She was a pretty, vibrant girl with a bright future before her. Her sister was a year younger than me, and I recall her saying later that she often felt suffocated by the restrictions her parents placed on her, feeling they needed to do so to protect her from harm. I recall passing the parents' car one day and noticing that they kept a type of shrine on the dashboard covered with pictures and small remembrances of their deceased daughter. The varying degrees of that family's pain will always remain with me.

It was comforting to find my yearbooks in the items retrieved from the Long Street site. The books are scorched and faded, a reminder of the harshness and the sudden change that can disrupt life, but also a reminder that discovery can come at any time. Just as I survived the awkwardness of those teenage years and moved on to face new chapters in my life, there are still possibilities open to me.

Reunion, 2019 - Can you spot me in the front row, 4th from the right?

Part of that naïve, insecure teenager lingers in me. There are many times when I still ask myself, *what will I be when I grow up?* I doubt my capabilities. Do we ever totally outgrow that insecurity? I can look back on those teenage years and hopefully see that no matter what our age, there is always time to learn and grow, and always time to extend the gift of friendship to someone new. It makes life pretty interesting.

3/17/14

Me and Liz

Author's Note: In June 2019, I joined several of my Bishop McMahan classmates to celebrate our 50th Graduation Reunion. Going to a reunion verifies that age affects all of us, and it does make us come face to face with our own mortality. I recognized many of the girls immediately, but some faces seemed to bear no resemblance to the teenagers I remembered. Our name tags included our senior pictures, which either aided the process of remembering who people were, or made me think, No, that can't be the same person!

I found myself sitting at a table with one of the nuns who taught me. Her name tag was flipped over, so I had no clue who she was. After talking with other girls, I discovered that she was my biology teacher. I finally turned to her and apologized, not because I couldn't remember her, but for being such a horrible student (may the frog rest in peace).

I was asked to be one of the speakers that night, not to commemorate my role as salutatorian of the Class of 1969, but as an author and a victim of the crash of Flight 3407. An array of newspaper articles was displayed on a long table to mark many events that were interspersed among five decades: Woodstock, the tragedy of The Challenger explosion, music legends, the horror of 9/11, and the unbelievable crash of an airplane in Clarence Center, New York. I touched very little on my tragedy, but instead read excerpts from my recollections of our high school years. I was relieved that the laughs I had hoped would follow some of my comments actually materialized.

A Hard Day's Night

I was almost 13 and about to embark on an adventure.

Basically, I had led a sheltered life. My world was confined to a few miles on the East Side of Buffalo, which included excursions to the Broadway Market and had just been expanded to include riding the NFTA bus to downtown Buffalo from our Herman Street home.

My Uncle Sid, a widower for some years, had married a nice woman, Ruth, from Kenmore. He resided in her home with her children, Ruthi and Billy. Ruthi was a year older than me and we soon became friends. Although we did not phone each other often, we corresponded a lot through mail. (You remember: take a blank sheet of paper, write all your important life-changing facts down, affix a licked stamp on the envelope, and put it in the mailbox that sat at the corner of Herman and Genesee Streets.)

Occasionally I was allowed to spend weekends at Ruthi's house. That in itself was an adventure for me, but that is not the main theme of this story.

In July 1964, while spending one of those weekends in Kenmore, Ruthi, her friend Margie, and I daringly stepped on to a NFTA bus on Delaware Avenue and headed downtown. No adult knew of this secret mission. We were headed to Shea's Theatre to clandestinely swoon over the much anticipated movie, "A Hard Day's Night," starring the amazing Beatles.

I loved the Beatles. On February 9th, 1964, I anxiously sat

on the floor in front of our television waiting to see the Beatles make their first American television appearance, live, on The Ed Sullivan Show. It was a dream come true for me. They sang 5 of their songs in two sets: "All My Loving," "Till There Was You," "She Loves You," "I Saw Her Standing There," and "I Want to Hold Your Hand."

Now, I was on this covert mission to see the Beatles' first movie.

We barely arrived in time and the theatre was packed. Luckily, we found seats very close to the screen. Along with hundreds of other girls, we screamed through the entire movie. At one point, apparently disgruntled boys stormed out of the theatre and smacked us on our heads. Although scared by this violence, I pushed fear aside and continued to enjoy the movie.

I felt like I had left childhood behind and truly stepped into my teenage years. I had become a part of Beatlemania. I cannot recall if we ever confessed to our mothers that we had embarked on this secret adventure.

Time swiftly flew by, and 54 years later, I again rushed to a theatre to see "A Hard Day's Night." Heavy snow made me consider staying in the warmth of my home, but as always, the Beatles were worth the slight chance of getting stuck in snow and being buffeted by cold, blowing winds.

The East Aurora Music Fest teamed up with the Aurora Theatre to enable local Beatlemaniacs to relive their youth. The Fab Four looked so young, and once again, I remembered why I used to daydream about George Harrison sweeping me off my feet. I happily joined in with the audience's opening screams, as the movie started. So many of the Beatles' great songs were included in the film, and most of us still remembered all the words as we sang along.

No boys hit me in the head this time around, but unfortunately, we had some very rude people behind us who never learned that loud talking is not acceptable in the theatre. Their mothers would

The cover has gone through some hard times, but it still sounds great.

not have approved. All in all, though, it was a great evening that I really enjoyed with my friends.

I have my original album of *A Hard Day's Night*. The cover is pretty battered, but the record still sounds great. There are several orchestrated cuts on the album, and I am sure as a teenager I cared very little for these renditions. Now I appreciate them for what they represent: the musical talent of four lads from Liverpool, with whom I was obsessed with during much of my teenage years.

1/29/19

Dancing

Dancing is poetry with arms and legs
~ Charles Baudelaire

I remember my first dance with a special fellow.

With a smile and a twinkle in his eye, he took my hands in his and I wrapped my arms around him. Stepping on his feet, it took me a moment or two to keep my balance, but he held me tenderly, and Dad and I swayed to the music.

My introduction to dancing had begun, and over the years, that rhythmic motion has provided moments to remember.

Dad continued to be my dancing partner, especially during the annual Dad and Daughter Dance at Bishop McMahon High School. Dads bonded with their daughters while guiding them over the gym floor. My freshman year I had to share Dad with my sister, Barb, who was a senior. To even things out, my Uncle Sid also accompanied us. Since he was my sister's godfather, this admittance to the event seemed acceptable.

Of course, proms were definitely opportunities to dance.

My first prom story actually began when I was a sophomore in high school. We moved from Herman Street in the heart of the city to Hagen Street off East Delavan near the city line. It was a big step for my parents, as this was the first home they had ever owned. Prior to that, their entire married life had been spent renting a house behind my grandmother's. The cost of $17,000 for the Hagen Street house was minimal, when compared to home prices today, but my father was concerned about how this would affect the family finances. It was really my mother who pursued the dream of owning a home.

To a teenage girl, this was a good move. For one thing, Bishop Turner, an all-boys high school, was right down the street. Some of the neighbors also had teenage boys.

The Murrays lived next door to us. Their son, Donny, helped me reach a teenage milestone. He surprised me with an impromptu "first kiss" shortly before my sixteenth birthday. This saved me from being "sweet 16 and never been kissed."

He invited me into his house and as we sat on the couch, he said, "I want to tell you something." He leaned over and gave me a quick kiss. I am sure I blushed, I think I said thanks and then I went home.

The incident was never mentioned again, and after that, we exchanged a hello or a wave, but that was the extent of our relationship. I had more contact with his dog, Penny, whom we lovingly provided with doggie treats over the fence, than I did with Donny. I sometimes wonder if he won a bet from the neighborhood boys after that kiss.

Then there was Tom Brych who lived diagonally across the street from us. Tom was a college man. He was adorable and I was smitten. He was around 6 feet tall, fair skinned, with brown hair and eyes that sparkled. I, on the other hand, was a scrawny 95-pound, 16-year-old with frizzy hair and a chipped front tooth.

I volunteered to help my father rake leaves or shovel snow because there was always a chance that Tom might come over and we would talk long after evening had fallen. I wish I could remember what we talked about. He was just a nice boy and I was thrilled that he spent time with me.

My junior year in high school arrived and with it the pressure of finding a date for the Junior Prom. The crazy thought popped into my mind that maybe, just maybe, Tom would consider going with me. As I walked home from the bus stop one day, Tom came over to say hello. Somehow, I blurted out, "Would you like to go to the prom with me?" To my great surprise, he said, "Sure."

Prom prep began. A long yellow chiffon dress with flowered bodice, along with long, white gloves were purchased; my mother made a hair appointment; and my friends and I planned after-prom events. But the bubble was about to burst.

Tom called a few days before the prom to inform me that he had mono. The prom date could not be kept. My mother and sister were very upset for me. If I'm truthful, though, I have to admit that I was relieved. The anticipation of being with Tom for an entire evening was frightening to me. I had never even gone on a date before. What in the world would we talk about? I would be so nervous I probably wouldn't be able to eat, let alone talk all night. So, while others fretted, I accepted this fate.

The evening of the prom, Tom's mother invited me to dinner at their home. I was given a corsage and a recovering Tom and I were left in the living room to talk. We joined his entire family for dinner. As anticipated, I was way too nervous to eat. I kept asking for milk to wash the food down. I laugh now when I remember Tom's dad saying, "Boy, you sure like that milk, don't you?" I appreciated that Tom and his family wanted to ease any pain I felt because I was missing the prom.

Over the years, Tom and I continued our casual friendship, but eventually lost touch as we went our separate ways. Then fate decided it was time for us to catch up. In 2010, Tom's daughter sent a teaching application to the Clarence School District where I worked in the Personnel Department. Their last name, Brych, wasn't common, so I thought she could be related to my Tom. He was her father, and after emailing back and forth, Tom and his wife, Carol, invited me to dinner at their home. It was an evening filled with reminiscing and laughter. As I was leaving, Tom motioned from the kitchen for me to come back. He pointed to the television, where music had entertained us during our get-together.

"Hear that?" Tom asked with a smile on his face, "sixties music. How about that dance we never shared?" There in the kitchen,

Reunion with Prom Tom

I was transformed once again into a 16-year-old teenage girl dancing with a college man. I knew why I had such a crush on him all those years ago.

Tom and our families keep in touch, and since he is such a good-natured guy, I do not think I embarrass him too much when I refer to him as Prom Tom.

I met my husband, Doug, at a ballgame in Getzville, New York, where I could not keep my eyes off of the curly-haired catcher. We seemed to click that night, and I anxiously waited for an opportunity to attend another game to make sure I had not mistaken that assumption. The following week, I was again watching his team play a game, and I eagerly followed the crowd to Lucky's restaurant on the corner of Transit and Clinton. The seat next to Doug was available, so I boldly claimed it. It was agreed that we would join some of the group at a disco down on Clinton Street. The place was crowded and hot. At one point in the evening my friend Cindy commented that I looked like a drowned rat, hair ringing wet with sweat, and perspiration dripping off me. Cindy and her husband, Gene, soon left, but Doug, apparently not repulsed by my physical appearance, stayed on the dance floor with me. Later

Doug and me dressed for the '50s dance

he walked me to my car. The stars aligned, and we shared our first kiss. It was a slight brush of the lips, but held the promise of good things to come.

I have an old picture of Doug and me taken in the 1990s before a St. Columban School PTO dance in Loveland, Ohio. The '50s theme was reflected in our outfits, as I was dressed as Karen from the Mickey Mouse Club, and Doug was a slick, leather-jacketed cool dude. Of course, Doug and I did our share of dancing over the years, but that night was special, as we jitter-bugged and hip-hopped like professionals. I never realized he could lead me straight back into the '50s. We hit a dancing peak that night that never was matched again.

Dancing can signal a change in your children's status in life. I watched my girls embark on the journey from little girls to teenagers as I chaperoned a dance at their elementary school. The occasion was their first girl/boy dance at St. Columban School. I felt their fear as they waited to see if a boy would actually ask them to dance. I felt their relief as a boy shyly approached to ask for that dance. I felt their anxiety as they walked toward the dance floor, and I felt their joy in experiencing that first dance.

I continue to enjoy watching my girls dance with their guys. Unfortunately, over the years, I feel some of my sons-in-law seem more intent on checking their cell phones than dancing with

Kim and Doug dancing

my daughters. Dancing is not on their list of things they like to do.

White attending the wedding of one of my daughter Kim's friends in 2008, I knew Kim was waiting for her boyfriend to slow dance with her. Doug looked at me and said, "Maybe if I dance with Kim, Jeff will cut in." A photo of Doug and Kim dancing captured the moment so well. It is a photo that Kim keeps on her dresser today. Doug's strategy worked and Jeff did cut in to claim his lady. As parents, the happiness on our daughter's face warmed our hearts.

I did witness a spark of love and hope while watching my daughters dance at Lori's wedding on August 1, 2009. After the devastating events of February 12, 2009, that ripped our family apart, my beautiful daughters held hands and danced in a circle of unity to Reba McIntire's, "My Sister, My Friend" at Lori's reception. I knew Doug's spirit stood beside me, and we watched with pride as our daughters showed their will to survive and carry on.

That spirit of survival, love, and hope continues to make itself known to me in many ways.

In August of 2015, I attended a wedding reception for Kevin Kuwik. Kevin lost his girlfriend, Lorin, on Flight 3407. He has dealt with that loss by becoming a leader in the fight for airline safety in Washington DC, alongside Lorin's parents, and immersed himself in his job as a recruiter for college basketball.

Our girls dancing (photo courtesy of Sarah J. Carr)

I, and all the 3407 family members, have always hoped this young man could find love again. It is what Lorin would have wanted for him. The right woman did come along. She is accomplished, sweet, loving, and understanding of Kevin's tragic past. She is a good match for him, and it was wonderful to see Kevin start a new chapter in his life.

Those 3407 family members who have been at his side in the fight for air safety, were asked to join the celebration of his marriage. The bride and groom's Irish and Polish heritage reverberated through the reception hall. There was no way I could idly sit by. The music coursed through my body, and I joined this amazing group of people as we moved around the dance floor to polkas, jitterbugs, and line dances. Laughter and smiles lit our faces. Yes, the dancing took my breath away, but the courage and determination of the families of 3407 touched my soul. Our motto that night seemed to scream: *We will dance until we ache, and our sweat will become our tears. We remember, but we carry on, celebrating the lives of those we lost.*

Life has come full circle. Now I say to my grandchildren, "Come dance with me," as they cautiously place their feet on mine to begin their dance journey. I hope they will enjoy the beauty and emotional sincerity of the dance. It is certainly an important part of their lives.

3/6/16

My Children

My third daughter, Jess, believed in requesting birthday gifts early. Her next birthday was not until February 26, but in December of 2017, she told me she would like me to write a reflection of my thoughts about her running her first marathon in New York City in November. You would think that I had plenty of time to meet that request, but I was barely able to finish until a few days before her birthday.

It is hard to sit down and write about your children, to describe the amazing blessing they are to you, the love and pride that fills you because they came into your life. I found this process easier to undertake when I decided to write to each of them a letter.

I thank Jess for inspiring me to write this collection of letters to her and her three sisters. They are all the greatest gifts my husband, Doug, ever gave me.

Kimberly Anne:
The Little Engine that Could

Dear Kim,

It seems like only yesterday that Dad and I raced down the I-90 from Eden, New York, to Sister's Hospital in Buffalo. I was only 27 weeks into my first pregnancy and it appeared that I was in labor.

If this assumption was correct, could a baby even survive?

You did survive, and we were thrust into parenthood that Easter Sunday, April 19, 1981.

I am having a bit of a struggle accepting the fact that you turned 40 in 2021. How did those years fly by so quickly?

Despite flipping through books and accepting advice from family and friends, dealing with a first child was like charting

Our little pumpkin Kim, 1981

Jill, Lori, Kim and Jess, 1988

an unknown course. The responsibility, care, and reality of being parents seemed overwhelming to us at first, but the amazing feeling of love for our little one somehow guided us along quite an adventure.

Girls on the Cincinnati Reds field

You captured our hearts.

Before too long, you became a big sister to Lori, Jessica, and Jill. As the oldest sister, you were our testing ground for what boundaries to set for our girls. That is a burden for the oldest child. Guidelines often start out being strict, but over time, younger siblings are allowed way more latitude in life. Parents just seem to chill out more with each child.

You loved school and we were pleased with your progress, but days before kindergarten ended, we received a call recommending that you enter a transitional first grade. That request was unexpected, but considering your early birth, perhaps you did need some catching-up time.

Some of your amazing qualities are your work ethic, resilience, and perseverance. In spite of your early educational struggles, you successfully completed bachelor's and master's degrees in early childhood and special education. Today, you provide preschoolers with the foundation they need to start their learning journeys.

Kim, I recall catching a glimpse of you and your friend, Liz, in seventh or eighth grade and asking myself, *When did they*

transform from little girls to young ladies? You both walked with such dignity and confidence. Perhaps you will tell me that you definitely did not possess those qualities at that time, but to my eyes, I saw evidence of those attributes in you both.

Liz and Kim, 2010

You attended Daeman, a private college in Buffalo. Unlike your sisters, who all attended state colleges outside of Buffalo, you were able to live at home and commute to classes. At the time you were considering where to go to college, Dad and I questioned whether we could afford the cost of a private school. Timing is everything. Dad had purchased a "penny stock" (common shares of small public companies that trade for less than one dollar per

Kim's graduation photo

share) and the value surged. That windfall, the scholarship you were awarded, and a loan resulted in the green light that signaled a right-of-way to Daeman.

I remember when you traveled to England in 2003 with a group from the college. During that visit, U.S. forces invaded Iraq. It was frightening for me to have a child so far from home, and I prayed that you would return home safely. You told us that your group did see protesters questioning the invasion, but that you were never in any danger. It was a great adventure for you and was definitely a highlight of your college experience.

I mentioned in *One on the Ground* that Dad found an English Bobby teapot for you at the flea market. Following the crash, bits and pieces of that gift resurfaced among the retrieved items. My thought was to throw them away, but you salvaged them. You and your husband, Jeff, tried in vain to piece them together.

Patty Cancilla, a Roycroft Master Artisan, was touched by that story. She contacted me and asked if she could create some jewelry

Jewelry created from the bobby pieces

for you from what remained. A beautiful necklace and bracelet now symbolize the love Dad had for you.

Kim, you have continued to remain close to several of

Jeff and Kim's wedding included vintage cars

your college friends who stayed in the Buffalo area. It has been wonderful to watch you and these young women build happy lives filled with husbands, children, and careers.

You found the right man through a friend's boyfriend. The first time I met Jeff Lipiarz, he and you were walking toward me between rows of cars at a summer food and antique car event in Clarence. I later learned that one of Jeff's hobbies was restoring antique cars. A parade of vintage cars transported you and your wedding party on a beautiful summer day, July 10, 2010, when you became Mr. and Mrs. Lipiarz.

Jeff is a jack of all trades, a handy fellow who can fix anything. He is also a caring and hands-on dad to Lydia, born August 4, 2012, and Curtis, who completed your family on April 21, 2014.

Since you are my only daughter who has remained local, you and Jeff have become two of my go-to helpers, especially when it came to unraveling the aftermath of the crash of Flight 3407. You were instrumental in dealing with the many storage sheds that contained items retrieved after that tragedy and helped me dispose of the ruined remnants. I know this was not an easy thing for you to do.

Lydia, Kim and Curtis, 2020

I am very thankful that I am able to participate in Lydia's and Curtis' lives and that you and I have many opportunities to enjoy mom and daughter times, too. Whether it is a night out for dinner and a show at Shea's Theatre in downtown Buffalo, or our annual lunch and shopping excursion to the Elmwood strip in the city, I cherish the opportunities we have to be together.

We have tackled road trips to see Lori and her family in Lexington, Kentucky, and stopped in the Cincinnati area for reunions with your grade school friend, Liz, and high school friend, Renee.

Kim, your love of searching for treasures at garage sales and flea markets reflects the passion your dad had for those hunts and that always makes me smile.

That tiny baby who arrived 40 years ago has brightened my life and was the first one who taught me the meaning of the word "mother." I am proud of the beautiful woman you have become, inside and out, who juggles being a wife, mother, and teacher so well.

Although I may grapple with the reality that you have turned 40, I can acknowledge that our history together is an important part of my life, and look forward to our many escapades yet to come.

Happy Birthday, Kim.

Love,

Mom

4/19/21

Lori Beth:
Trail Blazer

Dear Lori,

You changed Kim's status from only child to big sister when you arrived on November 20, 1982.

I was yet to go a full nine months with a pregnancy. As you know, Kim had arrived at 27 weeks, but at least this time I was only a month early.

You were simply known as "Baby Girl Wielinski" since we did not decide on a name until a few days after your birth (probably because we were focusing on boy names). You were the complete opposite of your big sister. You were dark haired with brown eyes, compared to Kim's blond, blue-eyed appearance. Of all the girls, Lori, you resembled your dad the most. Remember when you first saw Dad's high school senior picture? You exclaimed, "Oh my gosh, it looks like me!" Apparently, you were anxious to look at the world, and emerged with your face turned upward. This caused considerable bruising of your face. One doctor thought you were an Indian baby because of that coloring.

You had the distinction of being born with two bottom front teeth. Natal teeth are very uncommon and appear in about one in every 2,000 to 3,000 births. Once I saw an article that claimed those born with teeth are highly intelligent (which would apply to you), and even indicated that Albert Einstein was born with them. The teeth were wobbly and to remedy that problem, they were removed.

As with all my babies, you probably weighed between five and six pounds when we brought you home. I have to guess the weight.

I was diligent when it came to recording events in baby books, and chronicled details from birth-to-five. This obsession to keep

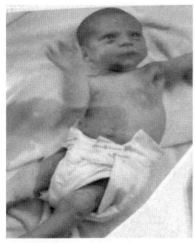

Baby Lori

detailed records of my daughters' early years resulted from the lack of information in my own baby book. Unfortunately, not one page turned up in the salvaged items following the crash.

Your Grandma Schoenwetter received little "Mission" magazines when Aunt Barbara and I were little. She would say, "Eat your food. There are children starving in Africa." We could turn the pages in those

magazines and actually see the children she referred to. Lori, with your bruised, baggy skin, and tiny frame, you certainly resembled those mission babies.

You filled out nicely, though, and we soon referred to you

Lori in her Buddha pose

as "Baby Buddha." There is a wonderful photo of you sitting on the couch in a white and yellow sleeper, your round little body positioned like a Buddha statue.

To start kindergarten in Ohio, a child had to turn five by September 30th, which meant that because of your November 20th birthday, you were almost six when

Kim kissing Lori

you started elementary school.

You were always an above-average student and part of a special gifted group at St. Columban. You were a great soccer player too. I will never forget one cold, rainy evening when you scored the only goal for the Clarence High School Varsity team, which turned out to be all they needed to win the Sectional Championship. Your love of the game continued after graduation, and you at one time even played on a team with your co-workers.

The title "trailblazer" can easily be bestowed on you. You were the first sister to go out of town for college (SUNY Geneseo and Rochester Institute of Technology), and the first, and only one, to join a sorority. You were also the first to move in with a boyfriend, obtain a job out of town, buy a home, get a dog, and get married.

You spent a year in the dorms at Geneseo before you and some of your sorority sisters moved to a house in the town. Although

Sorority sisters

you told me you do not remember this, jokingly, you girls referred to yourselves as the "10s" who lived at 10 North Street. Maybe I never heard all the stories of what went on in that house, but I do recall that the 10s had to pay for repairs to a commode there.

Your residence during your final two years at Geneseo was

at the sorority house. If walls could talk, I believe I would get an earful of escapades! Dad, Kim, and I once stayed there overnight. We made the rounds of night spots, and I cannot say if I was impressed or dismayed at the fact that several bars counted you as one of their regulars.

You and a boyfriend shared an apartment in Rochester when you studied for your master's degree. There was some turbulence during that time between you and him, and eventually the relationship ended. Not only were you learning about business, but you were also receiving life lessons.

Following graduation from RIT, you found a job in New Jersey. I remember you calling me to tell me that news, while standing in New Jersey directly across from the former site of the World Trade Center. Shortly after your arrival, I again received a call to say how nervous you were about taking the subway from NYC to your job. It was a time when there were continual talks about a possible attack on the subway system. I mentioned that if you hadn't wanted to deal with such possibilities, you should not have moved to such a "hot spot." I did worry, though. Your adjustment to living in a big city took some time.

You shared an apartment with two Geneseo friends in Brooklyn and Dad and I helped you move to the upstairs quarters on a very hot summer day.

Instead of receiving one of those late-night phone calls, I heard from you one morning about a harrowing after-midnight experience. Severe abdominal pain had sent you to an emergency room. Your roommate, Jill, was starting a teaching job in the morning, so not wanting to wake her, you decided to drive yourself to the hospital in Jill's car. You sat in an emergency room, located in what one might call the "seedy" part of town for hours. You finally decided to leave and informed me that at one point, while waiting for a light, you noticed an apparent pimp trying to get your attention. Wonderful! You made it safely home, avoiding any other undesirables.

In the morning, Jill asked you where you had parked the car. Unfortunately, you hadn't noticed that you parked in a bus zone and the car had been towed.

Jill found another method of transportation to her teaching job. You visited a doctor and then went down in the

Lori with roomate Jill

pouring rain to where the car was impounded, paid a hefty fine, and retrieved the car. Welcome to life in the Big Apple, and thank you for calling your mother <u>after</u> the fact!

My future son-in-law, Chris, was a fellow student with you at RIT and your friendship with him eventually led to romance. While you were in Brooklyn, Chris was in Vancouver, Canada, working for Toyota. It was basically a long-distance relationship with occasional long weekend visits by both of you.

The thrill of living in Brooklyn, shuttling back and forth to New Jersey every day, was wearing off. When Chris was transferred to Lexington, you followed. Luckily, your employer asked you to continue on with the company. You were able to work from your apartment and made trips back to New Jersey when needed.

As a mother, of course I hoped this live-in situation would result in an engagement. Finally, Dad informed me that Chris had approached him and asked for permission to marry you. I was thrilled. Chris was a nice guy from a good family (you girls always laughed at me when I said that, but it is important), he had a steady job, and most importantly he loved you.

Special occasions and holidays passed and still no ring. What was he waiting for? Fathers seem to be more patient about such things and Dad just said, "He'll do it when he's ready."

On an ordinary weekend, Chris finally made it official. You moved to Bellevue, Kentucky, soon after the engagement and picked a wedding date of August 1, 2009. The need to be organized resulted in your creating a book outlining all the preparation needed for the perfect wedding. All three of your sisters borrowed that book for their wedding planning.

Then the unthinkable entered our lives on February 12, 2009.

This time that late-night phone call came from me. I think the first thing I asked was, "Is Chris with you?" It would have been devastating to tell you I didn't know what had happened to

Chris and Lori

Dad if you were alone. Luckily, Chris was there for support.

You drove all night to arrive in Buffalo the next morning. Amid tears, you told me that you could postpone the wedding, but I assured you both that your wedding would still happen. It seemed important to have something positive to focus on.

No matter what steps were taken in preparation for the event, one thought was always present, *Dad won't be here for the wedding.*

He had planned ahead for our girls' weddings. After selling a considerable number of collectibles in 2008, we opened an account to cover costs. Following the crash, I had difficulty discovering where the money had been deposited. Finally, a Key Bank statement arrived in the mail for a Certificate of Deposit. The original date of the deposit coincided with the time of the sale, and the amount totaled our agreed-upon contribution for you and your sisters. That action released me from any financial burden, and allowed all of you to have memorable weddings.

We had no idea how our emotions would handle this first wedding. The evening before the big event, sisters, bridesmaids, and the mother-of-the-bride gathered together in the hope of relieving ever-present tensions. Your sisters and bridesmaids presented you with a photo album that rekindled many happy memories.

You also gave me a book, *Dear Mom…Thank You for Everything* by Bradley Trevor Greive. Previously, I had given you his book, *The Blue Day Book*, during a rough time in your life. You shared that little book with your roommate, Jill, on days she, too, felt down.

The "Dear Mom" book was filled with animals and captions depicting times moms deserved to be thanked. One showed a little mouse stuck between two tree branches stating, "Whenever I got into a bind, you were always there for me." On that page, you remarked, "I think the picture says it all," referring to the time you got your leg stuck between two tree limbs. Our neighbor, a Boy Scout leader, came to our aid. One of the best pictures showed a panda bear with the caption, "Thank you for letting a chubby-cheeked 2-year-old run wild among your most precious possessions," and you referred to yourself as "Baby Buddha."

Before we knew it, we stood poised at the back of Nativity Church bracing ourselves for the walk down that aisle. I did not trust myself to look at those in attendance. There was a 100 percent chance that everyone was thinking of Dad and many would be crying. How heartbreaking that he would not be walking his daughter down the aisle due to such a freak accident.

With our eyes focused on the priest and Chris, we took that bittersweet walk.

It can certainly be said that the beginning of your lives as Mr. and Mrs. Chris Tiede was a much-needed remedy for the pain inflicted on our family less than six months before.

Chris and Lori (photo courtesy of Sarah J. Carr)

After two years of marriage, you and Chris were ready to seriously pursue parenthood. Unfortunately, it was beginning to appear that motherhood was something that would not come easily to you. How my heart ached for you both. There appeared to be no quick remedy to this problem.

Listening to your trials and tribulations via phone wasn't enough. This called for some one-on-one time with Mom, so off I went to Kentucky. I could not provide the remedy to magically help you become a mother, but I could be a sounding board and support you. I could hug and kiss you, and tell you to hold on to hope.

By the time I arrived in Kentucky, though, you greeted me with the news that you were pregnant.

You waited several months before revealing the gender of the baby. I was driving home from work when you called me. It was a good thing I had pulled over, because the news that a baby BOY would finally be added to our family brought a surge of joy, especially after Dad and I had four girls, and now I had one granddaughter.

Caden Douglas Tiede arrived a few weeks prior to his due date on October 2, 2012.

Chris still worked for Toyota, and shortly after Caden's birth, your little family suddenly found yourselves transferred to Nagoya, Japan, for a year.

Chris, Lori and baby Caden in Japan

Chris, Lori and Caden

Due to the difficulty you had experienced with the first pregnancy, you felt that conception of another child would again take time. Therefore, you were very surprised when you discovered your family would be expanding. Your second son, Rowan, was conceived in Japan, but was born in the United States.

I had the opportunity to visit you in Japan, and then you and Caden returned to the states and lived with me for several months before Rowan's arrival on August 6, 2014. Chris managed to arrive home from Japan on August 5. His, or maybe I should say Rowan's, timing was perfect.

You moved back to Bellevue shortly after Rowan's birth and then became permanent residents in Lexington. Your job status continued to rise for several years, culminating in your achieving a Director of Project Management & Client Services position.

Lori's professional picture

Dad did not achieve that pinnacle until later in his career, so I know he would have been so proud of your advancement in the business world. However, you decided to put work on hold so that you could spend more time with your boys. I am glad you could make that decision as everyone is enjoying the benefits of that arrangement.

Lori running

You found an additional passion and have become an avid runner, accepting the torch your dad carried during his life. It appears that yet another generation will obtain pleasure from that pastime, as your boys often join you when you run.

Just as I had immersed myself in volunteering at your and your sisters' schools, you also are vigorously participating in your boys' school activities. It brings back to me those fun times of taking part in fundraisers, leading art projects, and of course, working on the St. Columban newsletter every month.

I am thankful that you and Chris share a special comradery with other Toyota couples in the Lexington area, which provides support and friendship for all the families. You are also fortunate that Chris' parents moved to the area to ensure that the bond of family can remain strong. I am very thankful that they are there to lovingly back you up on so many occasions.

Luckily, I am able to see all of you several times a year for birthdays and holidays. Our get-together for Thanksgiving in 2020 was especially welcomed, after being separated for so many months during the pandemic.

I need a steady stream of love and time to bond with each of my girls. I am so proud of the beautiful and strong women you have become. Sometimes, it is the only remedy I need to keep me

Lori with the boys

going. As the years march by, it seems to be a remedy you and your sisters also need. I am thankful for that.

Love,

Mom

11/20/21

Jessica Clair:
Marathon Woman

Dear Jess,

Happy 33rd Birthday! As you requested, here is your birthday gift.

The years fly by so quickly and you and your sisters refuse to stay little. Despite my desire to stop the progression of time, especially as your growth reminds me of my own swift aging process, it is wonderful to see my girls evolve into amazing adults. But, if I am honest with myself, watching you all transform before my eyes is one of the joys of parenthood. You have developed your own personalities, and yet, I occasionally catch a glimpse of Dad and me in your spirit and drive to achieve success.

Jess, you inherited my silly gene, which I received from my dad. There have been times in my life when I have laughed so hard that I ended up on the floor, doubled over, and unable to speak as snorts escaped my nose. I have witnessed you in that same situation. Unexpected change in your life has made that ability to laugh a lifesaver.

Did your zest for running come from me? Definitely not. We know that passion came from your dad. Perhaps I am unwise to begin writing this piece on the anniversary of Dad's death. Then again, what better way to remember and honor his memory than to recall your running journey that would lead to fulfilling

First marathons for Jess (2017) and Doug (1982)

your goal of participating in the New York City Marathon on November 5, 2017.

Dad never forced running on you girls. He seemed content to support your other athletic choices. I do recall you and Jill accepting his suggestion that you run a mile race at the Mariemont High School in Ohio when you were young. You both successfully ran over the finish line and I can guarantee that he was proud of his girls.

You began your journey into running in a way similar to his. You were both in your early twenties. He did not begin to run until he was deployed to Vietnam in 1970. Running was a good way to stay in shape during that time, plus an ability to run fast certainly could come in handy in a war zone.

It wasn't until 2007, while you were working for the Oneonta Country Club, that you considered running your first 5k race. The manager of the country club, who also had become your friend, urged you to give it a try. You called Dad and he was happy to share some of his running tips with you. A man with a love for making lists, he no doubt sent you a diagram that included a breakdown of the miles you should run each week in preparation for the race.

You completed the race, but the running bug had not really infected you yet. After his death, you decided you could honor your dad by participating in more events. I was surprised, though, when you told me you wanted to run the Cincinnati 10k Turkey Run in 2009. It was only a few months after the crash, and I was not sure I could emotionally enter that running atmosphere so soon after losing him. In addition to that fact, I was concerned that you had never run that distance before. Once again, I found myself in the familiar position of a fan on the sidelines. Your excitement and nervous anticipation, along with a thousand or so other runners, crept into my heart and soul.

When I finally connected with you after the race, I remember

how you tearfully told me, "I just wish Dad had been here with me."

That running bug was starting to work its way under your skin.

You became friends with Lauren, an avid runner, and with her encouragement, you ran your first half marathon in 2014 in Washington D.C.

Jess completing her first half marathon

Running was becoming an important part of your life. After watching Lauren and her husband, Justin, run the 2015 New York City Marathon, you made a decision to challenge yourself to run a marathon.

Unfortunately, that decision came on the day you learned that the progression of your life was about to change. To put it bluntly, it came at a time when "the shit hit the fan," and you discovered that your husband's version of the future differed from yours.

I like to think that having the goal of running a marathon helped you release the many emotions that divorce caused. You became a stronger version of yourself, both physically and mentally.

You decided 2017 would be "game time." Even when you were not picked in the lottery for the 2017 marathon, you decided to participate in the "9+1" program. By running in nine races organized by the New York Road Runners Group, and volunteering at one race, you qualified for the 2017 marathon.

People refer to "God winks" as surprising experiences that seem to be a sign of divine intervention. We had our share of those winks during your training for the big event.

While going through the storage units, I discovered a training book Dad had purchased, "Make the Marathon Your Event," by Richard Benyo. My enthusiasm to give you the book was apparent when you came to visit and you were barely in the door before I thrust this find into your hands. "Are you trying to make me cry?" you lamented, but I could tell you were thankful to have something of Dad's. You especially liked that he had written goals and anticipated times in the book margins, just as you had done in a training book you purchased. That brings us to the "God wink" moment. The book you bought was "Marathon, the Ultimate Training Guide," by Hal Higdon. Richard Benyo had dedicated his book to Hal Higdon. To me, that is more than a coincidence. I see God's and Dad's hand in the discovery of his book in those storage units.

Another surprise was finding a picture of Dad taken during his first marathon in 1982. That photo provided inspiration to you as you continued your training. It was not always easy, but you worked hard and you faithfully stuck to the program.

The marathon took place on a Sunday. I arrived in town on the Thursday before the event. That night, we took the ferry into Manhattan to pick up your race number. The minute we walked into the New York City Marathon Expo, tears welled up in my eyes. It was impossible not to think of your dad. So, there we were in the middle of this huge convention center, hugging and crying. We felt his spirit around us, but oh how we wished he could have physically shared this experience with us.

Lori and Jill arrived on Friday. I received some ribbing from you girls, as I refused to drive to the Newark airport to pick Lori up. Hey, once I park my vehicle in your parking garage, I refuse to drive through the crazy New York City area until I head home.

Saturday morning, we took an Uber into Manhattan so Lori and Jill could run a 5k. You and I walked through the brisk temperatures to find an area to cheer them on. The tourist in me loved passing Grand Central Station as we walked down to Bryant Park. As we waited for the runners to arrive, we peered at tempting items displayed in kiosks, which thankfully for our pocketbooks, were still closed. A hardy group of skaters practiced their skills on the ice rink, a favorite destination for New Yorkers during the holiday season. How cool it was to watch skaters in front of the Manhattan skyline, including the Empire State Building.

You also took me to Library Way, where we could read inspirational quotes about reading, writing, and literature along the sidewalk leading to the impressive New York City Public Library. You had discovered that area on one of your training runs. You know your mother well. I loved it and easily found examples of why writing is so important to me.

Finally, the runners appeared. We craned our necks and tried to dodge the sun that blinded our view as we anxiously looked for Lori and Jill. As a longtime supporter at these events, it is always nerve-wracking trying to spot your runners. Luckily, Lori saw us and shouted out to us. Unfortunately, we missed Jill streaking by.

There was no time to lose as you guided me down to the subway. I found myself packed into the subway with little room to breathe. Thankfully, it was a short ride, and we hurried out and up a huge flight of stairs to the street. Who was running the race, Lori and Jill or us?

When we arrived at Central Park, you wanted to rush ahead to catch a glimpse of your sisters. I agreed to this suggestion, as I caught my breath and hoped I would eventually catch up to you. I reminded myself that if lost, cell phones can keep us connected these days.

We were all reunited and headed to brunch at P.J. Clarke's near Lincoln Center. Lori's college friend, Kristen, and your friend, Jen, and her parents joined us. It was my kind of place, lots of wood and a nostalgic feel of days gone by.

After lunch, it was fun just being a bunch of girls strolling through Manhattan. On a whim, we stopped into a nail salon where you girls coordinated nail color for marathon day, and I managed to get a head and back massage.

Basically, we were killing time as you wanted to hear Kathrine Switzer talk at the NYRR (New York Road Runners) *Run Center*.

Jess with Kathrine Switzer

Kathrine, who was the first woman to run the Boston Marathon as a numbered entry in 1967, had become your running idol. When doing one of your training races, you were amazed to glance to your side and see that she was running next to you.

At a water station, she even let you snap a photo of the two of you. You had mentioned to me that Kathrine is spelled without an e in the middle. It was forgotten when her mother filled out the birth certificate. I couldn't help but laugh at that fact. Your middle name is spelled Clair without an e because I forgot how to correctly spell it when asked to fill out forms at the hospital.

While we waited for Kathrine, we spoke to Bill Rodgers, a runner who is best known for four victories in the Boston Marathon. He took considerable time talking with us. At one point he asked if I helped motivate you in your running endeavors. That question stirred up emotions in me, as I shakily explained that Dad had been your motivator, but tragically he had died. I could see his compassion as he told me Dad's spirit and my own support provided all the encouragement you needed to reach your running goals.

Bill Rodgers signing books
with Jess and me

You fought crowds to reach Kathrine, but your tenacity was rewarded when you were able to talk with her and have her sign two copies of her book. As she spoke, I think we were all inspired by her story and determination to succeed. *I am woman, hear me roar*, rang through my mind.

Finally, back at your apartment, we decided to have a quiet evening. Lori tackled the job of making signs, refusing to let you see them until the race.

My psychologist tells me I should not hide all my emotions from you girls, that it is good for you to see that those emotions are a part of my life. Well, one of the hardest moments for me that weekend occurred that night.

Lori had been calling the Tiedes each evening around eight to do FaceTime with the boys. She kept trying to reach them with no success. We were all concerned, as call after call went unanswered. Fear gripped me as I kept thinking, "Oh my God, this is how the girls felt the night of the crash as they tried to reach us on their phones." It was such a terrible feeling of panic.

Relief came when we learned the boys had turned the sound off on their grandparents' phones, and we could finally see that they were okay. Caden blamed Rowan, who blamed "Another bad boy," whom he named "Jimmy!"

Although I had managed to keep my feelings of panic from you girls originally, once the crisis was over, I had to tell you what I was experiencing. I always tried to imagine what you girls went through the night of the crash, but now I can say I understand more fully the heart-pounding fear you all felt.

The theme for the marathon was "It will move you," and you were on the move early that Sunday. You woke up at 3:00 a.m. and were traveling by Uber by 4:00 a.m. to Staten Island for the start of the race. Although you were in the second wave, you basically arrived at the crack of dawn and had to wait almost five hours until your starting time of 10:15.

Lori, Jill, and I snoozed a bit longer and did not catch the ferry to Manhattan until 8:00 a.m. From there, we began the subway journey that would take us through the New York boroughs. Your friend, Max, joined the fan club too. Thank heaven Lori, Jill, and Max were with me. I know I never could have traversed that route on my own. It was decided that Brooklyn would be our first point to catch sight of you. My friend Cindy's son, Kevin, lived directly on the marathon course. He and his wife invited us up to their apartment until your expected arrival time. Their television was turned on, and at one point, I made a complete fool of myself when I shouted out that I saw you as they broke to a commercial. Sure enough, texting confirmed it was not you.

The anxiety I felt throughout the day was at a fever pitch. It was nothing new. I felt the same racing heart, scanning racer after racer, when Dad ran his marathons. You feel totally stressed out until that dot in the distance becomes your runner. If you do not see that person at the pre-designated time, you wonder, *Did I miss him/her; has he/she collapsed somewhere down the road?*

Jill, Lori, Max and me ready to greet Jess at the 6.5 mile point

A moment of relief settled over us as you appeared at the 6.5 mile point, smiling and looking good. Kevin's wife, who had just met us, must have thought we were a bunch of crazy women. We screamed out your name, blew whistles, waved a sign, and jumped

Ready for the handoff!

up and down. You handed us some items you didn't want to carry and were on your way.

You later told us that you had already realized at that point that you had started the race too fast, despite the knowledge that you should not do that. You had gotten caught up in the high of the marathon start, and you were swept up in the adrenaline streaming through all those runners. You could not seem to slow your pace down.

We proceeded to the subway and our next destination was near First Avenue.

All this subway travel certainly was different from what I experienced during Dad's marathons. The races in Buffalo started in the downtown area, and I had to get in the car and cross the border for the finish in Niagara Falls, Canada. I saw him at the beginning and searched for him at the end. The Columbus marathons were not spread out like the New York marathon, at least in my memory. I could easily walk from spot to spot to keep track of his progress.

The crowd size was multiplying quickly, and we finally saw an opening at the side of the road around the seventeen-mile mark. You still looked good when you ran past us, but this time you shouted, "This is harder than I thought!" Our stress levels suddenly increased as we became concerned about your well-being. I knew you would be devastated if you did not finish the race.

It turned out that your thoughts at that 6.5 mile had been correct. Your pace was too fast, and by mile 12 you were feeling extremely fatigued, and were mentally stressed about whether you could finish the race. We did not help your situation, as you were counting on us to have raisins or pretzels you could grab as you passed us. Not only did we begin to worry, but we also felt guilty about failing to provide that boost to you.

This need for nourishment didn't surprise me. After all, you were the baby who needed to be fed every two hours. It is hard to let go of some habits.

Our thoughts were filled with concern as we rushed to the 25-mile point in Central Park.

The crowd of spectators had become a mob. If there were approximately 50,000 runners participating in the 2017 marathon, with spectators the total number milling around had to reach almost 100,000 people. It was incomprehensible.

Adding to the problem of securing a good vantage point was the fact that a misty rain had been falling all day. We had ponchos, but after a while hoods were abandoned, so we all resembled drowned rats.

As we walked through Central Park, we passed the Metropolitan Museum of Art. All weekend we had seen the outside of such great places: Lincoln Center, Grand Central Station, the New York City Public Library, and the Empire State Building. I made a mental note to actually visit these magnificent landmarks during one of my trips.

We were beginning to see that security had been beefed up along the course. Even if you are not dwelling on it, in this day and age, thoughts of terrorism are always tucked away in a corner of your mind during public events. At one point, a "pop" pierced through the shouts of well-wishers. I was startled, and waited to see if it was gun fire or a firework. I was relieved that nothing else happened.

My concern that you would not finish the race disappeared, and I felt such relief as I saw the smile on your face as you approached us. Lori raised her last sign and was screaming, "If it doesn't challenge you, it doesn't change you." I now knew that you would finish the race.

It was impossible to see you physically cross that finish line, but we could watch your achievement on the New York City Marathon App. We watched as a little "JW" dot advanced closer and closer, until finally reaching its goal.

The next task was to reunite with you at the designated family reunion spot. It was one thing to make spectators walk blocks and blocks to reach this point, but I could not believe that the runners had to walk that far after completing a marathon. We hovered around the W section for a while, but my anxiety increased as you did not show up, and you had not texted us after finishing the race. I needed to see you and make sure you were okay. We strayed from our section, which complicated things a bit, but we connected by phone and finally I could relax when I saw you standing with your friend Jen's family.

What a day it had been for us all, and what a road you had traveled to achieve your goal.

A wet but happy reunion! (above) Max, Lori, Jess, me and Jill

I cannot express perfectly what it means for a mother to see her children succeed. Especially on your birthday, I look at you and see a little baby who started life with a heap of dark hair and your dad's dimples. I see you with crooked bangs, after you

Toddler Jess in bike attire

experimented with the safety scissors you received in your Christmas stocking. I see you in mismatched clothes, covered in dirt as you played with your sisters on the driveway in Ohio. I see you changing into a young girl, trying to make heads or tails out of the teenage years and discovering boys. In the blink of an eye, you were off to college, and found your own way without needing too much assistance from your mom or dad. Dreams did come true for you, but you faced the hard reality that "happily ever after" was not guaranteed for everyone.

After the crash, as I felt such a weight of despair, I told myself, "I will not let this ruin my life." I feel it is a message you now understand. You have found a source of inner strength you never realized you possessed. You have embraced and accepted change, and you forged on.

Completing the marathon not only honored your dad, but it defined who you have become: a strong woman who embraces life. I admire you, and I am inspired by you.

You requested that I write about my experience during your marathon journey as a gift for your birthday. That request touched my heart, because it tells me that you value my writing. I discovered that writing this piece was harder than I anticipated, but in doing so, I smiled a lot, shed a tear or two, and enjoyed reliving every moment. I hope you can sense all the love that is between the lines.

Love,

Mom

Originally written 2/12/18, updated   02/24/21

Author's Note: Jess ran her second NY marathon in 2019. In January of 2021, Jess said goodbye to big-city life and moved to Denver, Colorado. Life there is more conducive to her love of running and hiking.

Colorado is the perfect place for Jess

Jill Marleen:
Last, but not Least

Dear Jill:

The year 2021 is already quite a year of milestones and a big year for monumental birthdays. I turned 70 in July; Kim turned 40 in April; and you, my baby, turned 35 in May. But, in a few weeks, you will truly hit a new milestone as you become Mrs. Noah Ronald.

You have had a wild ride in the last few years, surviving in many ways. This seems to be the perfect opportunity to reflect on wonderful you.

Jill, you have heard the story many times that you were our surprise baby. I hope I have assured you that child number four was in our plans for a family. We just did not expect you to arrive only 15 months following the birth of your sister Jess.

So much for the myth that you could not get pregnant while breast-feeding.

Home pregnancy kits were pretty new on the market in 1985, so despite a negative result, a trip to my gynecologist quickly reversed the verdict to positive. I called Dad at work with the news, rather than tell him face to face. He accepted your impending arrival after the initial shock wore off.

I lined up a second crib and we prepared for another bundle of joy.

Even after delivering three other children, there were still possibilities for new pregnancy experiences. A few days before your arrival, I started having labor pains. We shuffled your sisters over to Debbie Lindsay's house next door, and headed to the hospital. I could not believe that after spending the night there, they advised me to return home. I had never heard of false labor before. You were just teasing us, and had decided to stay snug inside me for a while longer.

You were finally ready to meet us on May 27, 1986. Back at the hospital, my doctor had just examined me, and announced that since things were not progressing, he would head out for some coffee. He had not even gotten to the door when I yelled for him to get back in the room. Our daughter number four arrived safe and sound.

Jill, you were not a child who was content to sit still. Perhaps you were encouraged by your sisters, or maybe you just felt that you needed to catch up with them. You were always raring to go. When they were small, I could put Kim, Lori, and Jess in the playpen or crib when I needed a quick rest to regain my strength. Not with you! You were fast, and we soon realized that you had tremendous skills when it came to escaping these "cages."

This was especially true at afternoon nap time. I had barely reached the bedroom door when you climbed out of the crib and

Jill climbing out of her crib

were heading out the door. Desperate times called for desperate measures. I needed a reprieve for an hour, so I put you in the crib and made a mad dash to close the door, which I then held tight while standing in the hall. As anticipated, you lay by the door, crying at my trickery. I did feel guilty, but you quickly fell asleep moments later.

Please tell me that this action did not come up in any psychology session in later years.

As your sisters started their school journeys, you and I had plenty of quality time together. When I began writing

Jill in Santa suit

the newsletter for St. Columban's Elementary School in Ohio, you were the darling of the office staff, as well as the teachers when I helped out in the classroom. It is easy to see why.

Your turn arrived, and soon you headed to the Lakeview preschool, following in your sisters' footsteps. We were a part of that establishment for seven straight years. As with the other girls, both Dad and I enjoyed participating in the school's activities. He became a master at pumpkin carving every Halloween season at the Dad's

Mom's tea at Lakeview

Night, and one of my favorite events was the Mother's Day Tea. I have always loved this picture of you and me from that celebration.

Like your big sister Kim, we decided to give you an extra year of first grade. I think you benefited and enjoyed one year at Loveland's Lloyd Mann Elementary School, and then continued that experience at St. Columban.

You made good friends over the years, especially Natalie Johnson, who even visited us after we moved back to Buffalo in 1997. We met halfway outside of Cleveland for a kid pickup.

Friendships continued to bloom for you in the suburbs of Buffalo. Annmarie Dean became your lifelong friend when

Jill and Annmarie

you met in middle school. I love that you have been able to keep close, despite the miles between you.

It became apparent during those middle school years that you possessed athletic abilities. You tried lacrosse, soccer, and basketball. You really excelled at anything you attempted, but soccer and basketball became your sports.

One day, after attending the 4:30 Mass at Nativity Church, Mr. Layer, the high school varsity basketball coach, approached us and praised your talents. We were terribly touched by his remarks and so proud of you.

You would eventually play varsity basketball for him in high school. You and your buddy, Christina Biedny, were referred to as Mutt & Jeff, due to Christina's six-foot stature against your smaller five-foot seven-inch frame. You were quite the duo. Your three-point shots were magic, and always thrilling to watch. It was always awesome to see you mentioned or photographed in several editions of the *Clarence Bee*. Dad kept all the clippings.

You were a big asset to the varsity soccer team during all four

Christina and Jill

Jill showing off some soccer skills

years of high school.

You made several select soccer teams, and Dad and I were kept busy driving back and forth to tournaments. It was a great experience. Thanks for all those thrills and adventures.

In high school, though, you discovered boys. Dad said that revelation played a bit of havoc with your sports performance. Once your boyfriend broke up with you just before a soccer playoff game. You were devastated and spent hours crying in your bedroom. Dad shook his head and said, "Couldn't he have at least waited until after the playoffs?"

You did try out for soccer at SUNY Brockport, arriving weeks before the start of your freshman year. Quickly, you realized how competitive college soccer would be for you. I could see you were pretty miserable

Kim, Dad, and me supporting you at a high school game

dealing with the practice schedule and the demands that would be placed on you if you made the team. I think we were both thankful when the coach cut you early in the process.

You worked hard on your studies and enjoyed campus life. Once again, you were fortunate to form lasting friendships during those four years.

When it was time to decide on your college internship, you called your dad many times to discuss your options. You finally made the choice of the Pinehurst Golf Resort in North Carolina, which was highly approved by Dad, who had visions of visiting you and taking advantage of the opportunity to play golf on one of their famous courses.

In January of 2009, you had completed your studies at Brockport and in February were back at home happily preparing to start your internship in March. Fate had other plans.

I am taking a deep breath before I begin writing about February 12, 2009…

So much about that night appeared in the pages of *One on the Ground*. I will simply say here that our mother/daughter bond became more deeply entwined in ways we never could have imagined. Despite the devastation that surrounded us, we witnessed miracles that night.

We both managed to escape the destruction that encased us. You, unbelievably, reached the back of the house and saw me emerging from my hole (as you expressed it, "Like a flower popping out of the ground"). It was a miracle that we were able to find each other so quickly.

Never forget those miracles, Jill, and the fact that we are survivors.

I do know one thing, though, if anything would have happened to you that night… I cannot allow my mind to even think about that scenario.

In looking up the definition of the word survive, I have a hard time finding a meaning that accurately describes the feeling that jolts me when I refer to us as survivors. One word that did come up was "persist," to continue in spite of obstacles or opposition; to persevere (maintain effort, steadfastly, especially in the face of difficulties). That is what we did that night. We were somehow blessed with the strength to survive.

And so, we continued on.

Graduation Day, 2009

I proudly watched you graduate in May 2009 from SUNY Brockport, and then drove you to Southern Pines, North Carolina, to start your internship at the Pinehurst Golf Resort. You eventually accepted a full-time job at the resort. The adventures we shared during those years are also covered in *One on the Ground*.

You and Dan were married in May of 2011 here in Buffalo. Much to my surprise, I later learned that you were also married in September 2009. In order to get Army housing, you did need to be married. Since Lori and Chris were married in August of that

Jill, me and Kim at Pinehurst, North Carolina

year, you decided that another big wedding was not a good idea for the family emotionally. I can't imagine how hard it was for you to keep that fact a secret for so long.

I was overjoyed when you decided to come back to the Buffalo area in 2012. Dan was still serving in the Army in North Carolina, but you had found a job here. It was nice to have a housemate. You brought along Zoey, one of your dogs, and Piper, your cat.

Since I already had two cats of my own, the adjustment to Piper was not too difficult. I had never lived with a dog, though. That proved to be quite a learning experience, like the night I sat on the edge of my couch, and suddenly wondered if old age was creeping up on me and I had a leakage problem. The culprit turned out to be Zoey. Apparently, we had missed any signal she had made to inform us she needed to go outside to relieve herself.

Then there was the night when you were out of town and I was dog sitting. I had been watching a sappy Hallmark movie and felt the need to cuddle Zoey's warm body on top of my bed. No sooner was I on the bed than I wondered, *what am I lying on?* I cringed when I realized Zoey had left one of her "poop-logs" there.

Despite these setbacks, we all commingled well together.

During your time with me, there were fun evenings out with Kim for dinner downtown in Buffalo and shows at Shea's Performing Arts Center. Even doing our Sunday morning grocery shopping seemed special to me. We enjoyed the company of my neighbors, Jim, Lisa, Ryan, and Jillian, at a wine party one night. You needed to make our famous family fruit pizza for a work party the next day. Ryan escorted you across the street, just in case your wine consumption had exceeded a certain limit. The next day, you informed me that the pizza never did materialize, as you opted for hitting a pillow instead.

I was so proud of you when you stepped forward to help organize the annual 3407 run, and you continued to undertake that job even a year after you moved to Denver.

It was exciting to accompany you on your first house-hunting expeditions. I was rooting for the older homes we checked out, but you were more realistic when it came to home repairs and eventually had a new home built.

I knew it was time for you to leave and to resume your married life, but it was difficult to readjust to my life alone.

In a story I wrote called "Sunday Afternoon," I talked about a day I spent going through some boxes of items salvaged from Long Street.

> *I took a break from my perusal of the photos, grabbed a few recyclables lying in the kitchen, and opened a door of the mudroom armoire to store them. Runners talk of hitting a wall somewhere around the 20-mile point in a marathon. I encountered my wall as the door swung open.*
>
> *Jill had begun the process of collecting her "stuff," and after 8 months of being my housemate had moved to her in-laws preparing for her husband, Dan's, arrival home from the Army. The emptiness of that wardrobe confirmed the reality that life on my own would now resume.*

We did create some good memories in your Hamburg home: family celebrations and BBQs. Okay, I'll admit one of those

Me under the table
(blurry because you were laughing so hard)

memories includes me climbing under your coffee table, but I still say I was only being funny and had not had too much to drink.

Although that was a nice house, I never could go there and not think about an old movie called "The Stepford Wives," based on a Stephen King novel. If you have never heard of that, look it up. It is a story about a cloned community. The houses in your neighborhood were so close together, almost identical, and the streets were so narrow, it did give off a cloned atmosphere.

Farewell dinner before Denver move

I was pretty surprised when you told me you were moving to Denver, Colorado, in 2015. "Why there?" I asked. Your reply "Oh, we are into the outdoor life," seemed like a new revelation to me.

Saying goodbye was hard, but I reminded myself that survivors can adjust to whatever life hands them.

By relocating to Denver, though, you broadened my horizons. I had a real adventure when I traveled there by train, and even received a proposal to cuddle one night. You were a bit horrified by this, but I actually considered it flattering, although I did not accept that invitation.

By the time I made my second visit to Denver, your life was changing.

Did you hear that? It's another deep breath from me as I try to write this next part.

Married life had become challenging for you, and I could see why. There definitely were personality differences, and it upset me how you were treated sometimes.

I knew it had always been a struggle for you to find professional help to deal with the 3407 trauma you experienced. It was a relief for me to learn that you connected with someone in the Denver area who could help you. You discovered that it wasn't just the sorrow of 3407 that was causing your emotional problems, but it was also your marriage.

I truly feel you worked hard to save that marriage, but that ultimately divorce was the only answer that enabled you to heal yourself. It took strength for you to take that step. I'll go back

Thanksgiving, 2017

to that word persevere; you were steadfast in the face of difficulties.

Just months after your decision, I celebrated Thanksgiving with you in Colorado. I met another dog member of your family at that time. Riley was just a puppy, and Zoey was attempting to accept her new sister. Even though you had set up a network of gates to keep the dogs contained when we went out, somehow they always managed to escape during our absence. I still have a small scar on my left hand from where I burned myself while checking the turkey that year. And, I became addicted to *The Great British Cooking Show*.

Your happiness meter started to soar upward when you met Noah Ronald. (Don't laugh, but right now in order for me to remember his last name, I have to associate it with Ronald McDonald. Sorry about that, and I am sure that won't be necessary in the near future.) The two of you quickly clicked. Jess thought perhaps things were moving along too quickly, especially when you decided to move in together. I laughingly told Jess that she

was becoming the "mom" and I was becoming the "child," because it bothered her more than me. I just saw the happiness radiating from you. A happy child equals a happy mother.

I finally got to meet Noah when I joined Jess, Lori, and

Jill and Noah

the boys in Colorado to spend Thanksgiving with you in 2019. He easily passed inspection, especially because I could clearly see his love and respect for you.

We created so many memories during that visit: enjoying delicious meals prepared by Noah; visiting a spectacular light display at the Denver Zoo; Noah creating a sled run off the back porch for the boys, and you and Jess as it turned out; tackling a "Toy Story" 1,000-piece puzzle that Noah might have purchased for the boys, but it turned into a family project.

Thanksgiving in Denver 2019

Hmmm, Noah's name keeps coming up there. No wonder he made such a great impression on me.

Because of the Pandemic, 2020 was not the year we expected, but one highlight was Noah calling me to request my permission to marry you. That gesture may seem old-fashioned to some people, but it meant the world to me.

It's unbelievable to me that we have not seen each other in person for over a year and a half. Thank heaven for modern technology that has permitted us to stay connected all that time.

I find it bittersweet that Jess moved to Denver in January. I am happy that you and she are near one another and can share so many good times together. You can take care of each other, which is a comfort to me. But I am sad that another daughter is so far away. I am adjusting, though.

Soon, I will be with all my girls in Denver for your wedding! There will be so many new memories to cherish.

Another blessing, and yes, a miracle will be the arrival in January 2022 of another grandson. You and Noah will be great parents, and I am excited that you will experience the happiness of having a child.

My baby having a baby. Wow, that is quite a lot for me to take in. The circle of life continues, and I am so proud of the woman you have become.

You are a survivor, and will continue to persevere when dealing with whatever life sends your way.

Love you,
Mama

7/12/21

Postscript: Gavin Douglas arrived on January 10, 2022, weighing 9lbs. 2ozs. He is definitely one reason Jill survived that tragic night in 2009. Gavin was destined to add a branch to our family tree.

Noah, Jill and Gavin

My Grandchildren

"I know I will leave my work unfinished. I just hope I planted enough seeds in my children and grandchildren that they will continue."

~ David Robinson

A Little Bit of Heaven

Alone,
existing,
awaiting his arrival.

Thrill,
anticipation,
love at first sight.

Another life, another world,
a little bit of heaven.

See,
experience,
thru different eyes.

Learning,
growing,
life in his arms.

Another life, another world,
a little bit of heaven.

One, two
three, four
daughters in our arms.

Responsibility,
discovery,
parenthood a joy.

Another life, another world,
a little bit of heaven.

Gone,
lost,
an empty void.

Searching,
yearning,
tears and sorrow.

Another life, another world,
a glimpse of hell.

Life
hope,
renewed in my arms.

Twigs,
blossoms,
Grandma's delight.

Another life, another world,
a little bit of heaven.

~ Karen Wielinski

2/17/14, updated 10/15/19

Dawn

My grandson, Caden Douglas Tiede's, imminent arrival was announced when my cell phone alarm went off on October 2, 2012. I fumbled to turn it off and thought, *Is it time to get up already.* My grogginess cleared and I realized it was 1:30 in the morning and the call was from my daughter, Lori. She was scheduled to deliver her first child in six weeks. Now she was at the hospital awaiting a C-section as the baby's heart rate slowed with every contraction she experienced.

I was eight hours away and it had always been pretty obvious that unless Lori was going to be induced. I would not be at her side during labor. This assumption was correct, so I sat and waited. Lori's husband, Chris, called at 2:30 to say preparations were being made for the procedure. The mother in me wanted to just throw clothes in a suitcase and head to Cincinnati, but the practical me knew

Baby Caden with beloved Ginger

that if anything went wrong, I would not want to be on a dark interstate and have to deal with such news.

How long did C-sections take? Finally, at 3:30 a.m., Chris called with the good news that all was well. Lori was fine and Caden had arrived at 4 pounds, 7 ounces. He is the first BOY in a long line of Wielinski girls.

Driving in the lingering darkness of early morning takes more concentration, especially when you have been up since 1:30 a.m., left the house at 5:00 a.m., and find yourself dodging yellow warning reflectors, stretched out like Christmas lights, along road construction sites.

Lori had also made her entrance into our lives a month early on November 20, 1982. She turned out to be a Thanksgiving rather than a Christmas baby.

A strange phenomenon seemed to be developing; it appeared that my daughters were following in my footsteps.

My daughter, Kim, had delivered my first granddaughter, Lydia Frances Lipiarz, on August 4, 2012, at only 25 weeks' gestation. Unbelievably, I had delivered Kim at 27 weeks.

It is a strange sensation to see my daughters, my babies, having babies of their own. It made me reflect on my own first pregnancy.

One of the items salvaged from the Long Street site is a book given to me by a friend, Terri Watters, after Kim's birth. The cover encouraged the recipient to "Write Your Own Book." Inside was a glowing description urging me to fill the book with *Poems & Stories, Love words & Hope thoughts, Drawings & Dreams, Insights to Grow on & Reflections on the Wonder of the World.*

This directive was followed with these final words of wisdom: *A living, growing book—blank pages to plant ideas and nourish dreams.*

Wow, it just made you want to pick up a pen and start writing. I started to chronicle my pregnancy.

In *One on the Ground*, I referred to an entry from this journal.

I had given Erik Brady, a journalist with *USA Today*, a copy of an essay I wrote that included a reference to the fact that Doug's and my first serious attempt to become parents occurred during a baseball playoff game between the Yankees and Kansas City. Erik was gathering information about Doug and his collection for an article that eventually appeared in *USA Today* in July 2011. Much to my surprise, and perhaps horror, Erik decided to include that revelation in his story.

Erik thought it fit "right into the importance of sports in Doug's life." Perhaps, but can you imagine the ribbing I have received from that revelation?

"Were you under the bleachers?"

"We were home!"

As I read the entries in this little book, some thirty years later, I was reminded of forgotten facts.

Five months into the pregnancy, I experienced bleeding. It upset me, but I tried to stay calm. *We went shopping and to a movie ("The Jazz Singer"). The baby was always on my mind. The movie had some emotional scenes, and I cried. Actually, I was crying because I was afraid that I was going to lose the baby. The crisis passed, though.*

I listed some world events during this waiting period: *The Iran hostages were freed, President Reagan was shot in Washington, and the first space shuttle was a success the week of April 12, 1981.*

I was reminded that sports continued to be a mainstay in our lives: *We planned a mini-vacation to Canton, Ohio, to see the Football Hall of Fame for the weekend of April 25.*

Doug and I had decided to choose a name for the baby on Easter Sunday, which was on April 19 that year. But, by Good Friday, we were ready to make that choice. Kimberly Anne was chosen for a girl and Eric for a boy, a fact I had completely forgotten.

First pregnancies are a mystery; you really do not know what to expect. The next day, Holy Saturday, I experienced cramping. I was only 27 weeks into this pregnancy. Could it actually be labor?

Despite my discomfort, I still accompanied Doug on planned errands. We went to a flea market, had a huge breakfast, and picked up trees. Back home, Doug planted the trees, helped me with chores and made supper: nice, greasy Italian sausage. We watched *The Love Boat* and *A Salute to Fred Astaire*.

Doug went to bed, but was quickly awakened when I started bleeding. Panic was settling in as I realized this baby was on its way.

"You mean I could be a father by tomorrow?" Doug asked.

I could not answer that question, and wondered if a baby could survive so early in a pregnancy.

We lived in Eden, New York, and Sister's Hospital in Buffalo was at least an hour away. Doug tried to keep the conversation going during the trip, but I just did not feel like talking. "PLEASE DON'T TALK!" I yelled.

I tried to remember what I had heard about breathing techniques during labor. How I wished we had scheduled those Lamaze classes earlier.

My journal entries stopped at this point, and I never did finish writing about that chapter in my life. There was a happy ending though. Our first daughter, Kimberly Anne, arrived shortly after midnight on that Easter, April 19, 1981, weighing 2 pounds, 3 ounces. She spent the first two months of her life "catching up," and finally came home to Eden in July.

I have a possible explanation that might explain Kim's early arrival.

While I was pregnant, Doug grew a beard, not a discrete goatee, but a full-blown Grizzly Adams beard. It wasn't bad, and I got used to seeing him with that full face of hair. A week or so before Kim's arrival, he decided to shave the beard off. One night, he started shaving a bit off at a time. I laughed hysterically during this process, uncontrollable, rolling-on-the-bed laughter, complete with tears running down my checks. He looked so funny without the beard. His trademark mustache luckily was spared the shearing.

Could excessive laughter bring on labor? Medical experts would probably say no, but coming into the world as a result of laughter is a nice thought.

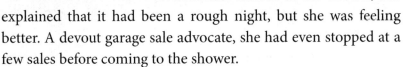

Kim's own early labor in 2012 resulted from an infection. Her journey on delivery day is quite a story, too.

Kim and Lori were both due within days of each other in November. A joint baby shower was scheduled for the morning of August 4, 2012.

Doug with his beard

When Kim arrived at the shower, she explained that it had been a rough night, but she was feeling better. A devout garage sale advocate, she had even stopped at a few sales before coming to the shower.

My protective mother antenna was in full operation, and I kept my eye on Kim throughout the morning. She seemed in good spirits, but by the end of the shower, her sisters and I all insisted that she call her doctor immediately.

"Don't wait until you get home. Call now!"

Her doctor was not overly alarmed, but suggested that Kim go to Sisters Hospital as a precautionary measure.

I faced a dilemma. Lori's in-laws were also having a shower for her that I planned to attend that afternoon in Caledonia, New York. My instincts told me to accompany Kim to the hospital, but she urged me to go with Lori. My other daughters, Jess and Jill, went with Kim.

Lori and I drove to Caledonia, approximately one hour away. We anxiously waited for an update from the girls.

The first update from Jess indicated that they were sitting in a waiting room with other women in active labor. The girls agreed that location did not soothe their anxiety at all. The second update swiftly followed about a half hour later.

Jess' shaky voice confirmed her concern, "Mom? I think you need to be here. Kim is dilated 2 centimeters and they are going to admit her."

Without hesitation, I told her, "I'm on my way."

I did not speed, as a ticket would only delay me. I tried to convince myself that everything would be okay. Things had changed in 30 plus years. If Kim could survive in 1981, surely advanced technology would guide her tiny baby into the world. "Tiny" was the key word. At her last check-up, the doctor had told Kim the baby was under 2 pounds.

As the evening progressed, the doctors could not determine if Kim was about to deliver, or just going through false labor. Her discomfort seemed to increase, and I prayed that things would turn out alright.

Kim's husband, Jeff, and I were on either side of Kim offering encouragement. It is not easy watching your daughter go through labor.

At one point, Kim looked up at me between contractions and said, "Mom, I don't think I can do this."

"Yes, you can," I encouraged, "Think about the end result."

What would the outcome be? I heard the doctor anxiously tell the nurse that she could not locate the baby's heartbeat, "I need that sonogram machine now!"

Finally, a tiny head emerged. Tears rimmed my eyes, but I stopped them in their tracks. I didn't want to get thrown out of the delivery room due to my hysterics. The tears signified not only my happiness due to the arrival of my first grandchild, but also the extreme sadness that Doug was not there to share this experience.

As for Jeff, there was excitement written all over his face. We had no time to even discover the gender, as doctors whisked the baby to a warming table.

The verdict was in, "It's a girl."

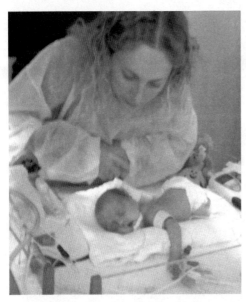

Lydia a few days after her birth

The doctor called Jeff and me over to meet the newest addition to our family, who later was named Lydia Frances. She made no sound, but her arms and legs were moving. She was rushed to the neonatal unit.

I felt pretty shaky, and went out to give the news to the other girls. In the beginning only two people could go back to see Kim, but the nurses finally relented and let us all visit. I felt a sense of pride as I walked behind my family: Lori, Chris, Jess, and Jill. I felt Doug was with us, too.

As for Lydia, she spent a total of four and a half months in both Sisters and Children's hospitals, arriving home in time for Christmas. She was the best gift we could have received.

Dawn gradually swept across the highway as I neared Erie, Pennsylvania. It was a new dawn, not only for this day, but in our lives. I had a granddaughter and now a grandson. They are our light and hope for the future, following the darkness of tragedy. Even a sleep-deprived grandma could appreciate that fact.

Three other grandchildren were added to our family tree. Curtis Lipiarz made his entrance into the world on April 21, 2014, about a month early. I was visiting Lori, Chris, and Caden in Japan at the time. When I landed in Buffalo a few days later, I drove straight from the airport to see my new grandson.

Rowan Tiede broke the pattern on August 6, 2014, and arrived only one day before his scheduled birth date. His dad had arrived from Japan the day before, which was perfect timing.

With Caden and Rowan, 2021

With Curtis and Lydia

With Gavin

Gavin Douglas our other full-term baby arrived on January 10, 2022. He did give us all a scare, when he developed pneumonia the next day. He would become my fourth grandchild to spend time in the NICU (Neo-natal infant care unit). Thanks to the wonderful doctors and nurses, he was able to go home a week later.

I am "Grandma" to Lydia and Curtis, and "Nana" to Caden and Rowan. My heart sings when I hear either name.

Originally written 2/2/13, updated 3/12/22

Initiation

My bathtub now sports a two-tone green turtle draped over the faucet, decorative iron gates bar entrance to the staircase and kitchen, and every item in my living room that seems to draw curiosity like a magnet has been delegated to whatever area of my home is free of tiny hands. Childproofing has become a way of life for me.

In the last two months, I have gained housemates. My daughter, Lori, and her son, Caden, ended their year-long stay in Japan and are adding a memory or two to the story of my life. The impending birth of Baby Boy Tiede, who apparently has a name that will not be revealed until his birth, brought Lori and her husband, Chris, to the conclusion that an American birth, surrounded by relatives, would be a wise choice.

What is that I hear? It is a motherly voice telling her daughter, "Whatever you do, do not get pregnant when you are in Japan." Well, these things have a way of happening.

Separation for the young family was difficult, but modern technology kept everyone connected. The good news that Chris would return to the states at the end of July was very welcome. Wielinski history continually seemed to repeat itself; babies just can't wait to join the family. Hopefully, though, this new baby would keep enjoying the warmth and comfort inside his mother and wait to arrive as scheduled in early August.

I am discovering that there is an initiation process involved in the grandparent club.

As a mother of four daughters, I am finding that this initiation is reached differently when little boys are involved. While bathing Caden recently, he turned to me with a solemn expression, which I found endearing. Lori's exclamation of "Watch out!" came just as he proceeded to pee in the tub. Did I learn a lesson? No. The next time there was no expression to indicate what was about to occur. Lifting him out of the tub, I was "baptized" with a stream of liquid. Welcome to the world of boys, Grandma. I survived that initiation, and was prepared at the end of the next bath. "Do you have to pee?" I asked Caden. He gazed at his little extension with some concern and up at me in total confusion. As I was not eager to encounter another spray from his appendage, I lifted him out, his back toward me, but there was no unexpected spritz.

I faced a more troublesome initiation from my granddaughter.

Gazing at my hands and feet that resembled "Lobsterman" or "Frogman," characters in a fellow writer's entertaining saga of a circus sideshow, I realized the rite of passage into becoming a grandma does entail some risk. My adorable granddaughter, Lydia, and I shared a childhood affliction known as hand, foot, and mouth disease, a common children's virus that causes sores in the mouth and a rash on the hands and feet. First of all, I think they need to rename this disease, as visions of "Mad Cow Disease" pop up in most peoples' minds. Although discomfort and unsightliness accompany the illness, unlike the fate of cows, recovery for humans is possible. Still, the thought of going mad did enter my mind once or twice.

When I heard Lydia had been exposed to the disease, I hit the internet for details. The "wisdom" I obtained assured me the risk was minimal in children and adults "rarely" developed the disease. I was gullible and believed this. Apparently, I was about to become a case study.

A slight sore throat and fever, accompanied by chills, brought the first omen of trouble. There was still no official word that

Lydia had contracted the disease from her encounter with a playmate, but per the internet, this was not a good sign for me. Sharing some food with Lydia and holding her as she napped for a good hour appeared to expose me.

I will not give a vivid description of what transpired during the following days. It is enough to say that it was not a pretty sight and very painful. The rash that set up residence on my hands and feet resembled an affliction of a poor teenager plagued by severe acne. Unfortunately, that brought back unpleasant memories of dealing with acne not as a teenager but in my early 20s. Talk about putting a damper on a girl's confidence. Just as I awoke in those days, hoping to discover that overnight my face was zit free, I now hoped the rash and outbreaks that populated my hands and feet would be gone. There were no miraculous cures in either scenario.

Do you know how your skin feels following a bad sunburn? Consider that sensation of tight, sore skin on hands and feet, and you will know how I spent about seven days. By day four, it was almost impossible to open a prescription bottle, and switching off a light inflicted discomfort. Even getting dressed involved alternatives that did not require the use of fingers; I resorted to a sort of hand shimmy to get the job done.

Calls to my doctor confirmed what my internet research revealed. There was no medication to speed recovery; it was a virus that had to run its course. I was concerned about passing the affliction on to others. "As long as no one touches you, they'll be fine." My doctor supplied no warning of what I could expect nor made suggestions for relief. Further attempts to read medical reports about adult reaction to the disease were fruitless. Luckily, internet comments by other adults who went through this ordeal offered me some assurance that my symptoms were within the norm, and prepared me for what would follow.

Lori and Caden were out of town that weekend, which eliminated some of the anxiety I would have felt if they were home. I refused the offer of another daughter and friends to stop over and assist me. "If you bring anything, just leave it on the porch. I am not letting you in," I replied.

On my own by day five, I was becoming a bit stir crazy and I craved fast food. Somehow, I did not want to admit that I even ate fast food, so how could I ask someone to pick up a burger and fries for me? I was desperate and finally crashed. Donning a pair of winter gloves, I made a fast trip to the drive thru at Burger King, hurried home, and savored a Junior Whopper and a Hershey's chocolate pie. I hung my head in shame.

My food supply was low, and at 6:00 a.m. on Sunday morning, I again grabbed my gloves and entered Tops Supermarket. I needed to pick up a few things and not have to come in contact with anyone so I went through the self-checkout. Of course, there was a hitch in that plan, and the attendant had to assist me. Did she wonder why on a hot summer day someone found it necessary to wear winter gloves?

I welcomed Lori and Caden's return home and relished the relief of no longer being alone. Isolation weighs heavy on your heart and gives you too much time to think.

Although I was no longer contagious, I did not return to work for a whole week. The peeling process had begun, and anyone I encountered took a step back in fear. Over a three-week period, I shed like an onion. I was amazed at the pieces of "plastic-like" skin that peeled from my feet. Enough said.

Initiation, indeed. I should mention that all three of my grandchildren had thankfully mild cases of hand, foot, and mouth disease. None of their parents followed in my footsteps. Most childhood diseases are controlled by vaccinations these days, aren't they? Since I seem to be susceptible, I did not want to deal with measles, mumps, or chicken pox.

A friend perfectly summed it up, "Childproofing the house is easier than childproofing the grandma."

I imagine there will be other moments of initiation as I

continue to follow the grandparent path. Will I avoid the unpredictable actions encountered during bath time? (I smile, as I remember Doug telling me that particular organ "has a mind of its own.") Will I refuse to hold Lydia close against my chest, even if I realize she is ill? I reply with a resounding "No" in both cases. Being a part of these little ones' lives is worth every temporary inconvenience I might experience. I embrace initiation into this special group.

7/10/14

Work:
A Whole New World

"A job is like a blank book and you are the author."

~ *Unknown*

Christmas Past

When girls attended Bishop McMahon High School, it was almost guaranteed that they would graduate with a job. Local businesses lined up to snatch those graduates. Thus, at 17, in July of 1969, I found myself traveling a few short blocks down Delaware Avenue to the National Gypsum Company.

I started out in the steno pool where, bored, I lamented the fact that I had not pursued a college education. Luckily, I finally emerged from the pool and was placed in secretarial positions for the credit and then advertising departments.

I'll admit that I was not the perfect secretary. My typing produced far too many mistakes and correcting those errors on ditto paper was impossible. Before Xerox came onto the scene, ditto paper enabled you to make copies of typed work. It was stained with purple ink and then put on a drum where methylated spirits of ammonia transferred the ink from the master template to other papers. The procedure was the reverse of carbon paper, as typing was printed on the back of the master. To make corrections on the text, you had to carefully apply a special solution to the back of the paper. This was not an easy feat, and in my case the results were messy.

My early secretarial days made me realize that perhaps those aptitude tests they gave us back in the sixth grade were a clue to where my talents really rested, definitely on the creative side. I didn't explore my writing abilities until I was close to fifty.

Coming from a private, all-girls Catholic school, stepping into the business world was an eye-opener for me, especially as I was pretty naïve in those days. Think about the television series "Mad Men," and you can envision the atmosphere I encountered at times.

Part of my education into the real world also resulted from sitting around the lunch table with other late-teen and 20-something girls. Monday lunches were especially exciting as we exchanged stories about our adventures in dating. A group of men sat at the table next to us, nibbling their sandwiches, playing cards, and perhaps getting a chuckle out of our gossiping comments.

The National Gypsum girls in the early 80s.

It is hard to believe that I have now known many of these "girls" for over 50 years. We still gather annually for a Christmas dinner and reminisce about the grand Christmas celebrations National Gypsum held for their employees at the Statler Hilton in downtown Buffalo.

Following the work day, the girls took turns squeezing into

the restrooms to change into our glittering party dresses. These restrooms included a lounge area with a large mirror that enabled us to catch a glimpse of our dazzling transformations after slipping into our Christmas dresses. Whiffs of laughter escaped the room as these newly created glamor girls headed out the door and into the cold night air.

I can still visualize some of the dresses I wore on those evenings. One was a long, sleeveless dress that was black on the top and had a flowing green floral skirt that I made on my Singer sewing machine. I accessorized the dress with dangling green grape earrings and a matching grape cluster necklace. Another year I chose a short, black sleeveless dress with a decorative gold band around my waist. I blocked the image of scolding McMahon nuns from my mind the year I wore a slinky black dress with a lacy insert that really resembled a slip more than a dress. I was young. What else can I say?

Cocktails and appetizers were served in The Terrace Room, followed by a prime rib dinner in the grand dining room. Tables were then removed and a band provided music for an evening of dancing. Inhibitions disappeared, as we twirled around the dance floor with our bosses and fellow workers, or once in my case, puffed on a cigar to prove I could be just like one of the guys.

It could be said that many of the antics occurring at the party were not remembered, or at least not spoken about, on the following Monday. It wasn't unusual to see one or more of the men leave the ballroom with a secretary. They might not be seen for the rest of the evening, having found a secluded corner in the hotel bar.

Guests were invited after the dinner, but seldom seemed to appear. I don't think I ever missed a Christmas party. I always went solo, but I finally was able to bring a date to the last holiday event in 1977, just prior to the company's move to Charlotte, North Carolina. My future husband, Doug, joined the bittersweet holiday celebration that year, as an uncertain future loomed ahead for the employees.

Although the National Gypsum girls who have remained my friends throughout the years do get together at other times of the year, it seems appropriate that we gather during the holidays. I do not think anyone orders prime rib, there is no dancing, we do not don long flowing gowns, and conversation tends to gravitate more around grandchildren than boyfriends. Oh, and I never smoke a cigar.

12/19/20

National Gypsum girls, Christmas 2021

Country Roads

The want ad indicated a part-time opening at WXRL Radio, 1300 AM.

We had been back in Buffalo for a few weeks, boxes had been unpacked, and the new house was basically organized since our arrival in December 1997. The girls were settled in their new schools, Doug was busy with his job, and I was bored. It was time to look for a job.

Flipping through the radio channels, I came to 1300 AM. Good Lord! Willie Nelson was singing "Mama Don't Let Your Babies Grow up to be Cowboys." It was a country station.

I was not a fan of country music. It always aggravated me that country music stations were the only ones that seemed to come in loud and clear on road trips.

Despite this loathing, the idea of working at a radio station lured me in, and before I could say "Hee Haw," I was on William Street in Lancaster in front of a house in the middle of nowhere, flanked by tall radio towers.

I was still in the process of getting reacquainted with geographic distance, and hadn't realized that our home in East Amherst was about 20 minutes from the station. It seemed like a longer trek than I wanted to take on a regular basis, but as long as I was there, I figured I might as well check it out.

A young receptionist greeted me, and I sat in a heavily wood-paneled room reminiscent of the '60s or '70s, with framed photos exhibited on much of the wall space. Escorted upstairs, I was interviewed by Bev, the station manager's sister. As the conversation commenced, I realized that the owner was actually Ramblin' Lou Schriver. I vaguely remembered him singing with his family band on the annual Variety Club Telethons.

The receptionist returned and introduced herself as Ramblin' Lou's daughter, Linda. We were also joined by Lou himself, a pretty imposing figure at well over six feet tall. The interview seemed to be going well, but I admitted to Lou that I really was not a fan of country music.

He smiled and said, "That's OK, we can convert you."

Thus began my education in country music with a pretty amazing man and his family.

As a result of that interview, I began working at WXRL about three days a week. When I left to pursue a full-time position in the Clarence school district in 2004, Lou called and asked me if I would be interested in working a few hours during the weekends. Since radio now seemed to be in my blood, I happily agreed.

The Ramblin' Lou Family Band today: Crista, Lou IV, Linda Lou, Lou V, Joanie and Luke. (photo by Lisa Boulden)

Affectionately known as "Western New York's Father of Country Music," Lou Schriver started WXRL 1300 AM over 50 years ago, and it remains the only family-owned-and-operated radio station in the Buffalo area. Along with running the station, Lou and his family band were a staple when it came to live performances, and annually appeared at the Erie County Fair, Canal Fest, One M&T Plaza, and numerous remotes.

The band consisted of Lou's wife, Joanie Marshall; daughters, Linda Lou, Lori Ann, Lynn Carol; and son Lou IV. Keeping with tradition, the grandkids soon were added to the act.

As babies, they were brought to the station while their parents worked. It wasn't unusual to have a toddler appear in my office and secure a spot under my desk. Little hands produced works of art to decorate the walls.

The family worked, performed, and vacationed together. That in itself was pretty rare.

My main job involved typing the log sheets that served as a guideline for the DJs to correctly air commercial spots. Voiceover experience can also be added to my resume, as I did a memorable (debatable, perhaps) spot for one of their sponsors, Milk for Health. Complying with son Lou's request, I did my best "sultry voice" for Extreme Chocolate Milk.

Although popular country hits were included in the station's format, a steady stream of "oldies, but goodies" filled the airwaves each day.

In addition to the music that was played during Lou's weekday and Saturday "Grand Ole Country" shows, I was exposed to syndicated programs "Country Gold," and "Classic Country."

Lou continued to promote the entertainers who paved the way for today's artists. He provided opportunities for fans from Western New York to enjoy the talents of Eddy Arnold, Buck Owens, Roy Clark, Waylon Jennings, Johnny Cash, BoxCar Willie, and Willie Nelson. Many of those shows were booked at Buffalo's renowned Kleinhans Music Hall. Lou recalled a few concerts which had to be canceled due to the "tipsy" state of Johnny Cash and Willie Nelson.

Lou also presented anniversary concerts at the Riviera Theatre in North Tonawanda. The Family Band opened for country greats. Attending shows starring Whisperin' Bill Anderson and Ray Price, I was surprised by how many of their songs were familiar to me.

My country music education included "new" country, as I listened to shows like the "Weekly Country Countdown," and "Overdrive Truckers Countdown." Yes, I did say truckers. Who would have imagined that I could enjoy this type of music, but country music tells a story you can actually understand, compared to some of today's other genres.

Shania Twain, Faith Hill, and Tim McGraw were just starting out when I came to WXRL. Of course, I still lacked knowledge. I first thought "Brooks and Dunn" included Garth Brooks and another artist, not the highly acclaimed duo of two men.

Speaking of Garth Brooks, Doug and I were able to see him in concert, along with Brad Paisley and Willie Nelson, thanks to WXRL.

I had just arrived at the station on September 11, 2001, when DJ Scott Cleveland told us that a plane had hit the World Trade Center.

"A small plane?" I inquired.

His answer was, "No, a commercial airplane," sent chills up and down my spine.

Lou brought out an old, black-and-white television and we watched the terror that ensued. I called Doug and together we wondered what in the world was happening. All programs were suspended and just that somber news filled the airwaves. It was one of those moments that will stay with me forever.

Another somber moment during my time at WXRL occured when Doug called to tell me that he had lost his job. How degrading to be given a box, instructed to only take "personal" items and be escorted from the building. That change in our lives resulted in my decision to seek a full-time job elsewhere, downsizing houses, and moving to Long Street. Little did we realize what that next chapter in our lives would bring.

On one Saturday morning, I sat at my desk as Lou announced that his annual "Tribute to Hank Williams" would be broadcast during his "Grand Ole Country" show later that day. He started these tributes following Hank Williams' death on January 1, 1953.

The country oldies had been spinning all morning. Gene Autry had been yodeling, Ernest Tubb was "Walking the Floor Over You," and Johnny Cash told the story of "The Night Hank Williams Came to Town."

Lou's day show was being broadcast from his home studio on Grand Island that day. His grandson, Raj, stopped in to tell Lou how excited he was to see a "dinosaur peeking out" of his stocking that morning.

Listeners heard how Lou enjoyed his favorite limburger and onion sandwich, and had smoked herring, called a "Blind Robin" by some, on New Year's Eve. They also were encouraged to patronize one of his sponsor's restaurants, where he always recommended their French onion soup.

The "Tribute to Hank Williams" had begun. The stories of "My Bucket's Got a Hole in It," "Hey Good Lookin'," and "Love Sick Blues" were retold.

Over the years, I have taken more notice of those old, framed photographs that hang in the waiting room of the station: Lou's daughters with Vince Gill and Garth Brooks; Lou with Charlie Pride, Bill Anderson, and Johnny Cash; and most amazingly, shaking hands in a photo with Elvis, circa 1955.

Lou had an impressive career. His name resides on the "Walkway of Stars" in the Country Music Hall of Fame in Nashville, and he

Lou and Elvis

has appeared on the Grand Ole Opry stage. He was inducted into the Buffalo Music Hall of Fame and the WNY Broadcasting Hall of Fame.

Lou's listeners were loyal, which was apparent from his sold-out Christmas Shows, tours, and cruises. Even as he reached his 80s, he continued a grueling schedule of concerts, "Traveling with Friends," and radio remotes.

In addition to country music, Lou provided his listeners with religious, Polish, and German programs. The station supported the local community with broadcasts of the Lancaster High School football and basketball games, and remotes at Nellie's Restaurant in Arcade, Southgate Plaza in West Seneca, the Shrine Circus at the Hamburg Fairgrounds and in the past, Earl's Drive-In in Chaffee, New York. The music of local country artists was highlighted each weekday morning, as Lou encouraged their endeavors.

His family remained his top priority and was always an integral part of his life.

Buffalo lost one of its legends on January 17, 2016, when Ramblin' Lou Schriver died. His legacy lives on, though, as his family continues to keep WXRL on the airways. They still spread those country vibes with their spinning of the classics and their band concerts throughout Western New York.

For over 25 years, I have shared good times and bad with the Schrivers. They have supported and encouraged me. Isn't that what being a family is all about? I appreciate their willingness to consider me a part of their WXRL family.

Lou's prediction was right, my musical horizon has expanded, along with my understanding and appreciation of country music, thanks to quite an experienced teacher. Lou had and now his family continues to preserve the soul of country music in its

purest form, and they will not forget those original artists who forged the way for today's contemporary country sound.

Don't touch that dial; keep it tuned to 1300AM!

7/10/18

Rambliin' Lou and me at the Christmas Show 2014

Scott

Scott Cleveland, a disc jockey at WXRL radio, died suddenly on Friday, March 20, 2015. He was 53 years old. There was no wake or funeral service. He would have agreed that those rites of passage were not necessary.

His real name was Howard, but when he started out in the radio industry in the mid-'80s, he dubbed himself Scott Cleveland. There are those in the media who feel a radio name is necessary to keep their life more private.

I was just a secretary at the station, and not an on-air personality, but once I did record a commercial spot. Scott decided I should be known as "April Fresh." The name seemed more appropriate for a stripper at The Kit-Kat Club, or the sultry voice at the other end of a questionable escort service phone call. We can all use a bit of make believe in our lives, so I accepted the name.

I would describe Scott as someone with a quirky personality, a bit unusual. He didn't believe in celebrating holidays, and spent those days working at the station. He was allergic to poultry, so his Thanksgiving dinner was a can of Chef Boyardee ravioli. He wasn't what you would call a snappy dresser. He usually wore a blue short-sleeve shirt, and its thin, worn appearance probably served as testimony that he had purchased it during his college days. He often looked like he had just rolled out of bed. I vaguely remember him with hair, but one summer he sported a buzz cut and the style remained for all seasons, no muss, no fuss, and good if you did just roll out of bed and had to run to open the station.

Scott had an unusual hobby. Thursday was his day off, and he would hop in his car to seek out post offices. He had amassed an impressive collection of postmarked envelopes, a tribute to zip codes.

His companion on these journeys was his trusty dog. In recent years, that would have been Darby. Scott and Darby had set their sights on a new goal: to have Darby "dump" in a variety of state parks. The number was growing. Like I said, Scott was quirky.

Speaking of companions, I must mention a stuffed version of Opus the Penguin from the cartoon strip "Bloom County." This penguin was well-worn, and in my eyes, that condition testified that he was well-loved. Opus perched on the radio control board, but Scott scooped him up at the end of the day before he headed home.

Scott was a jack-of-all-trades at the station. He was the morning DJ. He deftly handled production duties, worked the controls during Ramblin' Lou's "Grand Ole Country Show" on Saturday mornings, and smoothly ran the boards on Sundays to bring religious programing to a group of listeners who perhaps were advanced in years and unable to attend services. Scott was the energetic voice hosting "Polka Jamboree" for 3 hours on Sundays, and he also collected the trash. During that collection, he rummaged through the trash to salvage paper that still had recycling powers, perfect for radio lingo scribbled on its blank surfaces.

If I happened to work on a Sunday, I would find Scott at the front desk tackling the *Buffalo News* crossword puzzle. Once or twice, Darby would tag along, never letting a bark escape, just sitting beside Scott. Around 11:00, Scott's friend Ron would visit. Their conversations were mainly muted from me, but occasionally I heard them reminiscing about the good old days and the radio personalities I remembered growing up with in the '60s and '70s in Buffalo: Joey Reynolds, Danny Neaverth, etc.

Their talks might include information that appeared in Scott's "Linkedin" account, information that provided a hint of Scott's radio personality:

- Mass Communications major at Buffalo State from 1979 – 1983… "The initials ain't B.S. for nothing."

- In radio for 20+ years, including WHLM/Wilks-Barre/ Scranton; WKYN/St. Mary's, PA; WNTS/Buffalo, WYSL/ Buffalo; and WXRL since 1994.

- Lots of ideas for production, on air and most of all, having fun "Morning Mania/Production dude."

- Night jock… "It was the '80s…I had big hair and a big mouth!"

He also could have added that he managed the "Buffalo Drive-In" on Harlem Road in Cheektowaga for many years before it closed in 2007. Scott called it: "The biggest motel in the area."

After his shifts, Scott always signed off by saying, "BGYBGB." He was secretive as to the meaning of those letters. The mystery can now be revealed, "Be good to yourself; be good to Buffalo."

Two visions of Scott will forever be imprinted on my mind: He was the one who somberly informed me that a plane had crashed into the World Trade Center on September 11, 2001. Then there is a vision of Scott standing outside the door of the station. I had stopped there early in the morning on a Friday to drop something off. He opened the station up every day, and as his car was not parked outside, I assumed he was not there yet. I left a bag on the door knob, but just as I was ready to drive away, Scott opened the door, and with a grin he said, "What, you're not going to say hello?" We chatted for a few moments. That was the last time I saw him.

Scott never did open the station the following Friday, March 20. He had died in his sleep. His death came as a shock to me. There had been no warning, no preparation.

Mike Pasierb, who is host of the "Rockin' Polka" shows during the weekend, paid tribute to Scott during "Polka Jamboree" the following Sunday. As there was to be no wake or funeral service, I think those who worked with him needed that closure. Many of his co-workers and friends called in during that three-hour program with remembrances of his dedication to and love of radio.

Because of the lack of a public remembrance following Scott's death, I felt I had to write down my thoughts on a quirky, yet unique man. We encounter people in our lifetimes who act and live totally contrary to what we might consider normal, yet we often discover that even unlikely characters can touch our lives.

I cannot judge the total nature of this man, but his antics made me smile, and I thank him for that. I will remember and miss him as I say, "BGYBGB."

7/10/18

The Dungeon

When I worked for the Clarence School District, my New York State Civil Service title was Senior Clerk Stenographer. On the official "examples of duties," this job required a person to "take and transcribe dictation, answer telephones and greet callers in person, make appointments, perform general clerical work in an office involving the tabulation of figures, filing, completion of forms, etc., type forms, form letters, and standardized reports, maintain personnel and payroll records, and utilize enhanced computer systems and equipment in the completion of assigned clerical tasks."

Tests were required to enable your name to be put on a county and local canvas list. When I started in the position, the available lists were depleted, so I was told that I could be hired, but I would need to take a test at some point.

The thought of taking a test was daunting as I had not studied or taken a test in years. I thought that I could pass such a challenge, though. However, I was later told that I would have to be one of the top three people on the list to keep my job. Now that was a worry.

To make a long story short, I did take the test, and managed to be one of the top three candidates in the Clarence district.

By the way, strangely, dictation was not part of the exam, and in fact I rarely, if ever, had to take shorthand doing my job.

Job duties sometimes are not always set in stone, or Civil Service requirements, as evidenced by my exploits in the dungeon.

We referred to it as the dungeon, because it was basically in the bowels of Clarence High School. A network of twisted paths snaked through its dark and dusty avenues. Pipes and machinery to keep the school running smoothly resided there, as did old files and basically anything that wasn't being used to educate the kids any more.

Many of my co-workers cringed at the thought of going down there to retrieve old records.

"I'm not going down there alone," they fearfully lamented.

I offered to accompany them on their journeys and often headed down on my own. I enjoyed digging for things and considered it an adventure.

One must have the "official" key to enter these chambers. It was years before I was granted the privilege of having my own key. Once the door was unlocked, I was faced with a descent down steep concrete steps. Seasoned employees told me there was once a "smoking room" for the teachers next to the staircase. That must have been something, a small concrete, windowless room filled with smoke!

Before reaching the room reserved for payroll timesheets and old employee files, my hands had to grope along walls in search of light switches to illuminate the dark passages.

Once I decided to remove files from the over-packed cabinets, box up former employee records from the '60s through the '80s, and introduce employees from the '90s and early 2000s to the dungeon. It was quite a project and required stretches of time alone among the spirits that resided in that cramped room.

A blue La-Z-Boy chair had been delegated to that file room. Before I started working at the district office of the school, the superintendent's longtime secretary was unfortunately stricken with cancer and the chair was purchased to provide a comfortable spot for her to relax when her energy level was low. She had refused to use it. I never was tempted to sit in that chair.

I didn't often encounter other people in the dungeon, but

once I came upon a man who informed me he was replacing mouse traps.

"We've caught some pretty large mice down here," he proudly told me.

Now, that really comforted me. I did hear that years ago a cat was found roaming through the passages, so apparently that feline was able to sustain itself if it met the mice before those critters crossed paths with the traps.

Another room directly across from this archive room included ledgers which were roughly twenty-four inches square. These dusty books dated back to the '50s and '60s and showed payroll entries pressed into yellow sheets by some dinosaur of an accounting machine. I once spent several hours perusing these pages and felt the need to breathe some fresh air to clear my lungs afterwards.

A wooden chair equipped with leather straps sat in a corner. No doubt it was once used to enable a special education child to sit up straight. It looked like an uncomfortably cruel device, almost like an electric chair. I was glad that it had been tossed in the dungeon and was not used by a child now.

There was a wonderful metal wash tub sitting on sturdy legs with wheels. It would have made a great conversation piece in a garden filled with beautiful flowers, or filled with ice cold beer and pop for a summer party. I was tempted to sneak down to the dungeon at the end of a school day and whisk this forgotten tub away to my backyard. Although I never went through with my scheme, who would have missed it?

Sometimes it appeared to me that sounds and smells were coming from one passageway. Ah, it was "the roar of the crowd and the smell of the grease paint," a space filled with thespian spirits waiting for another set of actors and actresses to excitedly enter their underground retreat.

You had to walk down a hall with a sloped ceiling to reach the prop room under the school auditorium. Nancy, a co-worker and former Clarence student, told me that she used to slip out of study hall with her friends and escape down to this treasure-trove of theatrical paraphernalia. She and her friends felt like characters in "Alice in Wonderland," as they bent their bodies, becoming smaller and smaller to reach the entrance doorway. Once inside, it was possible to resume full height.

Rows and rows of costumes hung ready for the next performance. Shelves overflowed with shoes, hats, purses, and dishes. Tables, chairs, lamps, and suitcases of every size were scattered about.

Colorful spray paint graffiti filled the walls, ceiling, and floor. A sampling of phrases included:

"Hello all you beautiful people. I love you all," The Birds

"Laugh until you pee your pants"

"The crew's your pillar" (of course, written on a pillar)

"Dave's a dancin' fool" (accompanied by a whimsical dancing stick person)

"Life is like a huge video game; make sure you have enough quarters."

On one wall a testimony was recorded from "Jessica" and "Chaz," both performers between the years 1999 – 2005, listing the productions they starred in:

- *You Can't Take It with You*

- *South Pacific*

- *Blood Wedding*

- *Once Upon a Mattress*

- *The Many Loves of Dobie Gillis*

- *Mame*

- *Little Women*

- *Grease*

Empty snack containers had also been stuck to the walls: an Oreo box, Ice Breaker tin, and milk carton. On one of my inspections, a new bag of popcorn sat on a table, evidence that someone had recently occupied the room. Perhaps they, too, had been escaping study hall and were in danger of being discovered, forcing them to leave their goodies behind. Nancy and her cohorts had lookouts for the school principal or teachers in search of these renegades. Those delegated to those positions could give warnings by unscrewing a light bulb to provide the safety of darkness needed to escape via a back route.

Posters were scattered about: *Grease*, March 2003; *42nd Street*, March, 2004; *Fiddler on the Roof*, March 2005.

Glancing on the floor, I spotted a handwritten note: "Thanks for all your hard work in these shows over the years. You'll be missed. All the best for a good show tonight and for the full run of *LaMancha*."

This production of *"Man of LaMancha"* was an award winner for the school, receiving the top three Lipke Foundation and Shea's Performing Arts Center Kenny Awards in 2010 for Outstanding Musical Production, and Outstanding Performance by a Lead Actor and Actress.

I found it sad that the note was somehow relegated to a space where no one would see it. Hopefully, it was inadvertently lost in the shuffle of activity that evening. Soon the names and comments of yet another set of students would be enshrined in this space. When I explored this sanctuary, I noticed that a production of *Little Shop of Horrors* was scheduled to open in the spring.

As I retreated from the dungeon, I saw something lying on the floor, a green, studded leather jacket. I could imagine this being part of the wardrobe in the retelling of *Grease*, but Danny and the T-Birds certainly would have worn black jackets. So, what was the story behind the green jacket?

Hmm…maybe it was time for me to try my hand at writing fiction.

Inspiration can come from performing your job, even if you stray from the Civil Service requirements.

2/22/12

Thoughts on Homes

"*Where we love is home—home that our feet may leave,*
but not our hearts.."

~ *Oliver Wendell Holmes, Sr.*

221 Herman Street
Buffalo, New York (1951-1966)

So many material things were lost following the tragedy of Flight 3407. I am always thrilled and thankful when an item that I thought was destroyed is found. That was the case when I discovered treasures from my childhood at 221 Herman Street.

I held in my hands two crude drawings of our living room, a nostalgic pencil sketch of the back of Grandma Schwab's house, and a blueprint of our home's layout. I was the young artist who did these renderings back in the '60s.

My drawing of the living room

The living room was the size of what we would call a family room today.

This drawing depicts the entrance to the dining room with mahogany furniture that included a credenza. Christmas cookies were stored there. I sampled them discreetly, and secretly, before the holidays arrived. The glass cabinet glimpsed through the doorway stored Martha Washington and Betsy Ross dolls. We were never allowed to play with them, but admired them through the glass. A large table, surrounded by six chairs, provided a perfect setting for the good china used on holidays and for Sunday dinner. We always had a special dinner on Sunday. Although not visible in the drawing, Mom's plants basked in the sunlight that streamed through the large front window. Our Christmas trees were displayed by that window, including a silver one that reflected the glow provided by a color wheel rotating nearby.

Barb, Grandma, and me in the dining room

By the time I drew this picture, our piano was gone and my parents' music console cabinet occupied its spot in the living room. I was first introduced to music either listening to the radio or to old 78 records. Some of the records have resurfaced in recent years, including a few of my childhood favorites: "For Me and My Gal," "Too Fat Polka," "The Whiffenpoof Song," and "Lavender Blue."

The three channels on the television provided hours of entertainment for the family. *Captain Kangaroo* was a staple, along with *The Mickey Mouse Club*. We tuned into the *Ed Sullivan Show* every Sunday night. I can still sense the excitement I felt lying on the floor in front of the set waiting for the Beatles to perform in the U.S. for the first time.

The whole family assembled each week for *The Lawrence Welk Show*, *The Red Skelton* and *Jackie Gleason Shows*, Andy Williams, Carol Burnett, *Bonanza*, *Gunsmoke*, and so many other programs.

I believe my sister won a contest and the prize was the picture of the Blessed Mother that hung on the wall.

I recall that a crawl space was accessible from the living room. The Christmas decorations were stored up there and Dad had to climb the ladder to retrieve them. It's crazy, but I have dreams about that. We have company coming, and I am asking him to please bring them down so we can decorate before they come.

My drawing of the staircase

The second drawing includes a view of the staircase. We did not have many books growing up, but they were stored in the corner cabinet. Like many families of that era, there was an encyclopedia set, either bought from a door-to-door salesman, or purchased from the local A&P grocery store, one volume a week.

There were two religious children's books, which I do recall were bought from visiting missionaries.

I especially enjoyed a copy of *Little Women*, printed on rippled-edged paper and filled with beautiful illustrations. I still have it today.

In the drawing, the chair on the right was green and the perfect place for photo shoots on my sister's and my christening days and first communions.

On the left, a pink chair was more comfortable for afternoon naps. That chair was given to my cousin, Leo, when he attended

Mom, Dad, and Barb in the living room chairs

college in Toronto. Perhaps he still has it today.

A secret hiding place. That is what I felt beckoned if that door under the staircase was opened. The vacuum cleaner was in there, but so were our toys. My sister and I were content with the few toys we possessed: games like Monopoly, Go to the Head of the Class, Uncle Wiggly, and Concentration, Mickey Mouse Club coloring books; a few dolls, including my Tiny Tears; a puzzle, and cutout paper dolls of the Lennon Sisters and 101 Dalmatians.

The couch was placed in front of French doors that, if ever opened, led to a tiny alley and the neighbor's fence. I never saw those doors open, but perhaps before the fence existed they did provide access to the outside.

I have written about how special Grandma Schwab's house was to me growing up. I was so fortunate to have her living in the front house on Herman Street. I knew her for just 12 years, and I can only imagine how much I could have learned from her at different stages in my life and the stories of her life that she could have shared with me.

I captured much of what I remember about her house: the

picket fence, the back door to the woodshed that stored our bicycles and served as a work place for school projects, that window by her side door where she raised the shade to signal that she was up from her afternoon nap, and I even included a bit of the shelter where the garbage cans were stored.

Drawing I did in 60s of the back of Grandma's house.

Thinking about the many phases of my life, I could see my own childhood as I watched my four girls and now my grandchildren traverse their way through those early years. Watching my girls now navigate through the sometimes rocky sea of being wives and mothers, I recall those exciting, and at times challenging, days. All too suddenly, it seemed I had been flung into retirement just as my parents had, and I compare the differences a generation plays in facing those years.

Just the other day, I realized another shocking phase is starting. I will soon be as old as Grandma Schwab was at my birth! That is really hard for me to fathom, but when I look back on her life, I am inspired by the vitality and zest for life that she

My childhood home, 221 Herman , rear

exhibited at that time.

I was writing even back in those days. Accompanying the drawings was my "Farewell," which I wrote in 1966, when we moved from 221 Herman to Hagen Street.

> *The last pieces of furniture are being loaded onto the moving van now. Emptiness has filled the house. The time has come for that one final walk through the rooms where I have spent all of my childhood days.*
>
> *It seems funny walking through these barren rooms. It seems sad; all the laughter is gone. Wait, what is that? Yes, it is laughter and the sound of happy children. The walls have come alive with the voices of its occupants of the last 18 years.*
> *As I walk through the bedroom, I can see myself spending many an hour both by myself and with others in this small room. Wasn't it here that I thought over my problems? Yes, these thoughts will always remain in part here.*

The living room and the dining room are filled with the many happy parties held within their walls. They also hold the sad moments of the family, but these are few and soon forgotten.

The kitchen is filled with the smell of the hundreds of meals prepared within, and of the burned pies and potatoes which, by mistake, were ruined.

These things can never be taken away from this house. The years spent within it have been good ones. So, it is not with sadness that I leave it, for it will always be a part of me wherever I may go. The doors close now and await to be opened by its new occupants. I will no longer call it home, but in a small way, it will always be somewhat mine.

~ Karen Schoenwetter '66

Surprisingly, I can see hints of my current writings in these short paragraphs. I still like to insert questions in my pieces, and my sentiments, especially in the last paragraph could easily be included in today's pieces.

My cousin, Paul, and his wife, Eileen, rented the house after our departure. When Grandma passed a few years later, the property was sold. Sadly, at some point, a fire destroyed both houses.

I wanted to make sure I remembered the layout of that house, so, like an architect, I drew out the floor plan before moving to Hagen Street. Why? I thought perhaps some day I might be able to have the house rebuilt.

It was that important to me.

February 2021

Hagen Street
Buffalo, New York (1966-1977)

Hagen Street off of East Delevan near the city line became my next home. I lived there for eleven years and evolved from an awkward teen to a young adult. There were boys to dream about, proms that required a girl to find a date, life-changing decisions that needed to be made dictating what direction my life would take. On Hagen Street, I experienced many "firsts": first kiss, first car, and first job.

Many of those experiences were covered in "Dancing," but there is more to tell.

Although there was a front entrance to the house that led into an enclosed porch area, I cannot recall many people actually entering the house through that door. I recently found a nice example of that entrance, a picture of Doug, Lori, Kim, and me sitting on the

Being silly. Was I ever really that thin?

Doug, Lori, Kim & me

steps during one of our visits back to Buffalo after we had moved to Cincinnati.

The backdoor was our main entrance. Going up a short flight of steps, we entered the kitchen. Every evening, after my parents had split a beer, and enjoyed some crackers and cheese, my mother would set the kitchen table for breakfast. Was that one of Miss Manner's recommendations in the 40s, when Mom became a housewife?

That room, along with the dining room and living room were a fairly good size, which at that time nicely accommodated our family of four, and any other family and friends that gathered for celebrations.

Thinking about our courtship days, I smile remembering when Doug and I once left a family wedding early, and rushed to

Mom, Dad and Doug at an anniversary or birthday celebration in the dining room. I can't recall the occasion.

Hagen Street in a somewhat feverish state. Our rapture on the living room couch was cut short when we heard my parents' car pulling into the driveway! So much for exploring young love.

There were two tiny downstairs bedrooms off the living

Everyone looking "Merry & bright" during a Christmas Day visit, 1982. Mom, Dad, me, Doug, Lori (only a month old) and Kim.

room and dining room. I do mean tiny. A full bed and one dresser left little spare space for my parents to maneuver through the room.

Mom made the most of the guest bedroom. There was a small pull-out couch, my dad's dresser, a desk, and for a time the television was in that little room. One entire wall was covered with family photos. Many of those had been removed from the old photo albums I had enjoyed flipping through when I was a kid. Actually, Mom had made the decision to remove all those photos from the books and placed them in boxes. In her later years, though, she attempted to put them back in albums. I recall her telling us how overwhelming and nerve wracking that process was for her. I often think of her feelings, when I go through all the photos retrieved from Long Street or am searching for photos for my books!

I also remember that room for one "coming of age" remembrance.

Drinking with your parents and relatives would probably not be considered a cool activity when you begin your drinking experience. I did plenty of that, though. In fact, it was one Easter Sunday when I experienced my first hangover. A large family contingent had attended Holy Saturday services, and then went to The Lord Amherst in Snyder for drinks and food. I consumed two Tom Collins and a massive club sandwich. As my dad drove us home, I frantically asked him to pull over. I slide across the back seat and just opened the car door in time to vomit in front of a bar on Harlem Road. Easter morning my head ached and the dry heaves were my companion for most of the day. I swore I would never get myself into that position again, but of course, I have broken that promise a few times over the years. I have, however, never consumed another Tom Collins.

My sister and I had a huge bedroom in the attic, and we were allowed to paint it any color we desired. We chose a golden yellow, somewhat for the bold color, but mainly for its reduced price. It was a haven for music. While most kids my age were listening to the Rolling Stones, Grateful Dead or Chicago, I was listening to Rod McKuen—does anyone remember Rod? Ah, "The Earth," "The Sea," "The Sky." What was I thinking!

That was our get-a-way space, and often it made us feel like we had our own apartment. I loved that there was a built-in dresser and cupboard in the room, along with a huge closet. In one of those drawers, we had followed one of my dad's practices. On payday, we would slip money into white envelopes marked "car," "rent," "vacation," etc.

We purchased a sewing machine, and sometimes would whip up a dress one night and wear it to work the next day.

Even a fan did not seem to help us find relief from the summer heat in that room. I even tried to sleep with my head at the foot of the bed with the hope that a slight breeze would make its way into the room through the two big windows that faced the street.

I will make a confession here. I was somewhat of a stalker at those windows. Hidden, I hope, in darkness I would peer out at the boys across the street, as they gathered on porches and driveways, the red glow of their cigarettes breaking through the darkness.

It was great having a two-car garage on Hagen Street. Of course, Dad had the honor of keeping his car there, and my sister and I would take turns filling the other bay. We skillfully learned to back out of the garage and down the narrow driveway.

Backyard memories. Our little garden.

When not in the garage, we parked on the street. There were many times when considerable energy was required to dig-out a vehicle after a big-Buffalo snowfall, hopefully before a plow would come down the street to box us in again.

Riding our bikes still provided hours of enjoyment for my sister and me. Some Sundays, we would ride them all the way to Delaware Park, a good 3-mile journey.

The neighborhood provided me opportunities to walk to high school friends' houses, church, and even a Dairy Queen for an occasional banana split, but more likely a chocolate or cherry dipped cone or Dilly Bar. Mom's favorite was the Buster Bar covered in peanuts.

Enjoying a sunny day with my mom & Kim.

Yes, "coming of age" does sum up my days on Hagen Street. I was about to embark on my adult phase of life.

> *"How does one become a butterfly?*
>
> *You must want to fly so much that you are willing to give up being a caterpillar."*
>
> ~ *Trina Paulus*

6/7/22

Me ready to face the world.

The Southtowns:
Hamburg (1977-1979) and
Eden (1979-1983), New York

As an East Side city girl, the Southtowns were basically an area of suburban Buffalo that I had little knowledge about. We did visit relatives in Orchard Park and Langford, but I never imagined myself actually living in the arctic "snowbelt" associated with those suburbs of Buffalo.

My first taste of Southtowns living began when my sister and I moved to the Lakeshore apartments in Hamburg. We had spread our wings and flown the coop. Okay, so the definition of that phrase is to "suddenly or mysteriously leave," and our parents knew we were leaving, but it gives you the idea of our flight to freedom. It was 1977, and we were 25 and 28, and the adult ability to manage our own living space and lives was long overdue.

One word describes the experience: fun. Despite the fact that we held the full responsibility for cooking and cleaning, the freedom to come and go as we pleased put a whole new spin on life. We had a 30-minute drive to work in downtown Buffalo, but the drive along Lake Erie was always a unique experience. I once saw water-spouts (funnel-shaped clouds that connect to water) that alarmed me, until I learned they were not tornados. In the winter, the lake was transformed into a giant ice rink, speckled with brave ice fisherman.

Barb, Dad, and me in the Lakeshore apartment

Then, in the summer of 1977, my future husband, Doug, burst into my life. Living in an apartment proved to be very helpful when having a boyfriend. There was no worry about parents hovering nearby, and my sister was very good about giving us the space we needed to explore our new relationship.

So many memories were made in that apartment: peeking through the peephole in the door and seeing Doug after his three-week trip to Europe, running up the stairs sporting a new mustache, suede jacket, and jaunty cap; looking out the window and watching Doug's Monte Carlo, that he assumed was in park, roll down the parking lot toward a milk machine; proving that I possessed limited cooking abilities and presenting Doug with less than stellar meals; snuggling on the couch watching Joe Ferguson and the Buffalo Bills; and definitely venturing into the explorations of human relationships and falling in love.

Doug and me decorate the apartment tree

On the first anniversary of our meeting, it was there where I tearfully questioned where our relationship was going, and where I cried even harder when I learned I had ruined his plans for a surprise engagement announcement on my upcoming birthday.

While planning a wedding, we also discussed where we would live. We both grew up in the city, so it never dawned on me that a rural setting might be our first home. Doug was working in Gowanda, south of Buffalo, and I was working in downtown Buffalo, so we zeroed in on the Town of Eden, which served as a middle ground for both of us.

He discovered a house that he described as our "dream home" on Belknap Road in Eden. I can assure you that I never dreamt of such a home! It was surrounded by corn fields, and part of the road we had to travel on to reach it was a dirt road. It was a good-sized ranch house, but there was no garage door and we had to walk over a plank laid over a gaping hole of the porch to enter the house. Inside, the house was partially finished, but the majority was definitely a fixer-upper. I was stunned at his enthusiasm.

"We're going to finish all this?" I asked.

"Sure," he said confidently.

We started our lives as a married couple with little furniture. I had the bedroom furniture from the apartment, and it was at least a year before we added a living room couch.

Belknap Road house in Eden

I became his assistant in carpentry duties. I was educated as to the purpose of underlayment, insulation, priming, staining, baseboards, and louvered doors. I learned that cutting grass could reveal mice scurrying from their nests, and I used muscles I didn't know existed when I helped clean out a detached garage on the property.

Garbage removal

While working on forms as we prepared to lay a concrete path to the front door, I stepped right on a nail. Despite the delay that resulted from a trip to the emergency room for a tetanus shot, preparations were completed and Doug and a friend successfully accomplished the work the next day.

We spent many hours working to transform that

Doug prepping concrete for the front door pathway

Me and Doug working on door frames

shell of a house into our home. We often rewarded our efforts with a trip to the Eden Dairy Queen for mouthwatering burgers and fries. Those fries, with skins still clinging to them, were the best.

We came to appreciate the word "snowbelt." The wind whipped through those corn fields, and although we might not have had the piles of snow that settle on city sidewalks in the winter, we did have drifts that often blocked the roads. We kept shovels in

the trunk, and Doug often had to get out of his car and start to dig a path through the snow to arrive home.

Southtowners are a hardy bunch, though. We thought nothing of driving through that snow for an hour to watch the Buffalo Sabres hockey

Our first Christmas on Belknap

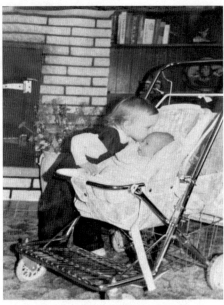

Kim and Lori, 1982. Doug built those bookshelves.

team play at the old War Memorial Auditorium.

Another memorable event took place when we locked ourselves out of the house one day. We ended up driving our car over to the bedroom bathroom, broke the window and I climbed in to open the front door. Obviously, I was much lighter in those days; I would not fit in that window today.

Belknap Road was where we brought Kim and Lori home after their births, and that truly made the house a home.

When I see moms pushing their baby strollers down the street where I now live in the little village of East Aurora, I can't help but remember when I would take my oldest daughter Kim around the block in Eden. It would take 30 to 45 minutes to walk around our country block as we stepped over railroad tracks, passed newly plowed fields, flowering gardens, and cows.

It was not an easy decision to leave the Buffalo area in 1983. We were adjusting to the country life. Doug was offered a position in Cincinnati, Ohio. Was a move worth leaving behind family and friends? Were we up to the challenge of facing the unknown?

It was time to rearrange our lives' puzzle pieces. We moved from the Garden of Eden to the town of Loveland, Ohio. To us, it seemed like we were going in the right direction.

10/25/21

Paxton-Guinea Road
Loveland, Ohio (1983-1997)

Our new house

In 2013, my daughter, Lori, and I turned into the driveway of 957 Paxton-Guinea Road in Loveland. We were about to step into the past. Our apprehension was real. What kind of reaction would result from this venture into a previous life?

Just days before, I had come to the Cincinnati area to visit Lori and attend a conference dinner. After dinner, several of my old friends gathered for a nightcap at a trendy nearby bar.

"Did you know your old house is for sale? It looks empty at the moment."

This comment piqued my interest, "Can you find out the realtor's name for me?"

The seed had been planted, and I felt an eagerness to walk once more through our old home.

Lori and I visit the Paxton-Guinea house, 2013

I realized it was almost 25 years ago that Doug and I first looked at the house. We were on a whirlwind tour of houses in the Cincinnati area. Doug accepted a position with USI Chemicals, where he would venture into the polyethylene industry. We left our two small daughters with my parents and the rush was on to find a home. Being a very exact person, and "map" man, Doug took a compass, set the pointed rod on his new place of business, and drew a circle within a 25-mile radius. Over a three-day period, we were introduced to a variety of Cincinnati suburbs: Goshen, Landen, Loveland, Maineville, Mason, and Milford.

Our "want" list was not too demanding: three bedrooms, a fireplace, trees, all situated in a kid-friendly neighborhood that included a good school system. Almost everything we were shown was a ranch style structure without a basement, which did not appeal to us. There was one 1880s home with a strange layout that required going through one bedroom to reach another. The need for updates flashed dollar signs before our eyes. Another older home, located in a village setting, looked very promising from the outside. Unfortunately, we could not go inside, as the basement remained flooded after some stormy weather. We crossed these older homes off the list.

Our allotted time to house hunt was drawing to a close. My head pounded and my spirits plummeted. Had we made the right decision to move away from Buffalo family and friends? The realtor wanted to show us one last property in Loveland. Who wouldn't want to live in a place called Loveland?

We pulled into a stone driveway that would have to be upgraded, but we were impressed with the red brick ranch. A small courtyard greeted us as we approached the front door. The place oozed with country charm and the owners had filled the rooms with tasteful antiques that were just our style. There were three bedrooms and two baths on the main floor. It lacked a dining room, but since we did not even own dining room furniture that was not a problem. The living room included a fireplace and an open staircase that led down to a barn-board paneled family room with another fireplace. Three other rooms in the basement provided plenty of space for our growing family and Doug's collections. It was love at first sight for Doug and me. We had found our new house.

Doug started his job and I was left in Eden to supervise and control not only packing, but two little girls. Kim was two and Lori was eight months old. Doug stayed in a motel prior to the Loveland house closing and the girls and I finally joined him to begin our new adventure. The girls slept considerably during the eight-hour trip to Cincinnati making the drive easier for me, but by the time we met Doug at work, I was anxious to reach the new house. I followed him to Loveland, and as we approached Paxton-Guinea Road, I became quite agitated when he did not turn down the street. He kept going straight. I was in no mood for delays, and if cell phones had debuted sooner, you can bet he would have received a call from one frustrated wife. When we finally arrived, he assured me he had simply forgotten how to reach the house.

Our furniture did not arrive until the next day, so we walked into an empty house. I learned a valuable lesson that day. When looking at prospective homes, keep your focus away from the furnishings of the current owners and concentrate on the bones of the house. As we entered, every blemish in the house seemed clearly visible. Carpets looked worn and dirty, wallpaper outdated, and paint color seemed all wrong.

Now in 2013, Lori and I were about to enter the house again: the courtyard once filled with vines and grass was now transformed into a pleasant stoned patio, which was definitely an improvement.

The inside of the house was another story. It looked like it had gone through some rough times. All carpeting, except in the living room, was removed leaving just the thin tacking strips of wood exposed. The living room carpet was disgusting, looking worn and dirty. Color schemes were definitely not appealing. A red ceiling in the kitchen definitely drew our attention away from the plain white walls. Obviously, red was the preferred color of choice by the current owners, as both bathrooms were completely painted red, and the master bedroom was a dark maroon.

Outside of those negatives, my heart soared as the house retained its charm for me.

The kitchen at the front of the house still had floor-to-ceiling windows and the blue tile backsplash we installed. I was sorry to see a porcelain chandelier gone. Echoes remained of all the meals and birthday celebrations we shared with so many people in that kitchen. Little girls playing with Playdough, coloring, and tackling school projects came into my mind. I could smell Spaghettios, macaroni and cheese, cabbage rolls, pork and dumplings, and more. The whiff of a bagel burned to a crisp in the microwave also resurfaced. The smell lingered for days.

Jess eating Spaghettios

I was pleased to see that Doug's mark remained in the living room. The beautiful molding that he painstakingly cut and installed still added class to the room. He was a perfectionist, and if it was off even slightly, down it would come until it was right. I recalled my surprise when he announced we needed more light in that room, and he brought out his sledgehammer and tore a hole in the wall for a new window.

French doors in the living room opened to additions we had built. Originally those doors led to a deck, but after returning from a home show, Doug announced that we would build a dining room. He did mean "we." Doug drew up the plans and the project began. I can easily remember the year. It was 1985. Shortly after the shell was finished, I realized there was more expansion in the works; our family would also be expanding. I was pregnant with Jill, daughter number four.

Despite my delicate condition, I continued to assist my "builder." I painted, helped put up borders and learned how to lay hardwood floors. Visitors also came to lend a hand. Doug's brother, Eddie, arrived with several friends to visit during a trip to Cincinnati for a bowling tournament. No sooner were they in the door than Doug recruited them to install a large bay window in the dining room.

The dining room framed (above); Doug working on Grandpa's Wing (below)

The plan for the remodel also included adding a room over the concrete cistern where water for the house was collected. There was no city water line on our property. Water was collected in a cistern. We depended on rain or water trucked in by a friendly guy named Gilbert. A manhole on top of the concrete cistern enabled us to insert a large stick to periodically gauge the level of water inside. We always welcomed any rain storm. The sound of water flowing into the cistern was music to our ears. Occasionally, we ran out of water and had to place an emergency call to Gilbert for a few loads. One time that stands out occurred when a large

Framed out Grandpa's Suite

contingent from Buffalo was in town for a Bills game and we completely ran out of water. Our guests took pleasure in kidding us about that event for years.

We referred to this new room over the cistern as "the sun room." A skylight bathed the area in sunlight. By the time Jill arrived, I enjoyed the warmth of the sun while rocking my youngest daughter.

The second addition came about five years later. "Grandpa's Suite," was added when my dad came to live with us. Once again, Doug drew up his plans, and we worked together to build a large bedroom, bathroom, and storage area off the dining room. We had the official ribbon-cutting at Jess's Communion party. Dad was thrilled with his private quarters.

Lori and I were transported back to those times of expansion as we now walked through the rooms. I remain amazed that Doug had the ability to visualize those additions and the skills to make them a reality. He was always ready to learn more. If something needed to be done, Doug searched for the answers and made things happen.

The visit to our old home was certainly stirring up memories.

We enjoyed stepping into the girls' bedrooms. Kim and Lori shared one, while Jess and Jill were roommates. Once, they secretly switched roommates, moving everything around and telling me about it later. It did not last long. They missed their old companions, and everything was moved back.

I purchased canopy beds for Kim and Lori with matching pink and white covers fit for little princesses. As they got older, they ditched the canopies.

Four little girls

When Jill arrived 15 months after Jess, two cribs occupied their bedroom. Two children in cribs and diapers at the same time was pretty crazy. One of my favorite pictures shows all four girls lined up in that room looking out the window, four little steps.

Our journey into the past continued as we made our way to the basement. The family room was always a cozy gathering spot, but during the Christmas holidays, colorful strands of lights twined through the banister and handrails to help create a fairy wonderland. A large wreath, complete with small wooden reindeer and festive red bows, greeted everyone at the bottom of the stairs. An alcove in the wall created the perfect setting for the crèche, and was just the right height for little people to gaze at the figures of Mary, Joseph, and Baby Jesus.

The basement provided space for many family activities. A

good-sized room (actually considered a bedroom by real estate standards, as it included a closet) served as the playroom. The door could be conveniently closed when the toys threatened to escape their designated area, or when the room resembled the aftermath of a small tornado (make that four small tornadoes). Periodically, Doug and I sent the girls into the room for a major clean-up. Hours later, they proudly displayed a well-organized line-up of toys. Alas, within days, the chaos would always return.

Doug had plenty of space for his collectibles in another room. He had a much easier time keeping his space organized. Sports cards were neatly placed in cabinets he had made. The original cabinet was the result of a woodworking project in grammar school. We kept our first computer, a Heathkit version Doug assembled, in that room, along with my sewing machine. The space also served as my sister's bedroom when she lived with us after her divorce.

Our property was situated at the end of a natural drainage slope, which unfortunately necessitated the use of a sump pump to avoid water issues. It seemed that a day could not go by without the sump pump kicking on. We lived in fear of power outages. Even though we had a backup battery operated sump pump, any extended outage meant big trouble.

Our worst experience happened one night when my sister lived with us. Not only was the power out, but lightning also struck our weather vane. What a night for all of us. As the water flowed from the sump pump hole into the basement, my sister, Doug, the girls, and I formed an assembly line from the basement "collection" room and up the stairs, feverishly transporting boxes and drawers of collectibles to higher ground. I will never forget Doug frantically saying, "I can't believe this. All these years I have been collecting and now it could all be ruined!" I have thought about that often, as I contemplate the collectibles lost or destroyed as a result of the crash.

After that storm, we discovered the previous owners had

installed foam padding under the basement carpeting, which like a sponge, absorbed the flood waters. The flooring had to be ripped out and replaced with an indoor/outdoor carpet. Calm was restored, and no collectibles were lost.

The basement returned to its status as a happy haven for laughing children, especially during birthday party sleepovers. I had a knack for entertaining gaggles of little girls. There was a craft of some sort, and the always anticipated "fishing" game. Numbered paper fish waited to be caught by the girls. A wooden stick with a line of yarn and magnet "bait" was easily cast to attract the paper-clipped fish. Everyone went home with a small gift as a result of their catch.

The girls spread out their sleeping bags in the family room, watched a rented movie, and sorted through fun party bags before finally drifting off to sleep.

Before leaving our visit to 957 Paxton-Guinea, Lori and I walked through the yard. The open fields that once surrounded the property were now filled with houses in a new development. The wood swing set was gone. Doug had added a sandbox to the set. We had to keep a close eye on it to make sure our cat, Spots, did not consider this an outdoor litter box. Doug also decided to enclose a "lookout" on the swing set, and created a clubhouse for the girls. Once again, his building skills were successful. Unfortunately, once the girls saw a bug or two in their retreat, they were not too anxious to use the club house.

A small storage shed in the corner of the backyard brought the recollection of animal tales. After delivering her kittens in a neighbor's attic space, Spots found a haven for her kittens in that shed, carrying them one-by-one in her mouth from the attic. A family of skunks also resided briefly under the shed. Luckily, they quickly departed. We watched out the window as a line of baby skunks followed mama's lead to a field across the street. One baby became distracted and lingered behind. We were concerned that he would be left behind, but he finally managed to catch up with his family.

As Lori and I walked back to our car, I warmly remembered our neighbor across the street, Mrs. Stevens. Mr. Stevens died shortly after we moved to Loveland, but Mrs. Stevens enjoyed our girls and loved watching the improvements we made to the house. She allowed Doug to practice his golf swing by hitting balls across the street to the large grassy lot next to her house. Only Doug would ask someone if he could do that. A novice golfer, I would endeavor to improve my skills too, but I was very concerned that my lack of control might damage a passing car or Mrs. Stevens' house. The girls loved to help us hunt for the balls in the tall grass. We had to be attentive to the general location of landings, as those cutting her grass were not pleased to encounter these obstacles. Yes, Mrs. Stevens no doubt found us very entertaining neighbors.

"You know, Mom, you could buy the house and move back," Lori told me during this visit.

Tempting, but as the ever elusive "they" say, "You can never go home again." Lori and I did prove that you can go home again briefly, both physically and mentally, but life moves on and there are new avenues to pursue.

I felt Doug's presence with every step I took that day. Our family had experienced much happiness in the Paxton-Guinea home, and what a building experience we encountered during those years, not only expanding the house, but building a family and a strong marriage.

My daughter Jess and I like to mimic a skit from an old "Saturday Night Live," where the characters kept repeating, "Good times, good times." That is a phrase that definitely describes our time in that home. Of course, what else would you expect in "Loveland?"

Author's note: My daughter Kim and I returned to Paxton-Guinea Road in 2017. We stopped to ask the current residents if we could take a picture of the outside of the house. They invited us inside. I felt no disappointment on this visit. No longer empty and in shambles, this time the house was beautifully decorated and obviously was well taken care of. The couple was renting the house from a friend. They had converted the living room into a dining room, and the dining room we had built had been converted into a sitting room. We did not go into the basement, as the house was once again up for sale and renovations were under construction. I left that day thankful, because the house where we had enjoyed raising our family was once more a true home.

Curtis, Kim and Lydia check out the backyard in 2015.

Lydia stands by a tree that we planted in 1985.

Everwood Court
East Amherst, New York
(1997-2004)

I definitely felt like I had gotten stuck with the short end of the stick.

While Doug had already moved to Buffalo to start a new job, I had been left behind to organize the contents of our home in Loveland, so that our girls and I could join him later.

He had reaped benefits from the new job. He recently returned from a trip to Germany. He was adjusting well.

Although I was excited about our return to the Buffalo area where Doug and I had been raised, I lamented leaving the friends and happy, fulfilling life I had enjoyed in Loveland. How could you go wrong living in a town called Loveland?

My mixed emotions about the move boiled over when Doug called and asked if I was watching the movers pack our garage contents, which included many of his sports memorabilia. They had been there all day. Had he expected me to stand over them all that time? Really? There were so many things I needed to do before our move, including farewell parties all the girls' friends had scheduled.

The girls and I finally set out on December 7, 1997, to reunite the whole family. Our minivan was solidly packed. The girls could barely squeeze themselves into it. Every time we stopped on the route, we opened the side door carefully to prevent things from falling out.

Our drugged cat, Spots, sat dazed in a cage. We had barely gone two blocks when I had to pull over to remove the poop she had just released as a farewell to her home.

Somehow, we survived the 430-mile trek that took about eight hours.

It was a real treat to be able to pull the minivan into a garage. That was something we had never been able to do in our other homes, since the garage was always used as a storage area.

Spots was still recovering from her sedation, so we left her in the garage. Hours later, when we went to check on her recuperation, we could not find her. There was nothing in the closed garage except the minivan. We looked underneath the vehicle, but could not locate her. I accused the girls of opening a door that allowed her to escape. Could it possibly be that after carting this cat from Ohio, she was now lost?

Around 2:00 a.m. I heard meowing and there she was in the garage. Of course, I had to apologize to the girls, and I can only assume that Spots had crawled up to some spot under the vehicle until she was ready to accept her new home.

Spots and me on the deck

The house on Everwood Court remained empty that first night, as the moving truck would not arrive until the next day. Even when the furniture was placed inside, it became obvious that we would have to purchase more things to fill up the 2,100

Moving truck

square feet provided in our new home.

It was a beautiful house. It had a grand entryway with a staircase leading up to four bedrooms, a separate bathroom for the girls, and a huge master bathroom. There were two walk-in closets in that master bedroom, along with a large storage area off one of the closets.

Although Doug had plenty of room to keep his collectibles in the full basement, he would also have a den, which included an entire wall of bookcases for displaying many of his prized possessions.

We barely used the formal living room. The large dining room had lovely stenciling and wainscoting.

The focal point of the roomy kitchen was an island in the center of the room. It contained stove-top burners and plenty of counter space. There was an indoor grill on another counter and a double oven in the wall, along with a designated desk space. We purchased a kitchen set to fill another area in the kitchen, where French doors led to a spacious deck. The laundry room was conveniently off the kitchen.

A step down from the kitchen was the family room, where

3 walls of windows framed the beautiful view of the yard and a grove of stately trees.

If walls could talk, that house would tell many tales of our family.

Our girls enjoyed their teenage years in that house. Since the basement was partially finished, their friends found it a perfect spot for their gatherings. Their laughter seeped through the closed door, and Doug and I could only imagine the trials, tribulations, and joys they discussed about their teenage activities.

The girls had their first boyfriends, the thrill of love, and sometimes the heartbreak of rejection in that house.

There was the excitement of proms and dances to prepare for during that time.

Three of the girls left for college from there.

Doug and I rode the wild rollercoaster, watching our little girls change constantly before our eyes.

I did not immerse myself in the volunteer activities I had pursued in Ohio and I quickly learned that I did not like just sitting around at home. Luckily, I decided to answer a want ad in the local *Pennysaver*, and began my association with WXRL Radio as a secretary.

Since it was a part-time position, I had plenty of time to explore our new neighborhood.

The Clarence Peanut Line was behind our house. Originally known as the Canandaigua-Niagara Falls Railroad, it became known as the Peanut Line when it was acquired by the Central Railroad and a vice president referred to it as "only a peanut of a line." At one time, it did provide transportation to downtown Buffalo, but that passenger service ended in the late '30s.

The tracks had long since been removed by the time we moved to Everwood Court, but the unpaved trail provided an easy means to walk a mile or so to Transit Road. Hot dogs and ice cream were rewards for taking the trail, as it ended right next to Pautler's Drive-in Restaurant. There was also a small shop nearby

Family photo

that was well stocked with Beanie Babies, which were all the craze in the late '90s.

Looking back, it probably was not the wisest choice for the girls or me to walk along that pathway. It did wind its way through housing developments, but much of it was flanked by trees and brush, where who knew what dangers lurked.

It was the perfect house for entertaining, and we welcomed our extended families and friends on many occasions. Ironically, we never seemed to congregate in the large family room. People usually gathered around the kitchen island, or outside on the deck or large wrap-around porch at the front of the house. I loved that porch, and one of my favorite photos of our family was taken on the porch steps. I always tell everyone that it shows Doug surrounded by the things he loved. He is wearing his Bills shirt, wearing his University at Buffalo graduation and wedding rings, and is surrounded by his girls and me.

When Doug's good friend, Jim Macie, and his wife, Betty, visited us, we learned of a most unusual coincidence. Jim and Betty had been to an open house at our new home when it was originally a model home.

Over the years, several of the girls' friends from Loveland visited us.

I drove to Cleveland a few times to pick up Jill's friend, Natalie. It was considered a halfway point, so her mom met us there, and Natalie stayed with us for a while. Jess' friend, Erin, flew to Buffalo to stay with us. A few of Kim's friends were driving, so they also arrived on our doorstep.

It wasn't hard to keep the girls occupied. Donning their bathing suits, they giggled contentedly as they sat in the huge jacuzzi tub or ran through the sprays of water provided by the sprinkler system on the front lawn.

It was good to see these friendships continue.

I wanted to know what memories my girls have from our life at Everwood Court, so in their own words, they recalled the following memories.

Kim: *"Having my own room with a walk-in closet, New Year's 2000, drinking too much wine watching the movie, Speed, by myself, the constant upkeep of 'The Pit,' babysitting for neighbors, riding our bikes all over the neighborhood, walking on the Peanut Line to Pautler's, the basement hanging out with friends, Dad breaking his*

New Year's Eve 2000

leg playing hockey, the huge pantry, a card being stolen from Dad's office, Spots disappearing when we first moved there, rolling the piano down the street, a blizzard in November."

Some further information may be needed in her recollection.

Doug and I were out to dinner when Kim encountered her first experience of being "buzzed." One of the other girls called us, and was concerned because Kim had positioned herself in the bathroom for quite some time. When we arrived home, we were not at first sure what had transpired, but slowly we pieced things together. She spent the night on the couch in the family room where I kept watch. I guess if you are going to experiment with wine, it's good to do it at home.

"The Pit," was a large area of tall trees on our property, and in the fall, leaves cascaded to carpet the area. Removing massive amounts of leaves once a year became a family affair. At times, those trees would sway in time to the harsh music of the wind, and we anxiously held our breath, hoping a gust would not fell one of the Pit's residents.

Doug loved to play hockey, and joined a group of young guys to play pick-up games on Sundays. I received a call late one night where an obviously concerned young man informed me that Doug was okay, but had been taken to the Emergency Room with a possible broken leg. I can still remember one of my first questions to the presenter of this news, "Which leg is it?" I know this might seem like a strange question, but I knew that if it was his right leg, he would not be able to drive. Since the girls' activities required a lot of chauffeuring, I realized this would not be a good thing for me as a driver.

When I arrived at the hospital, my worst fears were realized. It was his right leg, broken when a large fellow landed on him while fighting for the puck. Ah, the life of a jock's wife.

He recuperated for several weeks and then returned to work. Either I or a colleague from his work transported him back and forth.

Unfortunately, Doug hung up his skates after that. It was a difficult decision for him to make, but he felt he could not afford to lose work again due to a hockey injury.

Losing a few days of work did occur after another incident during our years at Everwood Court though. Doug had a habit of running during lunch time, and one day, stepped on loose gravel which resulted in a stumble. This time, the damage was to his face. He looked like he had been on the losing end of a prize fight.

Doug did believe that at some point a Mickey Mantle card had been stolen from his den. No accusations were ever made and it could never be proved, but Doug immediately purchased a lock for the French doors that opened into the room.

Although I never was a good piano player, I enjoyed having one in the house. When we moved to Long Street, there was no room for our piano and one of our neighbors wanted to purchase it. Somehow, it was rolled down Everwood Court one afternoon. I understand two neighbor children started lessons.

Lori: *"Bike rides on the Peanut trail, AOL/internet, 2000 New Year's Eve where I made headbands for everyone, playing the game 'Spoons' at Christmastime, my own room and repainting it (it was blue with glow-in-the-dark space stickers, and we put up the same border that we had in our room in Ohio), TV stand and TV in my room with a purple blow-up chair that smelled, staying up late watching TV in the basement (Brady Bunch with Loveland friend, Renee) and eating tons of Fudgesicles. Watching the winter Olympics when it was in Japan in the basement, my purple phone in my bedroom, dressing as Brittany Spears with Jess for Halloween, watching tons of MTV, especially TRL with Carson Daly, eating pizza rolls after school, practicing my soccer juggling in the yard, watching football and doing laundry on Sundays, sitting on the front porch listening to the Back Street Boys CD, being the only house in the neighborhood doing our own yard work."*

When Lori was that teenager watching the Olympics in Japan, she never could have imagined that one day she, her husband,

and seven-month-old son would be living there.

As an example of our yardwork, a cul-de-sac and the large tree/bush island was in front of our house. Stones covered the surface, and weeds easily poked out of hiding to clutter the island. We, along with other neighbors, took it upon ourselves to try and keep appearances neat, but it was a never-ending job.

Jess: *"Riding bikes to Paulter's and the store to buy TY Beanie Babies, Mom covering herself with a laundry basket to water the plants on the front porch because of the robins, basketball in the driveway, birthday parties with friends in the basement, going on AOL/internet and taking up the phone line."*

She would remember that robin incident! The birds built nests in the pots, and I made some strange attempts to water the plants. In the end, I just let the plants wilt away, and enjoyed the baby birds.

Jill: *"Jess and I watching endless hours of MTV and dancing around to music in our room, having sleepovers in Lori and Kim's rooms, Jess falling off the top bunk bed, playing Sonic the Hedgehog late at night, being creeped out by the unfinished basement, stealing Dad's candy (lol), all the celebrations for super bowls, holidays, and making peanut butter cookies."*

I do recall Jess falling out of the bunk bed. She was a bit sore, but thankfully not seriously injured. The bunk beds were taken apart the next day.

I have no idea what Sonic the Hedgehog was, but apparently it was a video game.

Jill also admitted that her candy thievery took place in all our homes, and she mostly sought out her dad's spiced jelly beans. Doug held on to candy, which I, as someone who feels compelled to consume candy within days of receiving it, could never understand.

I love that the girls shared their memories with me, and I am happy to see that those years on Everwood Court elicit fond memories for them.

We made life-long friends when the Southard family moved next door to us. When they first saw Doug working in the yard, they thought he was hired help. Both doctors, Eric and Kathy purchased their house about two years after us. They had two small children (who are now, unbelievably, college graduates) that were added to our girls' babysitting schedule.

I recall Kathy and me talking, in shock, following 9/11, and commenting on the eeriness of the silence that shrouded the neighborhood following the ban on airline traffic. Planes were always flying overhead in our neighborhood on their way to the Buffalo Airport.

Our families shared so many experiences together. There were birthday and graduation parties, and if household emergencies arose, we could always count on each other for a helping hand.

Another memory etched in my mind is a night when we placed our lawn chairs on the front lawn around 2:00 a.m., and enjoyed a light show in the heavens provided by shooting stars.

I love when Kathy tells me she considers me like "an older sister," and she and Eric have provided me with comfort since Doug's death. On the tenth anniversary of the crash of Flight 3407, when I had several engagements lined up over a two-day period, they opened their home to me. They encouraged me, fed me, and accompanied me to services on the anniversary date. Even their dog, Buddy, snuggled with me as I drifted off to sleep each night.

They are special friends.

Over the years, I have written many stories about the homes I have lived in. Everwood Court, though, did not appear prominently in those recollections. I do not know why that was the case. We lived there for about seven busy, happy years. Our departure from that home came unexpectedly following Doug's job loss. It was a difficult time for all of us and filled with uncertainty.

There was some regret when we left what definitely was an affluent lifestyle. Lori's boyfriend at that time summed it up as

House on Everwood Court

"going from filet mignon to baloney." Yes, space and opulence were limited on Long Street, but Doug and I felt it represented more who we really were.

Maybe I have hesitated to write about Everwood Court, because there is always an unanswered question facing me about that home. Where would we be today if we had not moved to Long Street?

I do not linger on that question. It is useless to wonder about the what and why of life.

Looking back on our time on Everwood Court, I appreciate what we had, the happiness it especially brought our girls during their pre-teen and teenage years, the bonding it gave us as a family, and all the good memories.

That is all you really need, and definitely not the short end of the stick.

1/25/21

Revisiting 6038 Long Street (2004-2009)

How do I grieve something that isn't mine anymore?
~ Denise Guido Forkin

Denise Guido grew up at 6038 Long Street. Her family lived in the quiet community of Clarence Center for over 30 years. Originally built in the 1920s, her parents bought the house in the 1960s and sold the property in 1999 to a young couple, who later sold the home to our family in 2004. When Continental Flight 3407 crashed into that home on February 12, 2009, Denise grieved. She had every right to feel a sense of loss.

I have never met Denise Guido, but I originally met her father, Dennis Guido, in 2008 during the annual Clarence Center Volunteer Fire Company's Labor Day Festival.

The festivities were held at the fire station located on Clarence Center Road directly across from Long Street. The inconvenience of dealing with a constant stream of people and vehicles passing by our house paled when compared to the excitement of the Labor Day weekend event. Music and the luring scents of barbequed chicken and chili drifted down the street. People arrived early on Saturday morning, large containers clutched in their hands, and patiently stood in line for that chili. Family and friends stopped by our house on their way to enjoy games of chance, visit vendors selling a variety of goods, or letting the kids try fun rides. We walked down for some food prepared by the firemen or local boy scouts and enjoyed the entertainment and a brew or two. The ease of having all this activity down the street could not be beat.

As we sat on our porch that day in 2008, Dennis walked by and introduced himself. Neighbors had spoken warmly of Mr. Guido, "the cookie man," a name bestowed on him because he was an Archway Cookie distributor. The kids in the neighborhood were always welcome at 6038 Long Street, and more than likely, cookies were passed around.

We invited him into the house, but he only looked briefly at the family room addition that we had recently finished. Perhaps he did not want to erase the memories he had retained of what the house looked like when he lived there. He was more interested in seeing if a large tree was still in the backyard, but it had been removed before we purchased the property.

After the crash, someone showed me an article about Mr. and Mrs. Guido that appeared in a local newspaper. They were standing before a painting of their former home at 6038 Long Street. It must have given them an eerie feeling to know their family had spent so many years at that address.

It was not until the publication of my book, *One on the Ground*, that Dennis Guido entered my life again. He had contacted the Clarence Historical Society to see if I could connect with him. We spoke on the phone, and he indicated he would like to show me that painting of 6038 Long Street and photo albums that his late wife had compiled. His

Visiting with Mr. Guido in 2017

Guido painting

Our painting by Kathleen Dworak

congenial personality made it impossible for me to refuse his invitation.

Dennis now lives in Silver Lake, a community of cottages that rim sparkling water in pastoral Wyoming County. As my friend,

Debby, and I enjoyed Dennis' hospitality, I once again found myself wandering through my memories of Long Street.

Mrs. Guido had the painting done of the house while they lived there. It depicts the house as it was when we bought it, including a group of bushes that obstructed the front of the porch. I couldn't help but smile as I looked at those bushes. Doug decided they had to go. Lori's boyfriend volunteered to assist in that process. Digging and pulling proved to be insufficient to get the job done, so the guys attached chains to the hitch on the old Chevy Malibu, wove them around the branches, crossed their fingers, and stepped on the gas. Success! With the bushes removed, the foundation was painted green, a touch of maroon was added to awnings and trim, and each spring impatiens provided a profusion of color at the side of the house.

As for the tree Dennis looked for in 2008, he did show me photos of that massive tree, which majestically had provided shade for the back of the house. The family room we added occupied that space.

It felt so good to see photos depicting the beautiful woodwork that highlighted the front hallway and living room, character that is often missing from homes today. I laughed as I saw the

The front room at Long Street

striped floral wallpaper in the dining room and matching drapes that Doug and I had quickly removed. After uttering, "I forgot how horrible that was." I quickly added, "I hope you didn't put those up?" My sigh of relief followed when he assured me that combination was the idea of an owner before the Guidos.

I examined with interest the placement of their furniture in each room, comparing it to our ideas on how pieces could be placed to make the most of the small space.

The dining room at Long Street

Denise's bedroom was at the front of the house, which had been Kim's room. Those photos caused a spine-chilling sensation for me as I thought of Jill sitting on the bed angled in one corner the night of the crash.

Dennis reminded me of an old safe and jukebox that they had left in the basement. They were told the safe was too heavy to remove, and although the jukebox had been dismantled, it still could not be maneuvered up the stairs. It was reassembled and there when we moved in. I had completely forgotten about those "blasts from the past." Knowing how Doug and I felt about history, it surprises me that we did not want to keep those pieces. We definitely sold the jukebox, although I cannot recall any difficulty the buyer had removing it. I felt the safe went too, but perhaps it was still in the basement, although I feel some comment about it would have been made during the retrieval of items from the crash site.

The basement was a hangout for the Guido and the Wielinski kids. Dennis also happily recalled the porch being a gathering place.

The photos definitely chronicled the many gatherings that took place at 6038 Long Street: birthdays, proms, holidays, and any occasion that could bring family and friends together. The pleasure of those attending the events remained etched in their smiles.

It confirmed what our family experienced at 6038 Long Street. It was a home filled with love and happiness.

At one point, Dennis admitted to me that he felt guilty. I was confused by that. His eyes brimmed with tears and his voice quivered, revealing the sincerity of what he told me. "I feel guilty that I waited so long to connect with you, and…I feel guilty that I sold 6038 Long Street and you eventually bought it."

I was startled by that second revelation, and hopefully I said the right words to relieve any guilt that torments him. Raising the question, "What if?" only brings unnecessary confusion and sadness. Everything happens for a reason and our doubts or guilt will not change anything.

Although I haven't met Denise Guido, I felt connected to her during my visit with her father. Many of the photos we viewed that day came from Denise's collection. Also included were diagrams she drew before leaving 6038 Long Street, showing the placement of furniture and household items.

I felt that was a remarkable coincidence. I did similar drawings when I left my childhood home on Herman Street. Perhaps the hope of preserving memories in that manner is more common than I thought.

Dennis asked me to sign a copy of *One on the Ground* that

Denise had purchased online. As I was doing that, I saw the quote she had written inside the front cover, "How do I grieve something that isn't mine anymore?"

Why shouldn't she grieve for the loss of 6038 Long? She grew up in that house and the memories she created there shaped who she is today. So yes, mourn the loss of that physical structure, but take comfort in the fact that the memories you created in that home live on and can give comfort.

Dennis and Denise gave me a gift. They helped reinforce my memories of 6038 Long Street by sharing their own memories with me and providing photos that allowed me to once again visualize our home.

2017

Kraus Road
Clarence Center, New York
(March 2009 - December 2009)

In the weeks immediately following the crash, my Aunt Agnes had graciously offered her home to us while she was in rehab, but finding a new home became an obsession with me.

We decided to move into a townhouse on Kraus Road in Clarence Center, New York. Kim and Jill were still living with me when we arrived.

It is true that this home held many moments of sadness and fear. There were revelations and discoveries around every corner during that time. Tears were almost a constant, and fear and panic were companions because the location, unbeknownst to us when we signed the lease, was directly on the flight path.

But, Lori's and Chris' wedding in August of 2009 brought some normalcy into our lives. Kraus Road was filled with exciting anticipation of the event. After her shower, our townhouse found itself overflowing with gifts. Later, all the ladies gathered the night before the wedding for a sleepover, and the next day there were plenty of "oohs and aahs" as Lori and her bridesmaids slipped into their beautiful dresses and had their makeup applied. So many wonderful memories happened during a wedding that had been planned before the crash.

Our cat, Belle, joined our family on Kraus, and she proved

Sleepover fun: Jill, Jill Morris & Lori

Lori in her gown

to be a very active kitten. We discovered she was terrified of the ceiling fan in the family room, so that remained silent during our stay. She found it necessary to nibble toes at night, which resulted in my not only closing my bedroom door, but placing a chair against it to avoid being attacked. She had great determination.

When coming home from work, I found her peering out the kitchen window anxiously awaiting my return.

Belle certainly entertained us.

We had chosen her from a litter of kittens born next door to my daughter Lori's house in Bellevue, Kentucky, which resulted in our choice of her name. Her sister had remained in Kentucky, adopted by a friend. However, due to a change in living

Belle

accommodations, Mia arrived on Kraus when Lori and Chris came to share the Christmas holidays with us in 2009.

We tried to keep many of our holiday traditions alive, as we came together for that first bittersweet Christmas without Doug. We received comfort in those customs, and also incorporated the addition of quite an array of pets attending the festivities, as cats and dogs were welcome too.

The houses were few and far between on our road, and country fields dominated the neighborhood scene. There were many times when I felt the weight of the world resting on my shoulders, and walking through that pastoral environment seemed to ease my stress.

Our nine-month stay on Kraus Road, as outlined in depth in *One on the Ground,* did become a home, despite all the sadness that surrounded our arrival there. Kim, Jill and I developed a special closeness as we gave each other comfort.

As the months passed, though, the girls lives dictated their need to spread their wings and fly. It was time for me to find a more permanent home.

8/30/22

Christmas, 2009

South Grove & Walnut Streets East Aurora, New York (2010-present)

Just Over the Horizon

Just over the horizon
It began to beckon me:
Bring all your tears and your fears,
I will help to set you free.

Walk along our tree-lined streets,
Leave cares and woes behind you.
Comfort like a longed-for hug,
On my streets will wrap 'round you.

Memories of childhood days--
Shops were but a step away.
No need to hop in that car,
Quaint homes to see along your way.

Friendship waits--inviting gifts,
Unwrapped to soon reveal
Those who wish to become
Part of your historic wheel.

Try something new--take a chance
Embrace what you discover.
Memories of what you lost
Remain, but yet grow dimmer.

Words that gather in your mind,
Unconstrained in written form.
Encouragement will guide you,
Ease the restlessness you scorn.

Just over the horizon
You'll find a peaceful aura.
A new life can be found--
Come live in East Aurora.

~ Karen Wielinski

9/22/13

The Five Senses

Do not ask me which one of these to lose:
Not see emotions flicker on the face,
Or miss the brilliant hues of fall and spring?
Not hear the laughter of a little child,
Or melodies that float upon the air?
Not smell the welcome offered by a meal,
Or whiffs of nature's fragrance in the air?
Not feel the warmth of a tender embrace,
Be it a hug or love's first magic kiss?
Not taste the succulence of summer fruit,
Or salty tears that drizzle down my face?
To lose a sense just makes no sense to me.

~ Karen Wielinski

Touch and Sight

"Nothing in this world compares to the comfort and security of having someone just hold your hand."

~ Richelle E. Goodrich

"The voyage of discovery is not in seeking new landscapes, but in having new eyes."

~ Marcel Proust

Hands

Let us celebrate the loving care etched in every line, crevice, scar, bump, and misshapen tendon of our hands. The occupation and even character of a person can be revealed by studying their hands.

I am drawn to these marvelous appendages, and find that I want to capture the many ways they touch my life. Here are some sights that were a delight to behold.

My first grandchild, Lydia Frances Lipiarz, arrived the evening of August 4, 2012, shortly after her mother's and Aunt Lori's baby shower. Obviously eager to join the family and use the many gifts bestowed on her

Kim with Lydia at Sisters Hospital, August 2012

that day, she was born at 25 week's gestation, weighing an unimaginable 1 pound, 12 ounces. A few days old, her mother Kim could only reach through the isolette to bond with her daughter. Lydia instinctively grabbed on to life, and her mother.

Caden Douglas Tiede arrived on October 2, 2012. He was a novelty in the world of Wielinski births, predominantly populated by girls. His dad, Chris, tenderly cradled his newborn son, a hand supported his small head, a hand that will support Caden as he encounters life's journey.

Chris and Caden, October 2012

Caden's outstretched hand tentatively reached out, "So, are you my dad?" A father and son's first bonding experience, captured for all time.

After four months in both Sisters and Children's Hospitals in Buffalo, Lydia finally came home a few weeks before Christmas. She was the best present ever. Her hands found a resting place on Grandma's hand. Grandma could not have been happier. Now, with her arrival, the house in the background of this picture is indeed a welcoming home of a young family.

Lydia going home for the first time

Caden's hand, so tiny in the picture with his dad, now rests on his mom. That is definitely the hand of an athlete. His Grandpa Wielinski, who loved to play basketball, often said he

Caden's hand on Lori

lacked the big hands that can make you successful at that game. Well, his grandson looks like he might be ready. Beneath his hand, mother's heartbeat offered comfort and lulled him to sleep.

Cousins Caden and Lydia are separated by hundreds of miles. This was only their second get together. Since their meeting at Christmas, they had both developed personalities and an awareness of the world around them. They seemed to

Lydia and Caden with their moms

accept one another as they joined hands in solidarity. "Hey, this is pretty special," Lydia's expression implies. To me, the wonderful smiles on their mothers' faces are special too.

Hands can be artistic, creating works of art, preserving

Belle and morning shadows

thoughts by the written word, or playing a part. Early morning sun, streaming through bedroom blinds, presented the opportunity for some shadow play and inspired me to write a poem.

> *Eyes open, it greets me,*
> *Rays of light projected*
> *Thrown forward on a wall*
> *Masterpiece unfolded.*
>
> *Image on a surface*
> *Clears cobwebs in my mind.*
> *Imagines come to life*
> *Dreams now reality.*
>
> *A dinosaur and bird*
> *Float and rest on canvas,*
> *Feel them bring joy and cheer*
> *Of childhood memories.*

What slides into my view?
Enters my illusion?
Pointy ears, curly tail,
Cat dares to join the play.

Proof that fun can be shared,
In fact adds dimension.
Thank you sun for your rays
Laughter starts a new day.

Curtis and Grandma

Me at the Vietnam Memorial

This moment brought such joy. Words can hardly describe the thrill felt by the feathery touch of such tiny hands, perfect in every detail. A bittersweet moment, though, as it produced a longing for a Grandpa who will never know that touch.

The first time I visited the Vietnam Memorial, I had three little girls in tow and another on the way. Perhaps a bit distracted, I could see the memorial but kept missing the exit, ending up in Arlington several times. When we finally reached our destination, I was impressed by the simplicity of the design, which clearly reflected the tremendous loss of life resulting from the Vietnam War.

On another visit to Washington, DC, in 2014, my companions were Jess' college roommate, Liz, and her friend, Milton. It was a cool, but sunny day in February, and we spent the afternoon walking through the mall area, stopping at the Lincoln, World War II, and Korean War memorials.

The sun was setting as we arrived at the Vietnam memorial. Once again, I was struck by the magnitude of lives lost. I also thought of Doug, and shared with Liz and Milton stories of his time in Vietnam.

I felt compelled to place my hand on the wall, and was surprised by the warmth that I encountered. I had not expected the heat from the sun to still remain. For me, I felt the sensation that radiated through my hand actually came from the very lives of those who died during that conflict.

My cat Belle is my shadow. In that respect, she seems more like a faithful dog. She follows my every move, which at times can be a

Belle on my keyboard

distraction. While trying to type on my computer, she often paces back and forth in front of me until finally plopping down on my arm. On this day, Belle decided the only way to get my attention was to hold my hand prisoner. It worked. Who could resist that kind of devotion?

The next picture was taken while my daughter, Lori, and her family were living in Nagoya, Japan. Caden seems mesmerized as he rests on his mom's belly, connecting with his future brother or sister. Was there movement beneath his hand? Did the murmur

Caden listening to his sibling

Rowan and Caden

of a faint heartbeat reach him? I like to think Caden started to bond with his sibling that day.

It was a brother! Rowan arrived August 6, 2014, looking very much like his mother. Since Lori resembles her dad, perhaps we will see a bit of Doug in this little guy as he grows. Caden is always being told to keep his fingers out of his mouth, so apparently he is passing that information on to his brother. That is what big brothers do: guide, teach, and love.

Lori gets some cuddle time with Caden, relaxing after a busy day at work, hands wrapped securely around him. "Look Mama, I can count to five," he proudly says. Togetherness is pretty special.

Lori and Caden counting

It was a picture-perfect day at Lori's in-laws' farm in Caledonia. Since their birth, cousins Caden and Lydia have been separated not by states, but by continents. Yet when they do get together, they know they are family. Modern technology plays a part in their connection. I have seen their excitement when FaceTime closes the gap between their worlds.

Caden and Lydia at the farm

Here, they link hands, guiding and protecting each other. Lydia is slightly ahead of Caden; that is her way. She tends to lead and he is happy to follow.

Hands reach out to receive and provide comfort. There was a birthday celebration this day in July for Curtis' sister and two cousins, Evelyn and Elizabeth. It was a long, hot day, devoid of naps and regular feedings, which is hard when you are only one year old. Curtis was upset, and no one else but Mom could soothe him. His hand on Kim quiets

Curtis and Kim

the little guy down and soon elusive rest silences the loud merriment surrounding him. Kim will cherish this moment and retrieve it from her memory some day when Curtis becomes a man.

Sorrow does enter our lives. At those times we must rely on our hands to help console our fears and heartaches. We reach out to others, embracing them and holding them with our hands. We try to express our regret and mourn even those whom we have never met.

At the 9/11 Memorial

I visited the 9/11 site with Jess, and my cousin, Leo, on the 4th of July. Before the crash of Flight 3407, visiting that sacred ground would have moved me. Now, I also have a personal connection to the tragedy of 9/11. Sean Rooney lost his life on 9/11 when Tower Two collapsed. His wife, Beverly Eckert, lost her life with the crash of Flight 3407. I have learned much about Sean and Beverly's life together during drives to Washington with Beverly's sisters. I felt the need to locate Sean's name on the memorial. As my hand traced his name, it was still hard for me to comprehend my new connection to yet another tragedy. Emotionally, I could not linger long at the site. Jess put her hand on my shoulder to provide comfort as we walked away.

Ideas blossom and ache to take form on a page. Sometimes the writing process is obsessive, but steady work, by determined hands, creates a finished product. My reward came while I relaxed on my porch, busy hands now stilled, thoughts transformed into written words, bathed in sunlight and accompanied by a furry guest, Zoey.

Relaxing with Zoey

Tracing Doug's name on Forest Lawn memorial

Another year, another wedding anniversary date, when this picture was taken, it would have been 34 years. Why do I even continue adding years to that beginning of wedded bliss? I visited the Forest Lawn Cemetery in Buffalo, New York. The only other time I entered this landmark cemetery was in November of 2009. A memorial was dedicated to those who perished in the crash of Flight 3407. Safely cradled inside this memorial are unidentified remains and those too small and numerous to give to the families—not a pleasant thought. I had no idea where the memorial was located. I asked people I passed, and they shook their heads, "What kind of memorial is that?…Oh, was that the plane crash in Clarence?" I felt a strong need to locate the memorial; I could not leave until I covered every acre of the cemetery. *OK, Doug, help me out here. Please guide me.* Suddenly, there it was—perhaps an answer to my plea. My hand traced the letters of my husband's name, and I remembered our wedding day.

If you look up the verb hand, the following words will appear: give, offer, supply, dispense, administer. Those descriptions express what our hands are capable of: giving or offering our support, supplying, dispensing and administering love. Hands are powerful instruments. We must use them wisely.

3/8/21

The Eyes Have It

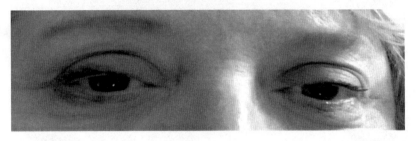

People say that eyes are the window to the soul. If that is true, when I look at this picture, I think I might be in trouble. This soul looks somewhat defeated.

Their appearance probably has more to do with the fact that I had just awoken, but these eyes certainly have seen their share of sadness in recent years. I do not want to focus on that aspect, though. Instead, I want to turn my sights to the visions that have brought joy.

A few sightings from the past quickly come to my mind.

One day, I had walked up and down the stairs in my home several times, yet it was not until late in the afternoon that I spotted a small leaf on one of the steps. That discovery made me smile.

The day before, a surprise visit by my daughter, Kim, and her two little ones had brightened my day. After yet another visit to the upstairs bathroom in her quest for potty training, three-year-old Lydia sat on the top step with Kim. For some reason, I thought of an old game we played as kids. It was called the stone game. The "leader" concealed a small stone in one of his or her hands behind their back, turned around, and asked the kids on the step, "Which hand?" A successful guess by the participants resulted in the reward of moving up the stairs in the hope of reaching the top and being crowned the winner.

I decided it would be a fun game to play with Lydia and Kim.

Lydia's eyes lit up during the game. This child, who often can spend large quantities of time connected to an iPad, and already has more knowledge of technology than I will ever have, was thrilled with this simple game. Her shining eyes and bright smile were a happy vision for me to behold.

What does this have to do with a leaf? Lydia had captured that small leaf as she walked from the car into my house, a treasure in her eyes. Her prized possession was dismissed and forgotten in the excitement of our game and her success at being the winner. When I spotted the leaf, I once again delighted in her joy.

My grandchildren certainly bring happiness to my eyes. My daughter Lori's oldest son, Caden, has a tendency to transfer the joy in his eyes to mine.

When I first visited their new home in Lexington, I was greeted at the door with his excitement. "Nana!" he exclaimed as he rushed out the door to me. Granted, he also showed that same exuberance when seeing the UPS and pizza delivery guys, but that special "Nana!" was reserved for me.

Caden also pulled on my heartstrings when he arrived at the airport for a visit with his parents. What a cute sight he was as he pulled his little suitcase behind him. The minute his eyes met mine, I was again rewarded with that "Nana!"

Viewing the world through my grandchildren's eyes is a benefit I received when obtaining the title Grandma and Nana. I experienced that point of view with my children, but I sometimes feel that the responsibility of motherhood does not let us fully appreciate the wonders our children discovered throughout their childhood. It is not until we become grandparents that we have the freedom of time to savor the true joy of childhood through our grandchildren's eyes.

Since my book *One on the Ground* was published, I often wonder if my grandchildren have any concept of my being an author.

When attending one of Caden's "Grandparents Day" celebrations, I watched as items he had selected to specifically represent me, were removed from a brown bag by his teacher. The first item was a toy egg. Caden had put that in the bag because, "I like when Nana makes us eggs at her house." The next was a toy pig, which was appropriate, as this nana has collected pig figures over the years. Then, the teacher pulled out a copy of *One on the Ground*. Before Caden could speak, the teacher said, "Oh, Nana likes to read…no, wait, Nana is the author!" The look in her eyes was priceless.

I was delegated to escort my grandchildren, Lydia and Curtis, to a birthday party at "Monkey See, Monkey Do," a bookstore, in Clarence. I love going to this little store, and time always seems to slip away when I wander around and my eyes take in the enticing covers of mainly children's books. They do, however, also carry adult choices. *One on the Ground* is included in their selections.

After the party, the children had time to walk around the shop. I happened to see Lydia stop by the shelf where my book rested. She pointed at my book, and proudly explained to her companion, the birthday boy, "My Grandma made that book."

That sight again pulled on my heartstrings.

I am definitely a person who shares pictures of my grandchildren with others, probably excessively. Pictures capture cherished moments and often can reveal the love shown in the eyes of others. That look may have escaped our view at the time the shot was taken, but the warmth of that love can be savored long after the shutter is closed.

Lydia and friend at bookstore

I am fortunate to have a photo that shows the

celebration of my husband, Doug's, birthday and my birthday. Doug's birthday was July 13, and mine is July 15. The photo was taken many years ago at my daughter, Jessica's, apartment in Oneonta, New York.

I always feel a rush of happiness every time I see the look of love in my husband's eyes. It comforts me. Yes, I was loved, and those are happy eyes.

Karen and Doug

Luckily for me, the eyes do have it and they not only provide a never-ending source of opportunities to create memories, but they also give me inspiration to write.

9/16/15, updated 11/9/20

Author's Note

On a visit to Lori's in Lexington, Kentucky, after I wrote this piece, I could see first-hand the magic of believing in my grandsons' eyes. I think perhaps this might have been the real Santa, as he seemed to mesmerize the boys. There is such love being exchanged between this trio, and Santa holding Rowan's hand is such an expression of tenderness. This sight exemplifies the beauty of childhood and the pleasures we can derive if we keep our eyes open for possibilities.

Taste

"To me, food is as much about the moment, the occasion, the location, and the company as it is about the taste."

~ *Heston Blumenthal*

Recipes

What material things would you miss if your home was destroyed?

For me, it was the little things: my daughters' baby books in which I lovingly recorded all their "firsts"; our wedding album, filled with memories of the happy start to our marriage; a wooden box shipped by my grandmother to my dad while he was stationed overseas during World War II, and upon his return filled with his memorabilia from Germany and France; beautifully illustrated old children's books; Christmas ornaments; my Grandma Schwab's scrapbook of Mayor Frank Schwab, and her small, worn little book of recipes. I could feel the warmth of her love by flipping through that old book and seeing her familiar handwriting.

It took a while for me to think about the recipes. They were part of our family's traditions, time tested and filled with memories. Would I remember the ingredients? Would I be able to continue making these dishes?

My daughter, Jessica, came to my rescue. She presented me with a binder filled with these treasured recipes, a simple gift that meant the world to me, a combination of measurements and ingredients that serve up delicious memories.

Four of Grandma Schwab's recipes remain a part of our family:

No Christmas is complete without **Grandma's Sugar Cookies**. When I was little and we lived in a house behind hers, we spent many hours watching her prepare those sugary treats, covered with a thin coating of icing and dotted with sprinkles. Grandma included anise in her cookies, which I omitted per my children's request. My dad always asked me to leave a few cookies without the icing, savoring the simple goodness of butter, eggs, and sugar. I even had her original cookie cutters. The shapes included Santa, of course, a tree, star, and bell. After a few visits to antique and flea markets, I was able to replace those cookie cutters.

Lori, Jess and Jill "helping" make sugar cookies."

Pork roast and Grandma's **Potato Dumplings** are my favorite meal and part of our Christmas tradition. A German form of exercise, grating was involved before food processors. The preparation is messy, as the mixture of potatoes, dried bread, eggs, and flour is not conducive to combining with a spoon. Floured hands usually have to be employed to do the mixing. Balls are formed and carefully placed in a large pot of boiling water. Jessica's gift included a picture of her and me engaged in this process on Long Street, a nice memory not only of cooking together, but also of the Long Street kitchen. People either love or hate the dumplings. My brother-in-law refers to them as "lead balls." Everyone is entitled to their opinions (even if they are wrong).

My dad gave me a handwritten copy of the potato dumpling recipe. It was soiled and torn from use, but I could never bring

Jess and me making potato dumplings

myself to rewrite it. There was the satisfaction and warmth of looking at a loved one's handwriting, retaining a piece of them.

Balls in a bowl

I regret so much that I no longer have that tangible remembrance of Dad.

Part of the marriage vow dictates that you have to at least try to cook things handed down by your mother-in-law. Doug's mom never wrote down recipes. She just gave you a general idea of what each dish consisted of, not many precise measurements.

All in all, my versions met with Doug's approval.

I had never been a fan of anything that included beans, so I definitely was not happy when Doug announced his mom was making chili. A hopeful future daughter-in-law would never admit this, so I resigned myself to the fact that I would have to eat at least one bowlful. It also helped that chili was sometimes served following a Buffalo Bills home game that we had sat through on a freezing Sunday. My fear of anything "bean" subsided and I came to like **Wielinski Chili**. I added my own touch to the recipe by adding potatoes and diced tomatoes, which was okay with my tough food critic, Doug.

Pigs in a Blanket was served to Doug on special occasions: birthdays and anniversaries. As with other Mom Wielinski recipes, tomato soup was an economical ingredient in this favorite. Cabbage leaves filled with savory ground beef, onions,

Pigs in a Blanket

celery, and rice were smothered in tomato soup, and baked until the tops were golden brown and crispy. Tradition now dictates that this dish be served on the anniversary of the crash.

Salmon Patties were another Wielinski favorite. Cooking involves trial and error, sometimes a lot of error. I knew nothing about salmon, so I received a lesson on removing bones in the canned version <u>before</u> blending the fish into leftover potatoes, onions, egg, and flour. Eventually, it was easier to forget the salmon with the bones and just open a can of tuna.

My sister, Barbara, introduced the tradition of having **Lasagna** every New Year's Day. I think she made it once and I have been making it ever since. The secret is lots and lots of mozzarella cheese.

Not all recipes came from relatives.

When I was 25 and my sister was 28, we decided the time had come to take the plunge, untie the apron strings and move into our own apartment. This decision was also hastened after spending a whole week housebound during the "Blizzard of 77." We moved out of the city and into the suburb of Hamburg. Our neighbors in the complex were Rick and Nancy Bohovich. Nancy had actually worked at National Gypsum for a time. Two of Nancy's family recipes were quickly added to my cookbook.

I have never met anyone who did not like Nancy's grandmother's **German Potato Salad,** boiled potatoes simmering in bacon, onions, and vinegar in a crock pot for hours. Delicious! A pot simmering on a charcoal grill in the park also worked well at the Wielinski Father's Day picnic each June. The brothers and their families always came together on that day. There was lots of good food, a few pinochle competitions, and many kids running around. Although that tradition continues, the girls and I cannot quite bring ourselves to attend often.

The Bohovich **Bread and Butter Pickles** were a summer favorite. Maybe it was because we were living in Eden surrounded by corn fields that I first felt the need to plant vegetables and can. Cucumbers were abundant, so making this recipe helped solve the dilemma of what to do with the bumper crop. As our family grew in Cincinnati, so did the bountiful choices; zucchini, beets, and even grapes entered the picture. I can recall Jill at an early age sitting on the kitchen table picking grapes off the stems. I made grape jelly only once. It was a long process that yielded only a few jars of jelly and didn't seem worth the effort. The pickles, though, were a constant project for many summers. They could be given as gifts throughout the year, if we didn't eat them all ourselves.

Chicken Broccoli Cheese is one of my daughters' favorite meals. The recipe came from a friend, Kathy Buckingham, in

Loveland. Her son, Scott, was born the same day as Lori. Kathy and I often got together with her two sons and my four girls for lunch and play dates. That was how I was introduced to this chicken dish, which proved a good way to disguise broccoli so kids would eat it.

There are recipes that I brought into the "Family Cookbook." Christmas morning would not be complete without a **Cheese Wreath:** refrigerated biscuits, cheese spread, bacon, and parsley fashioned into a wreath. We have gotten to the point now that two wreaths are needed to fill the family's appetite. We try to ignore the unhealthiness of this dish.

A **Fruit Pizza** and **BLT Pizza** have made the rounds. All four girls brought the fruit pizza into their Home Economics class for show and tell. A harried mother, doing too many things at one time, once mistakenly put the mayo/mustard spread on the fruit pizza and cream cheese/confectioners sugar spread on the BLT pizza. Luckily, there was time to scrape off the errors before final assembly.

For years I made fancy Wilton Cakes for the girls' birthdays, including Big Bird, Strawberry Shortcake, and Raggedy Ann, huge productions and so time consuming. Then my cousin, Gayle, introduced me to the **Oreo Ice Cream Cake.** This recipe simplified my life, just throw a half-gallon of vanilla ice cream in a pan, add crushed Oreos, Cool Whip, and fudge sauce, and ta-da, the cake was done. Time saved, which I needed to work on the lavish birthday/slumber parties the girls liked, complete with games and crafts.

So many recipes, but the all-time "critic's choice" goes to my **Peanut Butter Bars**. I found the recipe in a holiday magazine back in the early '70s. I made the mistake of making the bars in a cookie pan instead of the required brownie pan, but they have been made that way ever since. They are just the right combination of peanut butter, frosting, and chocolate and give the appearance of an upscale dessert. They have served me well at family gatherings, work, and social functions.

Many bits and pieces of paper were retrieved from the Long Street site. There are some that just make me shake my head in amazement when discovered. I find it hard to believe I am holding them in my hands. Part of the magazine where I originally found the peanut butter bar recipe survived, and within those salvaged pages, I found the recipe.

Jessica's gift has enabled me to continue our cooking traditions, another example of how life goes on despite tragedy. Recipes call for various ingredients, but there is one constant in them all, you must mix in a large dose of love. It makes a simple dish spectacular.

Find all of these favorite recipes at the end of this book.

4/19/12

Fish Fry or Fish "Tales"

I am proud to say that I am a Buffalonian. Where else can you click on the local news website and find not only a "Pothole Map," but a "Fish Fry Map?" What a combination. You can dodge those potholes and eliminate wasting any time getting to the fish fries.

Buffalo Fish Fry

A recent article in the *Buffalo News* by Michelle Kearns indicated that "if any dish has a chance of surpassing chicken wings as Buffalo's signature meal, it might be a plate of steaming fried haddock, Buffalo's fish of choice for a fish fry, with a heap of potato salad, coleslaw, and a roll." Lovers of this Buffalo culinary staple will be dismayed to learn that the "Atlantic haddock haul is down," which means the price for partaking of this tasty dish will no doubt go up.

Is nothing sacred? First gas, then milk, and now haddock fish fries will make us dig deeper into our pockets to satisfy our needs.

Fish Fries are a part of Buffalo life.

When I was a kid, growing up in the '50s and '60s on the East Side of Buffalo, it was a rare occasion when our family went out for dinner. When it did occur, we usually headed to a local gin mill run by the Gillouster family. We reached the "Family Entrance" by heading down a narrow alley. There never seemed to be a waiting line, and shortly after ordering, our fish fry would arrive. The meal was washed down with either birch beer or orange pop. Their coleslaw was the best, German-style, made with vinegar and a bit of sugar.

Of course, these family dinner outings always took place on a Friday. At that time, Catholics could not eat meat on any Friday; that restriction is now only required during Lent.

My sister and I rented an apartment in the late '70s in Hamburg and discovered a treasure trove of establishments that offered this traditional dish. My favorite was The Cloverbank Hotel. It was almost a given that you would have to wait at the bar, or on the front porch, for a good half hour or so before you could secure a spot inside the dining room. The wait was worth it, though, when that plate laden with fish, fries, and coleslaw was set before you.

I admit that I sometimes strayed from my loyalty to the fish fry at The Cloverbank. Their chicken wings were decadent and dripping with butter.

The craving for fish fries continued after Doug and I were married. One Good Friday, after working on our house in Eden, we visited The Armor Inn in Hamburg. We were starving after observing the Catholic rule of fast and abstinence on that day, which dictated that we could only have one full meal. A fish fry teased our minds all day, and we ignored the growl of our empty stomachs until dinner. Of course, there was a long line of people also waiting for that one full meal. We endured the delay by enjoying a beer at the bar. I kept wondering if the church allowed the drinking of alcohol on Good Friday, but what better appetizer to prepare the way for that fish fry. Actually the words "fish fry" are usually accompanied by the word "beer."

We said goodbye to the haddock fish fry when we moved to Cincinnati. Cincinnatians commit an act of blasphemy when uttering "fish fry." Catfish does not belong on a fish fry plate. We lived in Ohio for 14 years and were never able to find a true haddock fish fry.

We experienced fish fry withdrawal that could only be relieved by visiting Buffalo. Okay, we did go back to visit family too. My dad was a life-long member of the VFW Leonard Post, and he always treated us to dinner (on Friday, of course) when we returned. He understood the deprivation we endured, and he also liked to show off his grandchildren to his friends. We were thankful for the much needed antidote.

The Clarence Center Volunteer Fire Department always has their fundraiser fish fry on Good Friday. Tickets are sold in advance and go quickly. If you wait until the actual day of the event, you could be turned away at the door (fish fry rejection is very sad). It became a family tradition to gather together at 6038 Long Street and walk down the street to the fire hall. We enjoyed a delicious dinner and saw neighbors and friends. We felt like part of the community. I miss the tradition and the community.

Over the years, I have developed a number of "pet peeves" regarding the fish fry:

- The worst way to ruin a fish fry is to chomp on bones. From that moment on you tentatively poke through your fish to avoid another encounter. This is not enjoyable.

- A fish fry deserves to be served on a bigger plate. I do not appreciate dissecting my meal to look for the macaroni salad and coleslaw. I do not enjoy trying to retrieve food items that are about to fall off my plate onto a paper placemat or a questionable oil cloth. Could you please give each food item a little space to breathe?

- More places need to offer a half-fish alternative. Many of us do not want to consume a piece of fish the size of an oval plate. In my opinion, leftover fish never tastes good; plus my cats do not get table food.

- You really need to go to a bar for a great fish fry. It's a tradition, and *must* be part of the German culture.

You will have to excuse me now. I need to check out that "Fish Fry Map." Suddenly, I am very hungry.

P.S. I hope I don't find a bone in my fish!

2/28/14

Hearing

"I love hearing your voice...Yeah!! Even if it's only for a few minutes...For me it's just like a light hug from far off..."

~ *Crooked Corner*

Sweet Sounds

The sun had slowly slid out of sight and a sliver of a moon was surrounded by a sea of stars.

A murmur of soft voices, mixed with laughter was suddenly interrupted by a baritone voice, as the melodic and familiar sound of "Down by the Old Mill Stream" crept into the darkness.

One of my favorite parts of a Schwab family reunion had begun.

After a busy afternoon of sharing a bounty of talk, food, and drinks, Mom, Dad, aunts, uncles, and cousins all gathered in a circle to enjoy a leisurely evening of reminiscing and singing.

I am fortunate to have a CD of those sweet sounds. It was given to me over 10 years ago by my cousin Penny Schwab Koltesny's husband, Paul, following the crash of Flight 3407. For whatever reason, I had never listened to it until a few weeks ago, perhaps spurred on to do so after the death of another cousin, Paul Becker.

The CD covers two reunions, one in 1983 at Penny and Paul's home in Orchard Park and the other at Paul and Eileen Becker's home in North Boston, near Hamburg.

Paul Koltesny wanted to create an audio remembrance of the Schwab clan, how they were related or came to be part of the Schwab family.

Aunt Agnes & Uncle Leo in earlier days.

That summer day, my Uncle Leo Haug, a Buffalo policeman for 34 years, was approached first. "What's your story, Uncle Leo?"

"Oh, that's a long story (he chuckled). It was the happiest moment of my life."

A friend at a dance had introduced him to Aunt Agnes, my mom's youngest sister.

"She was much younger than I, she's four and a half years younger than I. What a beauty, if ever there was one, and I fell like a ton of bricks. It's been happiness ever since."

When my mother was introduced, I had to listen closely. Is that how I remembered her voice? It was several years before her struggle with OCD took control of her. Perhaps I had forgotten the excitement and happiness in her voice that I hear on the CD.

Mom was Nicholas and Clara Schwab's oldest daughter. The cousins referred to her as Aunt Marge.

"Glad I'm here and it's a beautiful day. Thanks for having us Paul…I miss Karen, Doug, Kim, Lori, Barbara, and Adrien. I'm sure that when I write to them, they will want to hear all about it. Karen and Doug just left three weeks ago (she reminded Paul that we had just moved to the Cincinnati area)."

My sister Barb and her husband, Adrien, were living in California at the time. I am sure it was difficult to be at the gathering without her daughters, yet her voice in this recording

Gathering probably in the 60s: Uncle Leo, Uncle Norbert, Grandma Schwab, Grandpa Haug, Mom & Eileen.

was upbeat and not sad. I am glad that she still felt capable of happiness at that time.

There was no hesitation on my part to recognize my dad's voice. He told Paul how he met Margie Schwab back in 1945 when he came home from the war.

Interspersed with laughter, he explained, "We went on a few dates, and the next thing I knew I was married! I usually kid about getting married, and when people ask me how it happened, I just tell them I guess I was shell-shocked."

My cousin, Paul Becker, indicated he was 40 years old, pleased to be at the "Koltesny Estate," and thankful to have the opportunity to say a few words. "I'm sure we will look forward to hearing this in the future."

The next generation of young cousins can be heard throughout the day, chattering and giggling like the pre-teen and teenagers they were at the time. In the background, you can faintly make out Uncle Leo telling stories. He loved to spin a tale or two and we loved listening to him.

Tradition also included a rendition of "Showboat" by my Uncle Sid, Dad's brother, who happened to marry my mother's sister, Maryann Becker, in their later years. You can hear the pride in his voice as he announced that they had now been happily married for 12 years. He robustly broke into song, "Here comes the Showboat, here comes the Showboat, puff, puff, puff, puff, puff, puff, puffin' along." Everyone joined in that refrain.

Various other cousins are on the recording.

Cousin Ann Becker Schuh couldn't believe that at the first reunion, her youngest son, Todd, who was now 18, had been in a playpen.

Her husband, Kenny, jokingly recalled how he had "picked up this broad at the Everglade Restaurant Bar. She looked pretty good and I married her 2 years later." He also remembered being together at another reunion as they watched the first walk on the moon in 1969.

My cousin Billy Becker, who had been living in Florida for 14 years, was visiting Buffalo that summer. "Love you all," he said as he left that night. By leaving a message he said, "48 years from now you'll know who we are. God bless. We're out." His tone definitely indicated he had some CB (Citizen Broadcast) experience.

At the end of the day, the singing included the sweet harmony of another old favorite, "Moonlight Bay."

It wasn't on the recording, but I still remember Uncle Leo leading us in "The Whiffenpoof Song," written in 1907. "We're poor little lambs that have lost our way, baa, baa, baa."

The singing was comforting, and I always felt a sense of love and pride being with my relatives.

One of my first dates with Doug was at a Schwab Family Reunion in 1977. Not only was I happy to introduce him to my extended family, but I wanted him to see how special these people were to me. They quickly accepted Doug into the family fold.

Doug and I had moved back to Buffalo and were guests at the gathering in North Boston in 1998.

My message for posterity included relaying how it was "Great to be with family. We've been back in Buffalo about a year now, and one of the benefits is how nice it is to see everyone."

Too blurry to say who everyone is here, but I can guaranty they are playing Jarts!

It was so good to hear Doug's voice as he said, "Even though I only know about half of you, it's good to be back in the Eden/Hamburg area, as we lived here for almost five years. Hope everyone has a good Christmas."

Several of Paul Becker's seven children were in town for the holidays. Nicole laughingly claimed she was the "coolest girl here." Alison said it was "great to see everyone," and Brent passed along the fact that he was 25, lived on the West Side of Buffalo, and thought it was interesting that the president was being impeached.

Paul himself was "looking forward to a wonderful year."

Cousin Ann's husband, Kenny, once more was interviewed. "I'm still married to Ann after 38 years...I'll never last to 50 years." Well, they had 60 years together.

Visiting from New York City, my cousin Leo Haug felt it was "great to be with everyone...we need to do this more often."

Yes, listening to this CD does make me lament the loss of loved ones long gone, but I can definitely say that hearing their dear voices resulted in more smiles than tears.

According to Klaus Schulze, German musical composer, "The human voice is the first and most musical instrument, also the most emotional."

Those sweet sounds unraveled so many memories and unleashed a rhapsody of music to my ears.

6/15/20

Brotherly Love

I knew little about brotherly love as I grew up with a sister and then raised four girls. I see that love beginning to manifest itself when my grandsons hug. Perhaps it leans more towards choking or wrestling, but the affection is there.

I also observed the love between my husband, Doug, and his six brothers. Three of those brothers were half-brothers, but I never witnessed any varying degree of love from Doug toward the men. They were loved equally.

The bond between Doug and his half-brother, Joe, was recently magnified for me when I discovered a unique treasure.

Doug had just graduated from the University of Buffalo in 1970, and as he put it, "I received my draft notice before I received my diploma." He left for Vietnam on July 13, 1970 (his birthday), from Travis Air Force Base in California. Part of the instructions he had received in preparation for the journey indicated that "the individual will arrive wearing combat tropical uniform and a jacket will be carried as comfort item." No doubt that jacket did not bring comfort, and he definitely did not consider his departure to a strange, foreign country as a birthday gift.

I recall him describing to me his arrival at the barracks. He had to kick his cot to entice cockroaches to vacate the premises. This was a far cry from the life he knew on Bailey Avenue in Buffalo's Lovejoy neighborhood. What emotions and fears he must have harbored in his mind during those early days in Vietnam.

Letters from home certainly lifted his spirits,

Doug, somewhere in Vietnam

and his half-brother, Joe, started sending Doug cassette tapes of all the Buffalo Bills games. Digging through storage units recently, I discovered a small box containing those tapes. The box also included a tape Joe had recorded himself for Doug.

The Buffalo Bills' eleventh season was in 1970, and it was also their first in the National Football League. It was not a banner year. They finished the season 3-10-1. On his tape, Joe said he almost felt that he had to apologize for sending such terrible games to Doug.

I can picture Doug standing with other hopeful soldiers at mail call. Who would be lucky enough to receive a letter or package from home? "Wielinski!" a voice barked. Doug probably waited for the perfect moment to listen to the tape, either privately or perhaps inviting his new friends, Warren and John, to join him.

Warren was a fireman from Milwaukee, Wisconsin. He met a girl, Eet, in Thailand, and brought her back to the states as his bride. I first met them in New York City in 1978, where Warren was on a sabbatical to concentrate on his art. They lived on the top floor of an old brownstone building, and I was shocked to see that their claw-foot bathtub sat in the middle of the kitchen. Eet and I struggled somewhat with communication, but we had a fun weekend. Oh, and yes, I did use that bathtub. Doug and I also visited them at their home in Milwaukee after the birth of their daughter.

John lived in Arkansas, and Doug, Warren, and he attended a few weddings of fellow soldiers over the years. Doug and I also traveled with three of our girls one summer to visit John and his parents. John's mom sent us updates every Christmas, and after her death, his sister corresponded for a while.

The tapes Joe sent arrived via San Francisco and cost 24 cents to send. The address included Doug's Social Security number. Can you imagine listing that on correspondence in this day and age? Doug would have carefully opened one side of the brown wrapping to release the tapes. After listening to them, probably

Buffalo Bills tapes in original wrappings

more than once, they could be slipped back into that protective sleeve. Over 50 years later, they now remain in those original wrappings.

I first listened to what Joe had personally recorded. "Ma" had contacted the local newspaper about forwarding papers to Doug in Vietnam. Joe indicated he would find out how brother Eddie's baseball team was doing. Brother Billy was using Doug's golf clubs and "playing well." Brother Jackie was recovering from surgery.

Joe discussed local politics, including former Bills quarterback, Jack Kemp, who was running for Congress.

To improve quality, a new tape recorder was sent to Doug. It was a bargain at only $24. Joe agreed it was a bit awkward talking into a microphone, "especially if there are others in the room," but he felt in the long run, it would become easier.

As for the Bills and the games, Joe indicated he had stopped the tape during commercials. He did include most of the WBEN 930 AM ("The place for sports on the Niagara Frontier") play-by-play commentary from Van Miller and Stan Baron. Joe admitted, though, that at times he cut off Stan's "jabbering."

This new guy O.J. Simpson was looking good, and Joe thought everyone should "keep an eye out for Al Cowlings."

I listened to part of the game played on November 1, 1970, against the Boston Patriots. The Bills demolished the Patriots 38-3. Starting quarterbacks were Dennis Shaw for the Bills, and Joe Capp for the Patriots. By halftime, the announcers felt the

Patriots had been "outplayed totally" by the Bills. In the third quarter, "tempers were short," and the Bills "never looked back."

As I listened, I remembered spending entire afternoons listening or watching football games. I did not start attending home games until 1973. Both Doug and I became loyal season ticket holders. I wonder if I passed or brushed Doug's arm while making my way through the bustling crowds at Rich Stadium before we met in 1977.

For me, the biggest thrill of this discovery was seeing a tape with the words, "Doug to home." I tentatively pressed the play button (on the only tape player I could locate, a Fisher Price children's tape player from the '80s). The quality of the recording was not good, and at first, I almost did not recognize Doug's voice. But then, I could make out the soft and low timbre of his voice.

He described how he spent his free time in the barracks reading books, or finding competitors to play pool or air-hockey games. He admitted that he wasn't eating much because, "Mess hall food isn't great." He had attended a movie night to see "*If He Hollers, Let Him Go*," and enjoyed a band called Go, Go Llams. Modesty had to be put aside, as "Mamasan" did her laundry while you bathed.

At one point, he had taken a military flight down the coast of Vietnam and described seeing "beautiful towns and villages." Before leaving the airbase, the pilot tried to make jokes, telling the men, "If you're going to get sick, throw up in your hat," and "If we crash, hang on."

Doug had stayed in a French Provincial Hotel where it was a two-minute walk to the beach. He had taken only his sandals and buried those in the sand. Some of the "locals would take everything." There were stories of how some soldiers, who had buried their wallets and clothes, looked on helplessly as they swam and saw their belongings being unearthed and snatched away.

Doug had been assigned to guard duty several times, which entailed four-hour shifts by himself. "You just have to keep alert as you don't know what to expect." He summed up his current reality by concluding, "I just have to take it as it is."

Another birthday rolled around, and Doug once more found himself heading back home on July 13, 1971. He once told me that his imminent departure was not discussed around the barracks, as it was considered bad luck to do so.

There was no welcoming committee present when he arrived in Buffalo. He had not told his family, as he wanted to

Joe

surprise them. Plus, the United States involvement in Vietnam was a hotly contested subject. Returning soldiers were not warmly greeted when they returned home.

Despite that fact, I know he would have been embraced with love when he walked into his Bailey Avenue home.

Tucked into his luggage were those tapes, a reminder of Joe's love for Doug. Joe was continuing college classes and working to support his young family. Although recording each game took time, it was an act Joe knew would bring the comfort of home to Doug.

Simple actions had expressed brotherly love.

7/6/17

Smell

"Nothing brings to life again a forgotten memory like fragrance."
~ Christopher Poindexter

Fragrance

Rain danced on my window pane,
as morning gently woke me.
It washed away yesterday,
and crisp air swirled around me.

Freshness brought back memories,
the sweet scents assaulted me.
A time gone by so quickly,
invited me back again.

Honeyed perfume greeted me,
as Mother pinned wash on lines.
It fluttered in the light breeze,
waiting to be gathered up.

Its scent had transported me
to Grandma's house on Herman.
A closet near her woodshed,
that smelled of Fels-Naptha soap.

Her cozy kitchen nearby,
enticing me to follow
the sweet-smelling creations
prepared by her loving hands.

Through the window a soft whirl
carried yet another scent.
The air laced with fresh cut grass,
as Dad pushed the old mower.

The fragrances of my youth
easily drift back to me.
They fill me with contentment,
as I inhale yesterday.

~ Karen Wielinski

3/8/21

Writing

"*The scariest moment is just before you start.
After that, things can only get better.*"

~ Stephen King

A Piece of Cake

Rick's suggested prompts rarely ignite an immediate story idea. If anything, they produce a moment of panic. "What can I write about that?" It really puts a person under pressure. If you are a good writer, shouldn't you be able to come up with a great idea? You know, it should be "a piece of cake," which happened to be a suggested topic one week.

That phrase basically means "something that can be done easily and pleasurably," and according to the Oxford Dictionary, it first appeared in Ogden Nash's "Primrose Path" in 1936: "Her picture's in the papers now, and life's a piece of cake."

For the majority of us, baking a cake isn't the easiest thing to do. Pitfalls you could encounter might include a lopsided layer or frosting picking up crumbs as you attempt to spread it on your cake. You get the picture. Sometimes you leap into a project that could possibly not be "a piece of cake" which brings me to my past life as a writer.

I did not write for my high school newspaper at Bishop McMahon, but I was in a group of kids who wrote for the Diocesan youth newspaper on a limited basis. I recall taking the Main Street bus to the Delaware Park area and interviewing some Monsignor. I have no recollection of what topic we discussed.

Being the co-editor of the yearbook really sparked my interest in journalism and the lay-moderator encouraged me to seriously consider going to the University of Detroit for their program.

Limited funds for college and the lure of a paycheck made me reject that idea, which may not have been the smartest thing I ever did. On reflection, though, going to college would have taken my life in an entirely different direction, but truthfully, I am glad I followed the other fork in the road.

The desire to write was tucked away and just waited to break loose. Opportunity knocked for me in 1987.

Our oldest daughter, Kim, had just started first grade and I attended my first St. Columban PTO meeting. The president of the organization mentioned that they were looking for a volunteer to do some publicity for the school. My ears perked up and I restrained myself from shouting, "Let me do it!" After the meeting, I rushed up to offer my services. There was no one else competing for the job, so it was mine. I could hardly sleep that night as all those writing ideas pushed forward to offer inspiration. Soon my first article appeared in the *Loveland Herald*. This would be "a piece of cake."

The local public school published a little newsletter each month. Why couldn't St. Columban do one? So, now I was a writer and an editor. The *St. Columban News* debuted in September of 1989. What could I include in the publication; how could I make it interesting each month? Maybe this wouldn't be "a piece of cake."

I walked around the school looking for ideas. A student council coordinator joined my staff. Each month we rounded up information and spotlighted one particular grade.

The first editions were done on a Heathkit computer Doug had put together. I ran copies off in the principal's office. Sometimes the machine would get so hot, I had to turn it off for a while. I lugged the copies home and hand stapled roughly four hundred of them. Life became easier when a new principal, Sr. Suzanne, arrived. She purchased an electric stapler and upgraded the copier. Sister ran the copies for me and recruited volunteer moms to sort and staple.

The news kept growing in content and size. One friend chuckled and indicated that it took her a long time to read these "books."

My need to write was being fulfilled and I loved every minute. There was always something exciting to report.

Astronaut David Walker provided high and low moments. Interviewing someone who had been part of four spaceflights (Discovery in 1984 and 1992, Atlantis in 1989, and Endeavor in 1995) was certainly exciting for me. This encounter proved to be one of my most embarrassing experiences, though, when I forgot to put film in my camera. Yes, I was a real professional! Luckily, others provided camera coverage that day.

A Russian reporter, Michael Salop, spoke to the students in 1992. He talked about differences and similarities in Russian and American lifestyles and his family's perils during a failed coup against Gorbachev.

"Events were blacked out, and continuous showings of 'Swan Lake' on the television actually became torture for us, as we longed to know the truth," Mr. Salop recalled.

A sense of humor helped during difficult times. He admitted that he admired Americans for their sense of humor, "They always seem ready to laugh, have fun."

My lengthy article on his visit did appear in *The Loveland Herald*, but unfortunately my name did not.

Getting recognition as a writer was not "a piece of cake."

Assignments enabled me to meet a survivor of the Holocaust, and I attended "School Newspaper Days" at the Cincinnati Museum Center with my student council reps.

The January 1992 issue was a special edition about St. Columban's history. The nuns allowed me to read their diaries, which provided a fascinating journal of events. It was also fun putting together the eighth grade "Prophecy" each May, as I looked into the future.

"Photographer" was added to my resume, as I took shots for the school's "Memory Book," started a "Spotlight" board and began adding pictures to *The News*.

Looking back, I wonder how I accomplished all this and still managed to take care of my kids.

The end was near, though. Doug's company announced plans to move the organization to Houston, Texas. For months we debated whether to move with the company. Recruiters contacted Doug regarding other positions. Two looked promising: one in Kansas City and the other in, of all places, Buffalo. The draw to return to our hometown and be close to family eventually settled any debate. We would move to Buffalo.

I experienced mixed emotions. I felt quite fulfilled with all my activities at St. Columban, had wonderful friends, and a good life that I was not eager to give up.

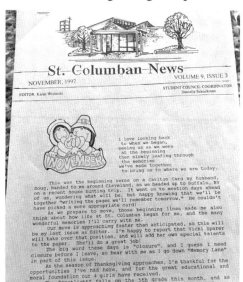

My last issue of "The St. Columban News."

My final edition of *The News* was in November 1997. After the crash, friends at St. Columban sent me a copy of that edition, a gesture that I appreciated, as all my copies had been destroyed. I wept as I read the first page for the sentiment it conveyed, but also because I had forgotten the following incident.

I love looking back to when we began,
seeing us as we were at the beginning
then slowly leafing through the memories
we've made together to bring us to where we are today.

This was the beginning verse on the card my husband, Doug, handed to me around Cleveland as we headed up to Buffalo on a house-hunting trip. It went on to mention days ahead of us, wondering what will be, but happy knowing that we'll be together "writing the pages we'll remember tomorrow." He couldn't have picked a more appropriate card!

I believe that stanza also summed up my feelings about leaving St. Columban.

The issue ended with a summary of my experiences as a writer and editor, but I had to include some humor too.

I couldn't quite believe it, but in my hand was a letter-- postmarked "Heaven!" Opening it cautiously, I found the following request:

Dear Mrs. Wielinski:

My name is Clarence…you may remember me from a movie called, "It's a Wonderful Life," in which I finally earned my angel wings. Jimmy Stewart got most of the fame out of that, but actually I think I was the real star…well, that's another story.

Anyway, since getting my wings, I've been given quite a bit of responsibility in our main Communications/Media Center, and I have to tell you, the last few months up here we've been working overtime trying to handle all the prayer requests coming into the system for the Wielinski family. An overwhelming amount came from St. Columban…and those nuns, especially Sr. Suzanne, really tied up the lines!

The Wielinski family thanks are coming through now, and I know things are looking up, but what's the deal with all these folks at St. Columban, and why are you, in particular, so thankful for them?

Eternally yours,

Clarence, "Angel 1st Class"

My history at St. Columban was explained to "Clarence," and I concluded:

So you see, Clarence, I'm thankful to St. Columban for letting me be a writer, editor, historian, photographer, and artist (through my involvement in the Art Appreciation Program (which by the way involved attending some great classes at the Cincinnati Art Museum) and hopefully a weaver of memories.

I've had wonderful experiences, made friends with great people: children, parents, and teachers. I've learned how to be more aggressive, how to speak up, get involved, take chances, and gained confidence. I've had fun and learned a lot. I feel fortunate that I had the opportunity to be part of St. Columban. Words can't describe how I'll miss this place, but I look forward to new experiences and adventures in Buffalo.

Put in a special request for thanks and blessings for all my St. Columban family.

Yours gratefully,
Karen Wielinski
P.S. By the way, the town we're moving to is Clarence, New York!

I loved the thought of being a "weaver of memories." Life changes, though, and we follow.

My days as "super mom" were over. Maybe I was burned out. It no longer was "a piece of cake" to be so active. I limited my involvement at the kids' schools. My writing days were again put on hold.

What a ride it had been for me, one filled with wonderful memories to savor. I can honestly say it wasn't a "piece of cake." I had the best "whole cake" ever, one any baker would be proud of. There were no crumbs in the frosting. It was worth all the effort I had put into it.

3/30/19

Newspaper Encounters

I am not sure exactly when my fascination with the newspaper industry began.

A memory flashes through my mind of becoming a reporter, editor, and distributor of my own little publication, after my sister and I received a portable typewriter for Christmas one year. I cannot recall what stories we covered, except that I did report on a fire in an old archive building in downtown Buffalo. Maybe I wrote it as a reporter sent to cover the event. Copies of the publication only went to my immediate family members, and as often happens with discarded paper, it dissolved in a junk pile somewhere in the City of Buffalo.

I am a fan of the movies, *My Girl Friday* and *It Happened One Night*. Both these classics revolve around the excitement of landing that big story. Other flicks would follow: *All the President's Men*, *The Paper*, and *Spotlight* to name just a few.

It is the quest to investigate, and piece together the clues that enable reporters to hand in their story minutes before the dreaded deadline that entices me.

In school, while many of my fellow students cringed as a teacher announced term papers, I jumped at the opportunity to get digging for the facts.

When it came to newspapers, I was on the outside looking in. Fate tossed me into the electrical current that swirls inside that industry, though, and I must say that I have been amazed at the

Rick on one of the writing group's May field trips.

people I have met.

Rick Ohler is a name that easily slips into conversations that arise regarding my writing efforts. I have no doubt in my mind that if it was not for Rick, I would not have published *One on the Ground*, and I would not still be writing today. For many years, he has been one of the *East Aurora Advertiser's* primo columnists and is the author of *Have You Lived Here All Your Life?...Not Yet!* For over 40 years, he has also guided fledgling writers to perfect their craft. His influence, and that of my fellow writers, has fine-tuned my writing, and also encouraged me to branch out of the comfort zone of my memoir genre.

Erik Brady, a sports writer for *USA Today*, burst into my life on January 24, 2011, when I received a Facebook message from him. At that stage in my life, I was very leery of anyone in the media. My attorneys had flashed the BEWARE warning in front of my face many times.

Details of our meeting in June of 2011, which led to the publication of Erik's piece that appeared in a July 2011 front-page story about my husband Doug, are outlined in the chapter, "The Story Behind the Story," in *One on the Ground*.

It seems so long ago, and researching my old emails, I smile at one message that I sent Erik on August 1, 2011.

Erik, for the last few days, I have been in a frenzy, or

shall I say obsessed, to write the story behind the story. Close your eyes and consider it arriving in a brightly wrapped package surrounded by a huge ribbon. I am so happy to present it to you with tremendous thanks.

I always felt that Erik was a person I was destined to meet. Not only was I impressed with his writing talents, but I liked him as a person. Although I probably only met him in person about 5 times, he is someone who impacted my life in so many ways.

In 2013, I was in D.C. with the Flight 3407 families on one of their quests to ensure that all aspects of the Safety Bill, passed in 2010, would be enforced. Owen Ullman, a news editor at *USA Today* and brother of one of my friends, had generously offered to give me a tour of the headquarters in McLean, Virginia.

At that time, I wrote:

Low cubicles filled the floors of USA Today. *Perhaps this concept allows employees privacy to work on their own pursuits, while making them readily visible to join their colleagues for "fast, breaking news." I loved it all, and appreciated Owen introducing me to writers, technicians, and graphic artists.*

It was good to see Erik. Although I would have preferred to give him a big hug, considering the professional atmosphere, I settled for a handshake. As we talked, my glance was drawn to Erik's cubicle. I liked the fact that it was not neat and organized. The helter-skelter of papers made me smile. I think that suggests someone whose ideas continually churn in their mind, and the necessity of transforming those thoughts into the written word sometimes results in a bit of chaos. I can understand that.

Somehow seeing his computer was important to me, as I pictured him working on Doug's article.

I left that tour in a state of awe. After getting a behind-the-scenes look into how a newspaper develops, I could not help but wonder how Doug's story had managed to appear on the front page of USA Today. *It still seems surreal, but what an honor for our family, and more importantly, a tribute to Doug's life. I will always be grateful for that opportunity.*

As *One on the Ground* was taking form, I sent an advanced copy to Erik. His reply:

January 24, 2017

The book looks great – and reads – great! What a pleasure to see all of your work on the page in a form that you can touch and feel. So happy to see it…Congratulations on this tremendous achievement. Just as Doug collected objects which taken together were worth a fortune, you have collected your thoughts and feelings into a work of art. It's priceless.

After I sent him a copy of the finished book, I could not have asked for a warmer reception.

February 13, 2017

I know that writing all this was good for you, a genuine cathartic exercise. I hope now you can see it is also good for the community, which can share in the despair of one terrible night and also in the beauty and the hope that your writing gives to you and your family and by extension to all of us in (and from) the Niagara frontier. God bless.

Although I really felt that Erik was a destined friend, I had to accept that we were work-related acquaintances. It was not easy for me to give up that comfort of friendship, which really was a special gift to me at that time. I can still enjoy his talent as a writer, though, as following his retirement from *USA Today*, he now writes for *The Buffalo News*.

Before and during the trial against Continental Airlines,

attempting to submit anything I wrote for publication was a "no-no." Everything we did was scrutinized by the defense attorneys, and writing, especially about my feelings, emotions, or recovery process seemed to provide fodder to fire the flame raging around us.

There were publication opportunities out there, and oh, how I wanted to be a part of those folks fortunate enough to have their work accepted by others.

When the trial ended in September of 2014, the barriers dropped, freedom returned, and I was able to scout out possibilities.

The thrill of seeing my work in print was granted on Friday, March 13, 2015, when "Buffalo fish fry just can't be beat" appeared in the My View column of *The Buffalo News*. I received an email from the editor accepting my submission while I was at work. I let out a shout and ran around the office spreading the good news.

Since that time, I have experienced that sense of elation 15 times, and my morale as a writer always increases when total strangers come up to me and say how much they enjoy the pieces in My View.

The Saturday edition of *The Buffalo News* at one time ran another column called, Women's Voices. It was through that vehicle that I met Bruce Andriatch, an editor at *The Buffalo News*. With his assistance, 6 of my pieces were published for that column with these titles: "Finding a slice of happiness after tragedy," "Rememberin' Ramblin' Lou," "Take a trip down memory lane at the Broadway Market." "A sense of peace, place riding the rails across the country," "Simple pleasures are the best holiday gift," and "Brotherly love seen in tapes from the 1970s." I also was **paid** for a review of the movie "Sully."

I am happy to say that many of those essays appear in "Pieces of My Puzzle."

Bruce had done so much for me. Could I possibly impose on him to read a draft of *One on the Ground*? Why not try? To my shock, he agreed to take a look at the book for me.

Since he was on vacation, I was instructed to take the manuscript to one of his colleagues. I nervously headed downtown to *The Buffalo News*. Clutching a large blue folder, I entered the building and encountered the security guard. I told him who I was coming to see, but he advised me that I could not go up to the offices.

"Just leave it with me, and I'll see that he gets it."

Reluctantly, I passed my future book, my baby, over to the guard, "I've put a lot of time and effort into this book. Make sure he gets it."

I impatiently awaited some news from Bruce. I was so anxious to see what he thought of my writing. I pestered him a lot about whether he had been able to start reading it. He was kind in his replies, and then on September 15, 2015, I had my answer.

> *I have been reading the manuscript and it is both gripping and – of course – incredibly sad. Your pain is palpable. I know you have said it was cathartic to put your thoughts down on paper, but you also need to know that it took a great deal of courage to do what you have done.*

Prior to publication of *One on the Ground* in March of 2017, I sent Bruce a proof for his review.

On January 25, 2017, he wrote:

> *I have to leave the building because I'm crying, which is a bad look for a hardened newspaper guy.*
>
> *I'm not sure I'm going to get all the way through this the way I normally read books, Karen. The writing is so good and the story is a page-turner. But because I now know you a little, I have lost all objectivity when it comes to you and your story….but if the rest of the book is written as elegantly and honestly as the first 30 pages, you will have done a magnificent job.*

I have visited with Bruce several times at *The Buffalo News*, and each time I walk through the vast room reserved for the writers, busily working on stories that will appear in our Buffalo paper, I still feel that surge of electricity that radiates not only through that room, but through me.

I can thank my granddaughter Lydia for giving me the opportunity to meet Sean Kirst. From 1988-2015, Sean was an award-winning columnist at *The Post Standard* in Syracuse, New York. Shortly after his departure, he joined the staff of *The Buffalo News*. When his heartwarming, human interest stories about everyday folks in the greater Buffalo area appeared in our local paper, I told myself I should drop him a note to let him know that he was a welcomed addition to the News.

I procrastinated, though, until he wrote about the Liberty Bank building in downtown Buffalo. I finally had a perfect reason to email Sean.

> *October 11, 2017*
>
> *First, let me say that you are such a great addition to the News staff. I understand Bruce Andriatch was a part of that. He's a great guy, and has encouraged and promoted my own writing endeavors, which I greatly appreciate.*
>
> *I am always happy to open my paper and see your articles. Today's Liberty Building piece made me want to share the fact that we have our own Statue of Liberty fan. My 5-year-old granddaughter, Lydia, saw her only from a distance when visiting her Aunt Jess in New Jersey, but apparently that made quite an impression on her. We often find Lady Liberty inserted in Lydia's drawings, and as you can see in the attached photo, she loved the ceramic plate Aunt Jess designed for her.*
>
> *By the way, I am part of a writing group in East Aurora...I am a great advocate of writing groups—in fact, that will be my subject matter at the Indie Day at the downtown library this Sat. I will be one of fifty local*

authors participating in the event. My book, One on the Ground *was published in March, and I would like to send you a copy, if that is ok.*

Anyway, thanks for your heartfelt stories. I look forward to reading many more.

I was amazed when I received a reply that same day.

I love the plate. But I especially love that plate because your granddaughter clearly has tremendous soul. And I have a hunch I know where that comes from…I'd love to read your book.

Lydia and Jess with the plate

I felt so honored that he would read *One on the Ground*. I couldn't believe how down-to-earth and kind he was being to me. My response reflected my excitement.

Wow, thanks for the prompt reply.

I will send a book to you tomorrow. Response has been good. Some people read it in a few days, although others find it difficult to read. When I mentioned that to one shop owner who had read it she replied, "Yes, but I felt that if you had the courage to write it, I could find the courage to read it." I appreciated that and it gives me goosebumps every time I think about her reply.

On October 24, Sean replied:

I was out of the office last week. Returned to find your book in my mailbox.

I didn't realize that was your family, or your experience, when we corresponded. I cannot imagine…but maybe I will when I finish the book.

I wrote for years about Flight 103 and Lockerbie, a tale in some ways, that would be all too familiar to you,

Take care. Thank you. I'm glad you're writing.

I was glad to hear that he had received the book and replied.

I wasn't sure if you realized who I was. The News has been very good about printing my stories (once the trial was over, I could start submitting pieces), and did wonderful excerpts from the book last February.

Some people read it quickly, some find that it takes a while to read due to the emotion. I'm just glad if they read it!

I could not help sending Sean an email or two.

I was just wondering if you had a chance to read any of "One on the Ground." Always looking for professional feedback.

That feedback came in November and I was relieved and appreciative that it was positive.

Got your note…Can't put it down. My only professional insight is that I already knew you'd endured unimaginable loss, but you've made me feel it 1,000 times more deeply.

Interspersed among these emails were phone calls we shared.

We talked about writing and the Lockerbie tragedy. I went back and read some of his beautiful pieces on Flight 103, and it seemed ironic that he, too, had a connection to the pain of airline tragedy. There were 35 students from the University of Syracuse on that flight, coming home to reunite with their families for Christmas. I could so empathize with his reports of their relatives receiving bits and pieces of material things that survived that bombing. Their stories reflected so much of my own joy at having such items returned to me.

I was thrilled when Sean asked if he could interview my writing class moderator Rick Ohler and me about our East Aurora group. We often frequented the local watering hole, Wallenwein's, after class and Sean met us there one night. I almost felt star-struck. I so admired Sean's work, and here he was taking time from his busy schedule to talk with us. A highlight of the evening for me came when there was a pause in our conversation and Sean broke the silence by saying, "Isn't this great? Just sitting here talking about writing." I agreed completely.

On January 21, 2018, Sean featured *One on the Ground* and our writing group in his column, "Grief finds release in writing class." I was so humbled by his sensitive reception to both the book and our group. He realized the importance of both to me.

These newspapermen are all pieces of my puzzle, and I feel it is important that I let them know that I appreciate the guidance, inspiration, and support they have given me through the years. Sometimes, we do not realize how our actions, whether big or small, can shape the lives of others.

Thank you, guys, for making me feel like a part of your newspaper world.

1/17/22

Inspiration

Creativity requires inspiration.

This thought crossed my mind as I entered the studio of artist Thomas Aquinas Daly during the annual Wyoming County bus trip Rick Ohler had organized for his creative writing groups.

Tubes of paint in an array of hues were scattered on easels and work benches. Some resembled toothpaste tubes, wrinkled and squeezed, but still kept to allow one or more dabs of paint to escape.

Copper dish art

A shallow copper bowl lay on a table, its rim decorated with an assortment of paint colors, no doubt placed there as a testing ground before a brush applied color to a blank canvas. The mixture of colors produced a patina transforming the bowl into its own piece of art. Paint tubes and brushes, haphazardly spread out next to the bowl, joined by photographs and a sketchbook, snapped and drawn by the artist as inspiration for future works.

An old wooden cubby was the perfect hiding place to store

cubby

CDs, business cards, camera lenses, matches, letters, and a catalog from Cheap Joe's Art Supply. Any one of those items could unleash a spark of inspiration.

On the wall death notices were not so much gathered together as grim reminders of mortality, but rather the remembrance of friends and relatives who had provided inspiration to Thomas during their lives.

An old poster provided me with a reminder of Buffalo's past, urging those seeing it to attend day baseball games at the old Offerman Stadium. Had that notice inspired the artist to capture a lone baseball bat casting its shadow against the wall in the painting now resting in a corner of the room?

Shortly after my visit to Thomas' studio, I visited my cousin

Cousin Suzy in her studio

Suzanne Barrett. She also is an artist who surrounds herself with a world of color to inspire her creations.

Again, those tubes of paint in her studio served as reminders of the extent of her creativity over the years. As I searched the canvases that filled the room, I detected the exotic hues promised on the tubes: Russian Blue, Violet

Window art and cousin Suzy's paints

Dioxzine, Burnt Umber, French Ultramarine Blue, and Alizarin Crimson.

The window in the studio flooded the room with light and could also be viewed as an artistic masterpiece. The blues and greens of a pond outside were illuminated by the picture-perfect sunny spring day. Sunlight transformed one section of the window screen in such a way that waves of blue created modernistic designs. Inspiration was found by simply looking out that window.

An array of Suzanne's Papier Mache dolls scattered around the room reappeared in several of her paintings as they joyfully assembled on the canvas in a colorful group.

Looking at these studios reinforced my belief that the items we surround ourselves with inspire creativity.

My corkboard

Lil' Dude

Just like these artists, I find a collection of inspiration in my
writing space. On a large cork board, photos of my husband
and girls inspire me to write stories of our life together. A paper

Japanese Geisha Girl reminds me of the adventures travel can bring. A copy of a check from *The Buffalo News* signifies that my words can be published and produce monetary rewards. An origami shirt fashioned from a dollar bill indicates how simple items can be transformed into works of art. A small stone figure, affectionately known as Lil' Dude, inspired me to design a tiny wardrobe of outfits for him to celebrate the months of the year, and yes, he became the subject of one of my essays.

May we never lose that thirst to find inspiration that urges us to create.

6/25/18

Good Things Come In Small Packages

As I weaved through the crowd, he caught my eye. Some people would say he exhibited a brooding or melancholy countenance, but to me, he appeared lost in thought, leisurely contemplating his future. His diminutive size made him blend into his surrounding, making it easy for people to pass by him without being noticed.

To me, though, it was love at first sight. He stole my heart. I had to make him mine.

As I approached his table at the Flea Market, his expression was hard to read that morning, or any other morning, as he had no eyes or mouth. I happily gave his owner three dollars for this miniature stone statue, reminiscent of Rodin's "The Thinker," rescuing him from the possibility of being stuffed back in a cardboard box and returned to a dark, damp basement.

I named him "Lil' Dude," a small name for a small fellow, and he was added to my menagerie of assorted pigs who resided on a shelf below my work computer. He would become a unique and special addition to that display.

I am not sure when I decided he needed to be embellished. The process started modestly enough, a Pilgrim or Santa hat adorned his head, depending on the season. Then, suddenly I began more elaborate productions. He even had backdrops.

A turkey could be seen lurking behind him, or the slopes of

Sochi, Russia loomed in the scenery, as I imagined him swooshing down mountains vying for Gold Medals. Fireworks exploded to celebrate the New Year or 4th of July. Dude arrived with his backpack and lunch bag at the beginning of the school year, and showed no change of emotion as he tucked his diploma under his arm in front of the graduating class in June. He celebrated spring by holding the ribbons on a Maypole, and enjoyed roasting marshmallows with his new sidekick "Pig" on a summer evening at the beach. Decked out in his costume of cat ears, whiskers and tail, the ghosts of his ancestors floated nearby.

Dude did not have the freedom granted to certain travelling gnomes, but my vision allowed him to travel to Times Square and Olympic competitions.

Many pets endure the placement of sweaters and Halloween costumes over their head and paws, and Dude never complained about his own adornment. Like furry creatures, he provides me with companionship, interest and amusement. He requires little maintenance, although at times it is difficult crafting his tiny accessories.

When I was about nine years old, I visited Santa and was handed a small wrapped package. Inside was a pad and pen neatly enclosed in an orange wallet. I felt very grown-up and special.

"Good things come in small packages," Santa ho, ho, hoed.

Dude makes me smile every day, so I would agree. Besides, who would disagree with Santa?

11/7/14

Shared Fire

It starts with a spark, a flash of light that stirs up excitement. Perhaps it came from a memory of the past, or was activated by something you saw, heard or smelled. It could have been extraordinary to you, yet unremarkable to others, but that spark awakened your senses.

Heat and light collided and resulted in a combustion of thoughts racing through your head.

That is how it begins, and as a writer, you hurry to express the experience not only for yourself, but for others. The urge is strong, and often you work at a feverish pace, afraid that you will be unable to fan the fire to satisfy the need you feel to put your words onto paper.

When successful, it is as though a meteor is racing through your brain. There are so many words that could describe the sensations you feel. It is exhilarating, intoxicating and puts you in a euphoric state.

Perhaps you do not experience those vibrations every time you attempt to write, but every now and then you hit the jackpot, and the resulting buzz almost seems like a miracle to you.

That is why we continue to write, hoping that we somehow have managed to share the fire that possessed us.

If we are lucky, an ember will remain to start another fire, too.

4/5/21

Letters and Notes

People ask me what material possessions I regret having lost due to the destruction caused by the crash of Flight 3407.

I quickly reply that I lament not having come across any part of the baby scrapbooks I diligently and lovingly put together for my 4 girls, and I regret losing an old wooden box where my dad stored letters from his days serving in Germany during World War II.

Thinking about Dad's letters, I recently recalled correspondence that I shared with several friends during my teenage years. I saved so many of those letters, but they too did not survive the wreckage.

One friend from high school who also worked at National Gypsum with me, moved to Florida in the '70s. We corresponded regularly, and I was especially envious of her replies, filled with the romance and adventures she experienced while taking a number of cruises with her parents. Some guy was always falling in love with her, and she did eventually marry one of those star-struck suitors. They have now been married for over 40 years.

I also corresponded with a friend who lived in Kenmore, which was probably only 20 miles from my home on Hagen Street in Buffalo. I spent fun weekends with her family on several occasions, and I am sure we talked on the phone, but writing letters seemed to be our main form of communication. The letters were filled with things that happened at school, our hopes for courage to talk to the boys we knew, and girly topics such as clothes, hair styles, and pop music.

If I still had those letters, what an array of ideas could have sprung into my mind and flowed onto blank sheets of paper. I know I would have been inspired to write stories that would have given you a glimpse into the '70s.

I believe I can best express my feelings through writing. Writing gives me the eloquence and depth I find necessary to express myself, something I believe I often fail to produce when just speaking.

There can be an easy flow of communication through emails, but I still feel more connected with someone if I am holding their letter in my hand. I suppose it is because they have touched the paper that a letter is written on, and made a pen flow over the paper with their hand to transform their thoughts into the letter.

The sad truth is that letter writing is becoming a lost art, but when it resurfaces, oh, the joy it can bring to me. I was recently given three special written treasures.

The Douglas Wielinski Memorial Scholarships are awarded at the Clarence High School each June. With the commemoration of the 10th anniversary of the Flight 3407 crash, I wanted to bypass my usual surge of emotion that hits me hard during the awards presentation and say a few words. In my mind, my attempt was less than stellar, as I struggled to repeat large font words that I had typed on a single piece of paper. My voice cracked, and several times, I motioned with my hands for the audience to please bear with me as I tried to compose myself. I was disappointed in myself, and after managing to congratulate our two winners, I escaped quickly from the auditorium.

The winners often send me thank you notes for their awards, so I was not surprised when recipient Maria Bienko's note arrived in the mail. Her words comforted me, though, as she expressed her take on my attempt to speak at the awards ceremony:

Thank you so much for granting me the Douglas C. Wielinski Memorial Scholarship. As you described what this scholarship meant to you in your speech on the night of the award ceremony, I couldn't help but to be moved to tears. The message you conveyed was very riveting, so when you called my name, I was immediately hit with a sense of honor and gratefulness. Being a life-long resident of Clarence and being involved in the community in several ways, I cannot express how thankful I am to have been awarded a scholarship that holds such great esteem not only in our community, but now also in my heart. Thank you for helping me in my journey to further my education. I appreciate it more than words can say.

I was shocked to learn that what I considered a less than stellar presentation had meant so much to Maria.

Then I received a letter from the other Clarence recipient, John Hewson, which also brought tears to my eyes:

Since I heard you speak and received One on the Ground, *I had known I received the most important scholarship that afternoon…I believe it was fate that I was given this scholarship. I was in elementary school when flight 3407 came down. I had heard the news but was too young for the details. As I grew older, I would ride my bike into town and often find that my destination was the memorial on Long Street. The memorial made me curious but each time I visited, I was afraid to step onto the property to learn more. I believe that in receiving your scholarship, God was telling me to appreciate, know, and love my community, to not be afraid to take those steps. You and Doug are to thank for this priceless lesson. The shared love for history between Doug and I have, and will continue to, impact my life…*

I so appreciated that these students took the time to write their thoughts in letters to me. They carefully had chosen words that expressed their heartfelt sincerity for receiving the scholarships.

I received another piece of correspondence, retrieved from the past, that also made me value the joy derived from opening a real letter.

While attending a retirement party for my former boss at the Clarence School District Office, I had a chance to speak with the Athletic Director, Greg Kaszubski. He too was retiring and he and his wife were in the process of sorting and discarding items in preparation for buying a second home outside of the Clarence area.

"I hope you do not mind me bringing this up," Greg began, "but I wanted to share something with you." His wife called him one day and said she had discovered something she wanted to show him. She would not give him any hint of what it was. She said it would be on their dining room table when he got home.

Naturally, his interest was piqued, and he was surprised to find that the item in question was a note that Doug had sent to him. Although the note is not dated, I would say it was written in 1998.

> *Greg:*
>
> *The summer soccer season was a huge success. But, I do recall the conversation we had in the high school gym where I asked you to find a spot on your team for Lori. This was so she could play with her age group and gain some friends. I'd like to thank you for making that happen. As you are now aware, Lori's very quiet and relatively new to Clarence. But, she seemed very relaxed and enjoyed playing with the team. Lori will see and play soccer at school in the fall with new friends which will make it much more enjoyable. I know Lori and myself will never forget winning the league championship, the Clarence tournament and the super trip to the World Cup and Philadelphia. Thanks for everything!*
>
> *Doug Wielinski*

I could sense how touched Greg was about rediscovering this note, and I realized he did not want to relinquish the original to me, but he did send me a copy the next day.

I love this note for so many reasons. It shows Doug's love for his daughter and his appreciation for Greg's help in finding a place for Lori on the team (Greg also helped find a team for Jill), the kindness Doug showed in taking the time to actually write a note, and also just the fact that it was written in cursive. Doug almost never wrote in cursive. I think he printed everything because it was easier and quicker for him. By using cursive, it shows me he put much time and effort in choosing his words for this note.

Let's keep the art of writing alive, so that we can give each other something to hold on to, something we can pick up and fondly read again without having to search through our electronic files.

By the way, if someone out there wants to become a part of my life, you may want to consider writing me a letter or two.

7/2/19, updated 10/7/19

The Dream

Note: written in 2016, right before One on the Ground *was published.*

I wearily raised my head off the pillow and tried to focus on the alarm clock: 4:45 a.m. I had been jarred from sleep in an attempt to escape the dream.

You may be familiar with this type of dream, the one where you cannot complete a task. Your fingers strive to dial a phone number. It might be an old rotary phone where your fingers just can't fit into the holes, or a cell phone where you repeatedly punch the wrong buttons. Frustration mounts as you try, try again to make a call, but your attempts are futile.

When I wore contacts, I dreamed that they were huge disks. I could not figure out how to insert these abnormal circles into my eyes. All attempts resulted in failure.

I used to have a recurring dream where I would get into an elevator, arrive at a destination, then find it impossible to return in that same elevator to my original location.

In tonight's dream, a writing class was being held at my childhood home on Herman Street. We sat around a table, and I anxiously waited for my turn to read. I was sure I had written a good story. Finally I began to read. I struggled to make out the words. I could not understand what was wrong. Words were jumbled. Some words were missing. The piece had been written on used paper, and I continuously turned the papers over in an attempt to make sense of it all. One woman, whom I did not recognize, adamantly criticized my work. Thankfully, the class ended. I left feeling totally dejected.

It is one of my fears; losing whatever it is that enables me to write. Writing is my lifeline. What would I do if I lost that ability to find comfort in my words?

I can see why that dream invaded my sleep tonight. The goal of having a book published has almost been met. The reality of that actually happening is pretty overwhelming at times.

Someone recently asked me what some of my favorite stories were in the book. I spent part of yesterday afternoon considering that question. I read aloud to no one except the cat on my lap. I needed to hear the words. I love some of those stories.

I asked a friend once if loving something I wrote made me conceited or vain. He replied that it just meant I had been inspired and fulfilled.

It seems only logical that tonight's dream crept into my slumber. It also seems that the only way to keep that horrible, confused piece of writing limited to a dream and not reality is to get my feelings down on paper. Hopefully, that will keep the joy of writing alive and well.

2016

Doug

"How dull my story would be if there had never been a you and me."

~ Karen Wielinski

Music

Music (noun), vocal or instrumental sounds (or both) combined in such a way as to produce beauty or form, harmony, and expression of emotion.

After we had known each other for a while, Doug asked me what type of man had entered my dream world before he came into my life.

I can't say any realistic man ever filled my dreams. Maybe Poindexter with the dorky glasses, a boyfriend choice in my Barbie game, might have drifted through my mind at one point. Then there was George Harrison of the Beatles (that dream always seemed to include him presenting me with a puppy for my birthday), and Alan Alda's Hawkeye often took up some of my dream time.

I have mentioned before that my piano skills were very limited, and I basically played for my own enjoyment, when no one was around. Some of my sheet music purchases came from the wonderful Denton Cottier & Daniels music store in downtown Buffalo. That business remained on Court Street for over 100 years and is now located in Getzville, New York, a Buffalo suburb.

There was something special about walking into the store, where pianos filled the showroom and were surrounded by impressive collections of vinyl records and racks of sheet music.

It was there that I purchased a bound collection of George and Ira Gershwin's sheet music. When I reached my twenties, the

Gershwin's music had the ability to move me. I couldn't help but dream while tickling "Someone to Watch Over Me" on the old ivories. The lyrics perfectly expressed what I was looking for.

> *There's a saying old*
> *Says that love is blind*
> *Still we're often told*
> *Seek and ye shall find*
> *So I'm going to seek*
> *A certain lad*
> *I've had in mind…*
> *There's a somebody*
> *I'm longin' to see*
> *I hope that he turns*
> *Out to be*
> *Someone to watch over me*

It took a while, but suddenly, and totally unexpectedly, a few weeks shy of my twenty-sixth birthday that dream came true when Doug entered my life. It was wonderful to have someone like him to watch over me.

Karen and Doug, 1977

On our fifteenth wedding anniversary, another piece of music spoke to me when Bette Midler sang "Wind Beneath My Wings." I searched music stores until I found the sheet music. I definitely did not play the piece for him on the piano, but I highlighted the stanzas that let him know what he meant to me.

Did you ever know that you're my hero,
And everything I would like to be?
I can fly higher than an eagle,
'cause you are the wind beneath my wings...

It might have appeared to go unnoticed,
But I've got it all here in my heart.
I want you to know I know the truth, of course I know it.
I would be nothing without you.

Perhaps this gift seems corny to some folks, but Doug brought love, excitement, adventure, and wonder into my life. Sometimes, it is hard to actually say those words to your love, so if a song sums up those feelings, why not let it do the talking? I should add that Doug did not laugh or say I was nuts. He loved me for who I was, even at my craziest moments, and accepted my gift graciously.

Music can soothe the soul, and it has brought me many moments of comfort. The soundtrack from "Sleepless in Seattle" was traditionally played on all family trips. Although listening to it now is laden with memories, Nat King Cole's rendition of "Stardust," can deepen my sense of loss, but also bring thankfulness for having those memories of Doug.

And now the purple dusk of twilight time
Steals across the meadows of my heart
High up in the sky the little stars climb
Always reminding me that we're apart....

Though I dream in vain
In my heart it will remain
My stardust melody
The memory of love's refrain.

I find myself again drawn to Gershwin as I hear,

The way your smile just beams
The way you sing off key
The way you haunt my dreams
No, they can't take that away from me.

I shared a history of musical interludes with Doug that "combined in such a way as to produce beauty or form, harmony, and expression of emotion." That seems to be a fitting definition of our life together.

2/1/22

Some Enchanted Evening

Enchanted: adjective, placed under a spell, bewitched, filled with delight, charmed.

I am sure it was not planned. It was a spontaneous decision. It took only seconds, but the memory is forever etched on my heart.

It was January 2009. My husband Doug and I had gone to Toronto where the U.B. Bulls football team was playing Connecticut in the International Bowl at the Rogers Centre. The night before the game, Doug and I explored the area around the hotel and stopped for a drink in a pub in Toronto's Flatiron Building.

We shared a familiarity that only couples who have been married almost thirty years possess. Without words, our looks and laughter revealed our innermost thoughts.

After our drink, we left and tried to find a restaurant for dinner. Nothing caught our eye, so we decided to head back to the pub.

The evening air was brisk as we retraced our steps. Surprisingly, for a weekend night, the streets were empty. It was as if we were the only two people in the area.

Our route took us through a small park. The trees were still lit by strings of tiny white Christmas lights. Doug stopped and kissed me. "I love you," he said.

His declaration was completely unexpected. The moment had a bewitching quality, and his heartfelt confession thrilled me.

As much as I appreciated that brief moment at the time, his sudden ability to change a weekend in Toronto into some enchanted evening took on more meaning for me when I lost him a month later.

Some memories stay with you forever, and as a song lyric proclaims:

> *And night after night, as strange as it seems,*
> *The sound of his laughter will sing in your dreams.*
> *Who can explain it, who can tell you why?*
> *Fools give you reasons, wise men never try."*

His memory continues to sing in my dreams, and I am so thankful for that enchanted evening Doug gave me so many years ago.

10/26/20

One More Day

As I was driving, "One More Day" by Diamond Rio drifted through the air. It made me start to wonder. What would one more day with you mean to me and what day would I want it to be? It did not take me long to realize that if you were granted one more day on this earth, Doug, I would have wanted it to be on Jill's wedding day, July 31, 2021.

Before the ceremony, you joined Noah, his dad and nephew in the game room upstairs in the wedding venue, while we ladies put the finishing touches on our formal attire downstairs. Your laughter floated down to us. I remarked to you later that I wondered why our room was small and we had to share a bathroom with the arriving guests, but the men had a sitting room, game room, and a private bathroom. It just did not seem fair. Your grin expressed to me that you thought that was just fine.

I sat in the front row as you led Jill down the staircase and proudly walked her down the aisle. Your baby was happier than she had been in a long time and a few tears threatened to escape from your eyes.

"Who gives this woman in marriage?"

Your response, "Her mother and I," filled me with pride, thankfulness, and love.

It was a lovely ceremony and the beautiful stained glass window in the background made the moment magical. Jill and Noah

Officiant, Jill and Noah

learned that the window was made in Paris, which added a special touch, since they had visited Paris a few years before. Their trip reminded me of our visit to Paris in 1994 to celebrate our fifteenth wedding anniversary.

As we walked down the aisle arm in arm after the ceremony, we recalled our own start as a married couple back in 1979.

Our expectations were high, and the reality of over 40 years together certainly indicated that those hopes had come true for us.

Just look at what blessings we have received. We are surrounded today by our four daughters and four grandchildren. It has been a while since we were all together in one place. I doubted that the smiles on our faces would ever cease that day.

You floated across the floor with Jill during the father/daughter dance and lovingly twirled our granddaughter Lydia around as she giggled in delight. You tried to mimic the wild footwork displayed by our three grandsons, but had to withdraw from that contest in fear of pulling muscles. I believe the kids danced away to every song that was played. It was so much fun to watch.

Late that evening, we were outside catching up with some of Jill's high school and college friends. It was good seeing them again and reminiscing about their parties at our Everwood Court and Long Street homes. We were beginning to realize that perhaps we did not know all the details and antics that went on under our roof. What great kids, though, who have kept close with Jill all these years.

Jill rushed outside to tell us that "our song" was playing. Since we had missed most of it, Jill had the DJ play Nat and Natalie King Cole's "Unforgettable" one more time. "It's incredible that someone so unforgettable thinks that I am unforgettable, too." It's true, you know, even after all these years, I can't believe that you chose me to share your life.

Yes, that's just how one more day with you would have been.

Fate prevented that scenario, but there is no doubt in my mind that you were present at that wedding. I, along with our girls and so many others, felt your spirit that day.

> *Unforgettable, that's what you are*
> *Unforgettable, though near or far.*

10/5/21

Felicia Spence photographer

Epilogue

"We need a safe place, a reserve of truth, a place where words kindle ideas and set ideas sparking off in others, a word sanctuary."

~ Allison Mackie

I Gather Memories

Gathering can be a word sanctuary.

I have been on a quest to retrieve memories. These snippets of the past never really leave me, but are safely tucked away in the recesses of my mind, just waiting to reveal themselves to me at some unexpected moment.

Following the tragedy of Flight 3407, memories tumbled from boxes of items retrieved from the crash site. Photos encouraged me to remember happy times. I felt that happiness swell inside me as photo after photo helped me recall friends and relatives who were a piece of my life. One photo showed Doug and me celebrating our July birthdays surrounded by little girls who helped blow out the candles. We looked sweaty from the summer heat, but we looked happy.

Blowing out our birthday candles together

I searched antique stores for replicas of items lost just so I could hold in my hand something from my past.

I found a Sebastian figurine of Lincoln, identical to the one Doug had given to me after our daughter Jess was born. I purchased Roseville pottery to replace the pieces my mother received as wedding gifts and had passed on to me. One day in an antique store, I spotted a plastic angel tree topper just like the one that adorned my parents' Christmas tree for so many years. I once more possessed items that triggered memories.

The majority of memories recall happy moments for me, but reality dictates that some will bring back painful remembrances. Sorrows have been gathered and sometimes understanding their intrusion into my life has been difficult.

I cannot drive down a portion of road in Clarence, New York without remembering an afternoon call from my daughter, Jess. The moment I heard her voice, I knew something was wrong. She wanted to do Face Time, and I sensed that this technological connection could not wait until I reached home. I pulled into a deserted parking lot and could see the pain reflected on her face. Amid tears, she told me her marriage was apparently in jeopardy.

Like the crash, the unexpected had happened again, and the next few months would mark a major change in all of our lives.

It has been difficult for me to receive notices of the passing of beloved family members and friends, suddenly having to realize that friendships are changing, feeling helpless to assist my children when they are hundreds of miles away from me, facing wedding anniversaries without Doug, and observing yet another anniversary of the tragic crash of Flight 3407.

I know I cannot simply gather memories from the past, and luckily, I can continue to add to my collection from new experiences.

My daughter, Jess, is a terrific aunt to her niece and nephews. She joined me in 2018 to celebrate Christmas with her sister Lori and nephews, Caden and Rowan, in Lexington, Kentucky. While

Lori ran errands, Jess and I became the designated babysitters. When the exuberance of two very vocal and active little boys became overbearing, my suggestion was to turn on cartoons. Aunt Jess had other ideas, though. Instead of "Paw Patrol" or "P J Masks," Christmas songs filled the family room, as Jess, the boys and even Sora the dog, exhibited their best dance moves for my entertainment. Their joy in sharing this activity eventually enticed me to get off the couch to join in the festivities. A wonderful family moment was preserved forever.

Jess, Rowan, Caden, and Sora dancing

Knowing that my daughter Jill would be staying in Denver, Colorado, for the Christmas holidays, I made sure that I sent her a few extra presents that year, as she would not be surrounded by family. A few days before Christmas, I was preparing breakfast in Lori's Lexington kitchen, when I had the sensation that someone was approaching me from the side. I could see Lori in the family room, so I assumed it was Jess. I turned briefly and momentarily went back to my breakfast preparations before I quickly realized it was actually **Jill** next to me! How do I explain my feelings? It was an explosion of joy, gathered and stored in the recesses of my mind.

When I pulled into a parking lot for lunch with my cousin Jan, a memory of the past began to push its way to the front of my mind. Although I had never eaten at Schnitzels, I knew I had been there before when it was LaScala, an upscale and pricey restaurant. I smiled.

In October of 2006, an unexpectedly early lake effect snow storm hit Buffalo, New York. The storm crippled the city and its surrounding suburbs. Thousands of people were without electricity for days. Our service was restored within a day, but Doug allowed a neighbor's parents to borrow our generator. They were very grateful for this favor, and thanked us by giving us a very generous gift certificate to LaScala.

We were escorted to a quiet table for two. The service was top-notch. I can't say that I remember what I had to eat that night, but I do recall Doug ordering something served with a hard-boiled egg embedded inside some sort of meat.

I can say with certainty, though, that it was the first time I ordered cognac. It made me feel decadent, mainly because it was so expensive. The warmth of that luscious liquid stayed with me as we retired to the bar area.

A Sabres hockey game was on. Doug talked sports with the bartender, and I took pleasure in watching their easy banter during the exchange. If you got Doug talking about history or sports, his enthusiasm was clearly etched on his face.

The miracle of birth, a new beginning, brings love and hope to me. The recent birth of my fifth grandchild, Gavin Douglas, is a shining example of how puzzle pieces can still appear to brighten and add comfort to my life.

Animals gather food to fortify them during the long winter months. In a similar manner, I gather memories that I can retrieve when I need inspiration and comfort. And yes, even bad

Special bonding time with Gavin

memories can provide those feelings.

Individual memories are gathered like pieces of a puzzle. When you connect them, they tell a story. Time may rob me of my ability to recall these memories, so that is why I feel it is important to transfer them into words on a blank canvas. In the future it could help me, or others, to remember the pieces of the puzzle I gathered to create my life.

1/11/19, updated 3/28/22

Sugar Cookies

Mix: 1 cup sugar
          ½ cup butter or margarine
          ½ cup shortening

Add: 3 eggs
          2 tablespoons milk
          ½ teaspoon vanilla

Sift and Add: 3 teaspoons baking powder
                  3 cups flour

Bake at 350 degrees for about 8 minutes or until bottoms start to get golden brown.

Let cookies cool, then frost with confectionary sugar and milk mixture.

Add sprinkles immediately after frosting.

Let dry before storing. When storing, put sheet of wax paper between layers to prevent sticking.

Potato Pancakes

7-8 Large potatoes (grated)
1 egg
Salt and pepper
About ½ cup flour

Grate in food processor. Mix all ingredients, adding flour as needed to make less liquid. You don't want them too floury. Fry in hot oil. Serve with applesauce.

Egg Pancakes

¾ cup flour
2 eggs
¼ teaspoon salt
½ teaspoon sugar
½ cup milk

Mix and put in small amount of hot oil to cook. Make like normal pancakes.

Potato Dumplings

4 Medium potatoes, grated
6 slices bread
1 ½ to 2 cups flour
1 tablespoon Crisco oil
1 teaspoon salt, sprinkle of pepper
1 egg

Lay bread out for 2 to 3 days to let bread dry out.

On the day you're making dumplings, crumble bread into big bowl. Add eggs and oil.

Grate potatoes in food processor and put in bowl with bread. Start to add flour.

Stir teaspoon of salt into water. When water boils, form small balls (with flour on hands) and let dumplings boil in water for 30-45 minutes (until they float on top). Don't let water boil over.

Chili

1# ground beef
1 large onion, sliced
2 cans tomato soup
2 cans kidney beans
2 cans diced tomatoes
2 cans potatoes (either diced or I buy them whole and cut them)
3 teaspoons chili powder
Salt & pepper

Brown ground beef and onions. Drain fat. Add chili powder, and salt & pepper. Let simmer for about 15 mins.

Put tomato soup in crock pot and add about a can and a half of water. Add kidney beans (I rinse), diced tomatoes – including juice, cut potatoes. Add ground beef and onions.

When pot boils, add corn starch to thicken (about 1 tablespoon mixed w/water)

Cook in crock pot for at least 4 hours.

Pigs in a Blanket

Cup of cooked rice (3/4 cup dry rice)
2 cans tomato soup
Pound ground beef
Onion
1 head of cabbage
Green pepper
Celery
1 can diced tomatoes; drained

Preheat oven to 350 degrees and boil water for cabbage.

Brown ground beef. Add onion, green pepper, celery. Cook until veggies are soft.

Once done, add diced tomatoes and about ½ can tomato soup, so mixture sticks together. Add cooked rice.

Boil cabbage until a little soft; 10 minutes. Drain water and let cool for a little bit.

Fill with beef mixture. Put some tomato soup in bottom of pan, then add cabbage rolls (seam to bottom).

Dilute remaining tomato soup slightly and pour over top. If needed, add more tomato soup to almost cover top.

Cook at 350 degrees for about an hour.

Salmon or Tuna Patties

Canned tuna or salmon
Small onion
1 egg
½ cup mashed potatoes (cold)
Flour

I use about three cans of tuna. Add enough flour to make the batter less liquid. Mix all ingredients and fry in hot oil.

Lasagna

Sauce:
1 ½ lbs. ground beef
1 clove garlic
½ onion – chopped fine
½ cup green pepper – chopped fine
1 bay leaf
Oregano to taste, 1-2 teaspoons
1 16 oz. can tomato sauce
2 6 oz. cans tomato paste
Salt & pepper to taste
1 Tablespoon parsley flakes

Brown meat, drain off fat. Add onion, green pepper and all other ingredients. Cook on simmer or low for 1 hour, stir occasionally.
Beat 2 eggs and mix with 3 cups ricotta cheese, 2 tablespoons parsley flakes, ½ cup grated parmesan cheese, 1 tsp salt, ½ teaspoon pepper. Set aside.

Cook 1 box (10 oz) lasagna noodles as directed on package.
Cut up 1 lb. (use 2-3 packages!) mozzarella cheese.

Put 3 noodles on top of a little sauce in large 13 x 9 pan.

Alternate layers – ground beef, ricotta mixture, mozzarella cheese, noodles, etc. Put mozzarella cheese on top with little sauce.

Bake at 375 degrees about 30 minutes. Let stand about 10 minutes before cutting.

German Potato Salad

7-8 Medium potatoes
1 Large onion, sliced
Salt & pepper to taste
½ Cup vinegar
¼ Cup water
½ Pound bacon

Boil potatoes, with skin on. Cool and peel. Cut in cubes.

Place in crock pot along with onions. Salt and pepper to taste.

Cut bacon and fry. Add vinegar and water and boil. Put bacon mixture (including grease) in crock pot over potatoes and onions.

Cook for 4-5 hours. Stir occasionally.

Can also be made in the oven. Cook at 350 degrees for about an hour.

Bread and Butter Pickles

4 qts. sliced cucumbers (8)

6 med onions, sliced

2 green peppers, chopped

3 cloves garlic

1/3 cup salt

5 cups sugar

1 ½ teaspoon turmeric

1 ½ teaspoon celery seed

2 tablespoons mustard seed

3 cups vinegar

Do not pare cucumbers. Slice thin. Add onions, peppers, and whole garlic cloves. Add salt. Cover with cracked ice. Mix thoroughly. Let set overnight. Drain. Combine remaining ingredients, pour over cucumber mixture. Heat just to boiling. Seal in hot sterilized jars.

Chicken Broccoli Cheese Casserole

Put 2 chicken breasts in water and boil for about 30 minutes. Drain water and allow chicken to cool a bit, then cut into small pieces. Thaw in microwave 1 package of broccoli pieces. Remove excess water.

Mix:

1 can cream of chicken soup

½ cup mayo

½ teaspoon of lemon juice

In greased casserole dish, put a layer of broccoli, then some chicken, then the soup mixture, and then some shredded cheese…repeat layers (use about 1 package of shredded cheese). Bake for 30 minutes at 350 degrees.

Cheese Wreath

3 tablespoons butter flavor Crisco
1 jar (5oz) cheese spread (I use the cheese in "squirt" container
that you put on crackers)
1 pkg. (10 count) refrigerated flaky biscuits
4 slices of bacon, crisply cooked and crumbled
2 tablespoons of parsley

Preheat oven to 450. Cut a 12" square of foil and press on
bottom and sides of 9" round cake pan. Place inverted custard
cup in center of pan (I use crumpled foil). Lightly grease foil
and sides of custard cup. Set aside.

Melt Crisco and cheese spread in small saucepan on low heat
and stir vigorously until smooth and creamy.

Spread to cover bottom of pan around custard cup. Cut each
biscuit into quarters and fit pieces into pan around the cup to
form "wreath.".

Bake at 450 for 14 minutes (top will be brown). Turn over
onto serving platter. Remove foil and cup.

Sprinkle with crumbled bacon and parsley. Serve warm.
Makes about 40 appetizers.

Fruit Pizza

1 package Pillsbury sugar cookie dough
8 oz. cream cheese
½ cup powdered sugar
Fresh fruit (kiwi, mandarin oranges, strawberries)

Prepare and bake cookie dough in pizza pan. Combine cream cheese and powdered sugar and spread on top of crust. Put fresh fruit on top of cream cheese mixture. Refrigerate.

BLT Pizza

1 package (8 oz) refrigerated crescent rolls
½ cup mayonnaise
1 ½ tablespoon Dijon mustard
6 bacon slices, cooked, drained, and crumbled
1 cup shredded lettuce
1 medium tomato, chopped
½ cup (2 oz) shredded cheddar cheese

Preheat oven to 350 degrees

Unroll crescent dough, separate into triangles. Arrange on greased 14" pizza pan with points toward the center.

Pat down dough w/fingers to 12" circle, pressing seams together to seal. Bake 12-15 min. or until golden brown.

Remove from oven; cool completely. In small bowl, combine mayo and mustard; spread evenly onto crust.

Sprinkle w/bacon, lettuce, tomato, and cheese. Cut into wedges to serve.

Oreo Ice Cream Cake

15 oz. package of Oreos
½ gallon vanilla ice cream
Jar of Smuckers fudge topping
8 oz cool whip
1/3 cup soft margarine

Put cookies in Ziploc bag and crush.

Mix crushed cookies with margarine and pat in 13 x 9 pan.
Reserve ¾ cup cookie mix.

Put ice cream on top, then fudge, then cool whip.

Sprinkle reserved cookies on top and pat down a bit.

Freeze.

Peanut Butter Bars

1 cup peanut butter
2/3 cup margarine
2 cups brown sugar
Teaspoon of vanilla
3 eggs, added one at a time

Mix above ingredients. To this add:
1 cup flour
½ teaspoon salt

Bake at 250-300 degrees in an 18 x 12 pan (cookie sheet size). Watch carefully, usually takes about ½ hour. Done when toothpick in center comes out dry.
After taking out and while still warm put on white frosting (just mix confectionary sugar and milk, making thin frosting)

Drizzle chocolate over white frosting (Melt chocolate morsels…about ½ cup…with 1 teaspoon shortening) for about 1-2 minutes.

Let set briefly and then put in refrigerator. Best if kept in refrigerator until ready to use.

Acknowlegements

If any woman dwelled on the pain of childbirth, there would be no such thing as siblings! Luckily, the pain disappears the minute we lay eyes on those little bundles of joy. The same can be said about the journey we take to reach the goal of placing a published book into our hands.

I recall the sense of fulfillment and joy I felt when *One on the Ground* was published in 2017, but I definitely forgot the commitment of time and energy that went into that endeavor. It all came flashing back to me when I started writing and compiling essays for this second book, *Pieces of My Puzzle*.

I reflected, once more, on this quote from Kahlil Gibran:

In friendship or in love, the two side-by-side raise hands together to find what one cannot reach alone.

I have traveled a long road to reach the goal of completing a second book, and it could only be reached due to the efforts of many people.

I am thankful for the continued support and love I receive from my four daughters: Kim, Lori, Jess, and Jill. They have agreed to let me share their adventures and life journeys from the '80s and beyond.

I have been blessed with five grandchildren: Lydia, Caden, Curtis, Rowan, and Gavin, who add delightful experiences and adventures to my life. I hope this book will allow them to know and treasure those who came before them.

Thanks also go to my Schwab and Schoenwetter relatives, a wonderful cast of colorful characters who provided me with a rich array of stories to add to my life puzzle.

Thanks to my sister, Barbara Fox for adjusting to my arrival in 1951, and for giving me an enthusiastic thumbs up for *Pieces of My Puzzle*.

My friend, and now editor, Debby Sullivan, painstakingly read, and reread this manuscript many times. Thank you for polishing my words, and preparing this book for publication.

Thanks also go to Librastream Publishing, led by Sallie and John Randolph, and Leslie Taylor of Buffalo Creative Group who magically brought the book to life and patiently placed hundreds of photos into the book. I appreciate that they all continue to have faith in my ability as a writer.

Special thanks to Christina Abt, who was kind enough to provide a blurb for the back of the book. A talented writer herself, I appreciated her reflections on *Pieces of My Puzzle*.

I purposely did not include a section about "Friends" in this publication, because I feared someone would be left out. You know who you are, and I hope you realize that I am thankful that you are a part of my puzzle.

Without the encouragement and support of Rick Ohler and the East Aurora Creative Writing Group, I do not believe that my efforts to become a published author would have been realized. I am very thankful that Rick provides a place for would-be writers to reach for the sky.

My husband Doug was, and remains, a big part of my story. He continues to inspire me, as I leave a record of the "Pieces of My Puzzle."

Hopefully my memories will enable those who read this book to get back-in-touch with their experiences in the '50s, '60s, '70s and beyond, and embrace and celebrate the many facets of their lives.

About the Author

Karen and her family 2021

Karen Wielinski is a freelance writer and speaker who has lived in East Aurora, New York, since 2010. Along with the love of her daughters and grandchildren, her involvement in a local writing group continues to be a source of inspiration and strength to her.

The Douglas C. Wielinski
Memorial Scholarship Fund

Doug loved to delve into history. Collecting allowed him to preserve the past, and he always loved the opportunity to share what he learned with others. He especially enjoyed bringing history to life for high school students by sharing his Viet Nam War experiences with them.

After the crash my daughter Lori said that since her dad had always loved history, it seemed only fitting that he was now a part of history.

The Douglas C. Wielinski Memorial Scholarship Fund was established in 2009 to provide assistance to students who have a genuine love of history. It is my hope that profits from the sale of *One on the Ground* and *Pieces of My Puzzle* will enable more students to benefit from this fund.

If you are so inclined to help in this effort, donations can also be sent to:

> The Douglas C. Wielinski Memorial Scholarship Fund
> P.O. Box 241
> East Aurora, NY 14052

Thank you for considering to honor Doug in this way.

~ Karen Wielinski